Beyond the Edge *of* Chaos

ADHD, Identity, and the New Science of Thriving

by Jon L. Thomas, EdD

Beyond the Edge of Chaos
ADHD, Identity, and the New Science of Thriving
1st Edition

Published by:
The ADHD College Success Guidance Program
ISBN: **979-8-9992946-0-9**

Library of Congress Control Number: [Insert LCCN once assigned]
Cover and interior design by [Insert name or "the author" if self-designed]

This book is available in paperback, hardcover, eBook, and audiobook formats.
Printed in the United States of America.

For inquiries, permissions, or bulk orders, please contact:
[Insert email or website—e.g., www.LivingCompassTools.com]

BISAC Subject Codes:
• PSY020000 – Psychology / Psychopathology / Attention Deficit Disorder (ADD-ADHD)
• EDU029180 – Education / Special Education / Learning Disabilities
• HEA046000 – Health & Fitness / Diseases / Nervous System (General)

First Edition: September 15, 2025

Copyright Registration Statement

To Pamela

My partner in every sense.
Illustrator of these pages, designer of their cover,
and the quiet artist of my life.
You have been the light when the path dimmed,
the anchor when I faltered,
and the grace that carried me through.
These books were born of your inspiration
and sustained by your love.
At the edge of chaos, you are the quiet heart
behind every word—
and the pulse that carries them into the world.

Acknowledgments

My deepest gratitude to my wife, **Pamela Thomas**, whose fine work has brought these words to life through her illustrations and design. Her creativity not only shaped the images throughout these pages but also gave this book its cover—the face by which it will be known in the world.

I am also indebted to **Danilo Salli**, **Sebastian Soto**, and **Gabriel Blake** for their careful editorial assistance. Each of you strengthened this manuscript with clarity, insight, and attention to detail.

To all of you—thank you for lending your gifts to this work.

Beyond the Edge of Chaos: ADHD, Identity, and the New Science of Thriving

- Reframing ADHD through systems thinking
- Canary in the coal mine metaphor
- Signal, salience, and the cost of misdiagnosis

- Edge of criticality, time blindness, and variability
- Span of apprehension and emotional sensitivity
- DMN/TPN dynamics and ADHD's non-linear signal-based learning

- State-switching, flow, and freeze
- The ADHD Underground Pharmacy (self-medication for state-change)
- Hyperfocus, crash cycles, and span of apprehension

- How deficit-based lenses mislead

- Why naming the problem determines what solutions even occur to us
- Reframing ADHD as a motivation and momentum disorder

- The MMO (Method–Motive–Opportunity) diagnostic framework
- The execution gap and ADHD's unique struggle with activation

- Identity-based motivation and personal salience
- The Crystal–Steel–Plastic prioritization model

- SASMA: Signal → Amplifier → Signal → Motivation → Action
- 10 signal types and common signal pitfalls
- Elijah and Tommy case studies
- Signal mapping worksheet and reflection tools
- DMN/TPN/salience network neuroscience
- Clinician- and educator-facing applications

- Introduction to SDSS (Signal-Driven Support System)
- 10 ADHD motivation types (fear, novelty, belonging, etc.)
- Motivation Compass and signal-matching strategies
- Clinician-facing section with annotated APA references

Author's Note—How to Use This Book

This book isn't just about college. Or work. Or executive function. It's about all of that—and more. Because ADHD doesn't show up in one place. It's not a single problem to solve. It's a way of sensing, responding, and moving through the world.

That's why this book isn't organized like a typical ADHD manual. It's not a checklist, or a how-to guide. It's something else: a compass. A system for tuning in, not just pushing through. A companion for navigating ADHD in real time—when the map doesn't match the terrain.

You'll find practical tools here—strategies to help you notice what moves you, regulate emotion, and build systems that actually fit. But you'll also find questions. Reflections. Patterns. Because thriving with ADHD isn't just about meeting deadlines—it's about tuning into those systems and learning to trust them.

You'll also find a different kind of framing. One that begins with "*What if?*"

What if ADHD isn't a failure of attention, but a difference in how we respond to signal?

What if the problem isn't motivation, but misalignment?

What if you're not broken—just operating on a logic the world doesn't yet understand?

These aren't rhetorical questions. They're working models. Philosopher Hans Vaihinger, in his 1911 book *The Philosophy of*

"As If," argued that we often live by fictions—ideas that may not be literally true but are **useful**. We act *as if* a theory, a metaphor, or a map is accurate—because it helps us move through life with more clarity and purpose. These fictions give us room to breathe. Room to act. Room to grow.

This book offers that kind of fiction. The models here—Signal Mapping, SASMA, the Compass framework—are designed not as rigid truths, but as tools to help you see your experience more clearly. They work *as if* ADHD is a signal-based operating system—because when you try living from that perspective, things often start to make sense in ways they never have before.

This book draws on both the science and the story of ADHD. You'll encounter frameworks designed to help you understand the underlying activation pathways that drive motivation. But you'll also discover the deeper story: the ADHD journey as a kind of quest—to reclaim agency, to rewrite shame, and to find your own way home.

Each chapter is written in layers—one for people with ADHD (students, workers, and curious minds), and another for the people who support them: parents, educators, clinicians, and coaches. You'll see those sections clearly marked. Read what speaks to you. Skip what doesn't. This book is designed to be flexible, like the minds it's written for.

You don't have to read in order. You can jump around, skip ahead, and return later. Use what works. Leave the rest. This book is meant to be lived with, not just read.

And while it's written for those of us with ADHD, it's also for anyone walking this road beside us. If that's you, you're welcome. You're part of this, too.

With wonder as our compass,
Jon Thomas

Disclaimer: Em Dashes, Emojis, and Similarities to AI

A funny thing happened on the way to getting this book into print.

Several of my colleagues and early readers pulled me aside—some with concern, others with curiosity—and said, "Hey... this has AI's fingerprint all over it." Their evidence? Em dashes. Emojis. White space. Syntax too smooth. Layout too clean.

At first, I panicked. Had I lost my voice to the robots? Was my style starting to carry the faint scent of machine learning? Had ChatGPT ghostwritten my soul?

So I did what any concerned and responsible human would do: I went back and looked at my first book—*Thriving at the Edge of Chaos*—written well before the bots took over. And sure enough, there they were: the same em dashes, the same visual rhythm, the same strategic emoji use.

It wasn't AI. It was just... me.

(Em dashes, by the way, are far better for brains with ADHD than semicolons. A semicolon politely whispers. An em dash kicks open the door.)

Feeling somewhat vindicated, I decided to test things—and asked ChatGPT for formatting suggestions for readers with ADHD. Its top recommendations? Use (even more) em dashes, break up dense text with whitespace, and yes... sprinkle in emojis.

That's when it hit me: maybe ChatGPT is modeling *me*.

So yes—AI has a fingerprint in the layout of this book,

but not in the writing. Think of it as the roadie who set up the lights, not the band on stage.

As for the illustrations—those are 100% the handiwork of my wife, Pamela Thomas. ChatGPT and Canva were involved, but mostly in the way a pair of electric scissors is involved in a haircut: they make it faster and sleeker, but you still want a human you trust holding them.

Pam drew, designed, tweaked, and occasionally rescued things from my "brilliant ideas" pile, transforming them into art that not only lives on the page but also deepens the story the words are telling.

Also, for the record: this book disagrees with the MIT article titled "ChatGPT Is Making Us Stupid." That article's response is included in Chapter 15: Critical Thinking—feel free to form your own opinion.

Thanks for reading,
Jon Thomas

P.S. This disclaimer has been reviewed and enthusiastically nodded at by Sam Altman. (Probably.)

✳ Introduction to Part I

A New Way to See – Rethinking ADHD from the Inside Out

In the 35-plus years I've worked with people who have ADHD—and the many decades I've spent learning to work with my own—I've encountered countless programs, approaches, books, memes, podcasts, and expert opinions claiming to explain what ADHD is, how it works, and how to fix it.

Some of them offer relief. A few deliver hope. Many just fall flat.

I've come to believe that happens because most of them are missing two essential pieces—ones I've discovered through years of trial and error, both professionally and personally.

The first missing piece is a deeper understanding of our unique ways of experiencing the world—how time, attention, urgency, emotion, and meaning behave differently in a brain with ADHD. When we don't recognize these differences, we often reach for tools that don't fit—and misread our struggles in ways that create shame, not progress.

The second piece is perspective—not just more information, but a different way of seeing. A shift in the lens itself. One that honors complexity, embraces both compassion and agency, and makes space for real change.

These aren't just nice ideas. They're the foundation for everything that follows—and for the tools, strategies, and systems that actually work for ADHD minds.

In this book, that foundation rests on what we call the **three pillars of thriving**—the key areas where ADHD causes the most persistent and painful challenges, and where the proper support can unlock the most significant growth:

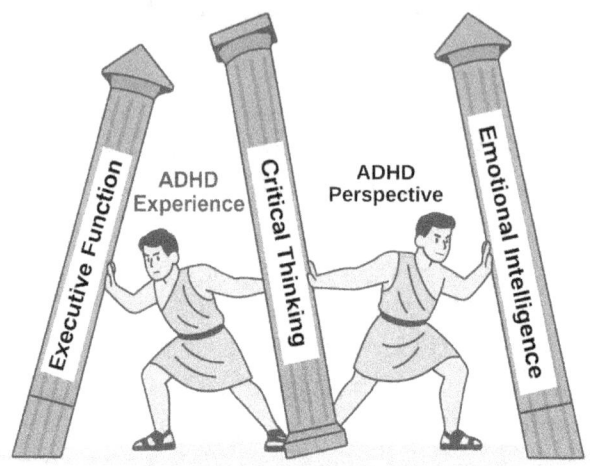

- ○ **Executive Function**—how we organize, prioritize, and take action
- ○ **Emotional Intelligence**—how we process feelings, feedback, and identity
- ○ **Critical Thinking**—how we interpret, assess, and adapt to complexity

These aren't just academic categories. They're the real-world systems that break down when ADHD isn't understood—and the same ones that come alive when we build the right supports.

I'm sharing these ideas with you now because I've seen what they can change—and even transform—in people's lives. I believe the only way you'll know that for yourself is by trying them, living with them, and seeing what becomes possible. That's what I want for you—and for everyone walking this path.

🗐 How to Read This Book (Especially If You Have ADHD)

This book is doing something unusual—and honestly, a little risky.

It's written for people with ADHD first and foremost. But it's also designed to help the people who support them: parents, educators, clinicians, and coaches.

To do both, each chapter is built in three layers:

1. **Bullet points up front**—a quick preview so you know what's coming and can decide where to focus.
2. **A voice for people with ADHD**—students, workers, and curious minds, with stories, metaphors, and tools in plain language for navigating life in real time.
3. **A voice for parents, educators, clinicians, coaches— and curious readers**—with deeper dives, science, references, and structured guidance to support real-world implementation and conversation.

You can read straight through, skip to what speaks to you, or return to it whenever a challenge shows up.

However you use it, the goal is the same:
To offer a new way of seeing ADHD—one that works.

Chapter 1

What Makes Us Uniquely Different—New View of Time, Emotion, and Neurodivergent Design

If you judge a fish by its ability to climb a tree,
it will live its whole life believing it is stupid."
—Albert Einstein

🔍 What You'll Get From This Chapter:

- How ADHD reframes our experience of time, urgency, and presence
- Why our learning thrives near the edge of criticality—and breaks down elsewhere
- The role of emotional patterning and urgency in motivation
- A foundational reframe of ADHD as a feedback system—not a broken one

📄 How to Use This Chapter

This chapter is designed with *three perspectives in mind*. You don't have to read it all at once—and you're free to skip to what's most relevant for you.

- 🧠 **For People with ADHD**—Students, workers, and curious minds: This section offers a new way of seeing

ADHD, built on emotional truth, time experience, signal awareness, and what makes sense when shame is removed from the lens.

- ○ 🖋 **For Parents, Educators, Clinicians, and Coaches—** This section explains how ADHD traits like time blindness, emotional intensity, and performance variability emerge from deeper signal-level dynamics—and how support systems can work *with* them, not against them.
- ○ 💡 **Key Concepts and Takeaways**—Throughout the chapter, you'll find metaphors (like the Geometry of Now and Criticality), neuroscience references, and scaffolding tools that preview strategies from later in the book.

> 💡 *Read it straight through—or come back to the part that gives you a clearer map. This chapter sets the lens through which everything else comes into focus.*

🧠 For People with ADHD—Students, Workers, and Curious Minds

🔄 A New Kind of Mirror
ADHD changes the way the world feels.
Deadlines land differently.
Emotions hit harder.
Time bends and slips.

And yet, most of the "explanations" you've heard—even the well-meaning ones—start from the wrong map.

They measure you against rules you didn't write, with tools that weren't built for the way your brain actually works.

Because ADHD isn't just a different way of behaving.

It's a different way of sensing, responding, and being in the world.

The things you struggle with—time, emotion, urgency, follow-through—aren't character flaws. They're artifacts of a differently wired feedback system.

This chapter isn't about proving you "fit."

It's about picking up a new kind of mirror—one that reflects your life in ADHD terms, not neurotypical ones.

Because once you see your patterns through the right lens, the struggle starts to make sense.

And once it makes sense... you can start to change it.

⟳ Time Blindness

The Geometry of Now—Why Time Feels So Strange

One of the most defining—and misunderstood—parts of ADHD is how we experience time. Not as a straight line—but as something slippery. Foggy. Impossibly close one moment, gone the next.

Ask someone with ADHD about the future, and they don't describe a timeline. They describe a thundercloud: "maybe later," "probably soon," or "oh no—that was today?" Ask about the past, and it's often vague, distorted, or weirdly emotional. It's not that we don't have a sense of time. It's that we don't see time the way others do.

FUTURE **PAST**

Here's something I've noticed after thousands of hours in the therapy room: when I ask neurotypical clients to gesture toward the past, they usually point to the left. Toward the future? They point right—just like timelines on a whiteboard.

FUTURE   PAST

Clients with ADHD? They point behind them when talking about the past, and straight ahead for the future, like they're staring something down. It's not lab science, but it shows up again and again: a different geometry of experience.

And it makes sense. If the past lives behind you, it's out of sight. You have to turn around to see it—and let's be honest, that's not always appealing.

You miss patterns. Forget lessons.

The rearview mirror is either foggy or missing entirely.

And if the future stands directly in front of you, it's not a neat calendar. It's a mess. A fog. A dense, undifferentiated blob of "stuff you're supposed to do"—but can't sort, prioritize, or plan for.

It's like building IKEA furniture—without the manual. Or the tools. While the clock is ticking. And someone keeps moving the screws.

This is time blindness. It's not a lack of awareness. It's a different operating system.

We don't walk beside time. We're in it—like fish in water. Like dancers in fog. And that makes time management strategies feel frustrating or even shame-inducing. Because they're based on a timeline we can't see.

But there's more here than dysfunction—there's design.

Cognitive linguists like Lakoff, Johnson, and Boroditsky have shown that most people understand time through spatial metaphors. Time flows. Passes. Moves forward. We picture it left to right. Past to future. That's how most brains organize experience.

But ADHD brains? They use a different map. One where the past isn't integrated and the future doesn't feel real until it's now.

That difference isn't just inconvenient. It's disabling—unless we build supports that make time visible.

And here's the kicker: without access to the past, we can't learn from failure. Without a workable map of the future, we can't prioritize, plan, or act in advance. We just improvise. Often brilliantly. Sometimes at a cost.

To function, we need ways to make the invisible visible—to give shape to the fog. That's the real task of time management for ADHD: not discipline, but geometry. Not effort, but access.

If ADHD reshapes how we experience time, then the edges—where urgency cuts through the fog—might hold real clues.

Let's go there next.

⚡ Learning on the Edge

We Thrive at the Edge of Criticality

"For it is not light that is needed, but fire; it is not the gentle shower, but thunder. We need the storm, the whirlwind and the earthquake in our hearts."
—Frederick Douglass

When the past is foggy and the future feels like a looming blur, it's no surprise that we look for clarity in the now—or more accurately, at the edge of now.

That edge—where urgency collides with action—is where many individuals with ADHD feel most alive.

You've probably been there: a massive project due in four hours, your focus finally kicks in, and somehow you knock out three days' worth of work in an afternoon. Or maybe the opposite—you had all weekend to send a simple email or finish a short reading... and somehow, it never happened. It's not laziness. It's that the *structure of time* didn't offer you the spark your brain needed to move.

One college student I worked with said it best:

"I can write a ten-page paper in three hours if it's due at midnight—but if it's due next Friday, I'll think about it *every day* and still not start it until 11:00 p.m. Thursday."

What sounds like procrastination is often something deeper—a brain that needs intensity, urgency, or emotional weight to access its full capacity. The problem isn't motivation or discipline. It's ignition.

In 2024, neuroscientist Dr. Keith Hengen of Washington University in St. Louis helped reintroduce a compelling idea: that the brain becomes a learning machine only when it reaches a special state called **criticality**. Borrowed from physics, **criticality** describes a system perched right between chaos and order—not frozen, not frantic, but poised for transformation.

Hengen's research shows that brains function best—gain the most information and integrate it most effectively—when operating at this razor's edge. Too much stability, and the brain resists change. Too much randomness, and it can't encode meaning. That tipping point? It's where the brain is tuned, alert, and ready—and if you have ADHD, it probably sounds very familiar.

Everyone performs better at the edge of criticality—but those of us with ADHD don't just perform there. We thrive there. That's not poetic language—it's functional design. And in my view, that's no accident.

My theory is this: minds with ADHD are constantly—often unconsciously—trying to get back to that edge state. The methods we use to get there are varied and sometimes unconscious: procrastination, chronic lateness, deadline-chasing, overcommitting, taking on emotional emergencies, even stirring the pot a little just to feel alive. And while these strategies can be remarkably effective at generating urgency—they often come at a cost.

The negative side effects can include:

o   Emotional exhaustion or burnout
o   Damaged trust in relationships (personal or academic)
o   Missed deadlines and missed opportunities
o   Shame spirals triggered by self-criticism
o   Perpetual cycles of stress and guilt

Here's the good news: awareness changes the game. When we recognize what we're really chasing—not the chaos, but the activation—we can begin to find healthier, more intentional ways to access it.

We can choose to enter that edge state on purpose, with support, preparation, and structure. We can harness the productive energy of criticality—without having to set ourselves on fire just to feel the heat.

And here's an essential part of that process: managing the cost of being "on." Thriving at the edge burns fuel—emotional, cognitive, and physical. It requires energy, emotional regulation, and attentional stamina. That's why we also need to learn to let go of the destructive methods we once used to achieve our goals.

In the chapters ahead, we'll introduce tools to help you track, monitor, and manage your internal resources: emotional load, energy fluctuations, and stress responses. These tools will help you access your edge when it serves you, and step back when it doesn't.

Because thriving at the edge is not about living in crisis. It's about dancing with the spark without letting it burn you out.

ADHD minds are often operating in that edge state by default. We're not wired for long stretches of calm, linear input. We're built for moments of ignition—urgency, novelty, emotional intensity. We don't ease in. We activate.

This doesn't mean we're broken. It means we're edge-oriented learners. The challenge is not that we can't engage. It's that we may need to hit that edge before we do.

Many readers may recognize this territory through another concept: the concept of **flow**. Psychologist Mihály Csíkszentmihályi defined flow as a deeply immersive state where time disappears, and full attention merges with action. Flow is beautiful, but fragile. It requires structure, matching skill with challenge, and emotional calm. Individuals with ADHD often experience flow—typically during hyperfocus—but we rarely choose when it appears. It finds us.

Criticality, on the other hand, is volatile. It isn't comfortable, but it's functional. It's the point just before flow, where alertness spikes, where decisions start forming, where signal breaks through the fog. It may not feel good, but it's gold for activation.

And here's where things get exciting. Unlike flow, which we mostly fall into, criticality is a state we can learn to recognize and even initiate. Through signal mapping, emotional amplifiers, and environmental design, we can begin to shape our edge rather than be thrown by it. We can use it to move into action. To begin. To engage.

This isn't about chasing chaos. It's about learning to stabilize while near the spark. When you learn how to ride the edge, you don't have to wait for panic or pressure to light you up. You can create systems that bring you just close enough.

We'll return to this idea later in Chapter 12, when we explore how Sprint Thinking—an adaptive strategy drawn from software development—helps ADHD minds structure their work to activate urgency, sustain momentum, and reach flow.

And that brings us to the next defining difference: **variability of performance**. If time is a fog and learning happens at the edge, then it's no wonder that our daily output can swing so wildly. The same brain that solves a crisis at 3 p.m. can forget how to answer an email at 3:05. Let's look at why our performance isn't just inconsistent—it's patterned, reactive, and trying to tell us something.

Variability of Performance

"You do it right once and they hold it against you forever."
—Dr. Russell Barkley

You finish a project early—once. You respond to every email in a single afternoon—once. And suddenly, it's the new expectation.

But for many students with ADHD, that success wasn't the norm. It was a moment of alignment—the right energy, the right spark, the right conditions. The next day? That same task might feel like a wall.

It's not laziness. It's not sabotage. And it's definitely not a character flaw. It's neurology—in real time.

In school, this might look like acing a quiz one week and bombing the test the next. At home, it might be the teen who cleans their room without being asked—once—and then can't pick up a sock again for months. The inconsistency isn't imagined. It's real. And it's demoralizing for everyone involved.

✧

 So what's going on?
Part of the answer lies in the complexity of ADHD itself. It's not a one-size-fits-all condition, and even effective medications can't smooth out every bump. Some of the most stubborn ADHD symptoms—like emotional volatility, activation delays,

or sudden disengagement—aren't easy to medicate, accommodate, or rationalize.

One of the biggest wild cards? Emotion. When emotional load is high—anxiety, frustration, excitement, even anticipation—focus often collapses. Add in inconsistent sleep, shifting motivation, sensory sensitivity, or sudden environmental changes, and you've got a brain that can pivot from brilliant to bewildered in minutes.

And here's another tricky truth: Not all motivation is transferable.

What sparks focus one day might fall flat the next—because motivation isn't one-size-fits-all, and it doesn't copy-paste. A specific cue, signal, or emotional hook might unlock engagement on Tuesday—but have no effect on Friday. This is part of what makes ADHD so frustrating: the conditions that support success can be hard to reproduce, and what works for one task may not translate to the next.

This is why we introduce signal mapping in this book: to track what moves us and when, so we stop trying to replicate results blindly and start building around what actually works.

🫠 It's not failure—it's feedback.

A 2022 study (Stevens et al.) identified key predictors of academic success for students with ADHD or learning disabilities. These included:

- o Academic regulation
- o Academic self-efficacy
- o Emotional regulation
- o ADHD symptom management
- o Academic and social integration

Notice the pattern? Sustained performance is built on internal architecture—not brute-force willpower. These aren't traits. They're systems.

That's also where emotional intelligence enters the picture—not as a feel-good concept, but as a learnable skill set. The more aware we are of how emotions shape attention, activation, and overwhelm, the more we can begin to work with them rather than be blindsided by them. Later chapters will offer specific tools to help students build this awareness and translate it into more consistent outcomes.

🔧 So what can we do?

First, we normalize variability. It's not a sign of failure—it's a signal. It tells us something about what supports are missing or what conditions we thrive in.

Next, we build systems that reduce randomness:

- o cue-based routines
- o emotional check-ins
- o flexible structures that respond to shifting energy, interest, and readiness

- environmental amplifiers that prime us for criticality or
  flow

We also learn to listen to internal variables—such as emotional state, energy levels, and stress load—because they shape how consistently we can show up.

The tools in this book are designed to help you do just that: track patterns, test strategies, and tune your environment until success isn't just something you stumble into—it's a rhythm you can build.

RSD, Sensory Processing, and the Challenge of Emotional Regulation

"You're just too sensitive."

If you've ever heard those words—and you have ADHD— there's a good chance you weren't being dramatic. You were being accurate.

Because for many of us, emotional and sensory sensitivity isn't a side effect of ADHD. It's central to how we move through the world.

Let's break it down.

People with ADHD often live with amplified sensitivity—to sound, touch, movement, brightness, temperature, and even internal bodily states like hunger or heart rate. This is called sensory processing difference, and it can shape everything from how we work to how we relate.

But here's the kicker: the same sensitivity that picks up background noise and flickering lights? It also tunes into emotional tones—real or imagined. We're not just sensitive to the world around us. We're exquisitely tuned in to the world within.

That's where Rejection Sensitivity Dysphoria (RSD) comes in.

RSD isn't a clinical diagnosis in the DSM, but it's a term that describes a very real experience. For many people with ADHD, a single disapproving glance, harsh tone, or even imagined slight can hijack the entire nervous system. One wrong word and the inner critic takes over. Motivation collapses. Focus disappears. The emotional weather turns stormy in a flash.

Here's the critical insight: RSD and sensory processing differences are two sides of the same signal amplification coin.

- o Sensory overload comes from outside in.
- o RSD overload comes from the inside out.

This isn't just heightened awareness—it's signal amplification. Our internal amplifiers crank up threat detection and rejection sensitivity to max volume, even when the input is small.

Both types of overload can distort our ability to respond, leading to shutdown, avoidance, overreaction, or freeze. And both are often misread as signs of immaturity, fragility, or a lack of grit.

What they actually reflect is a different kind of signal wiring—a nervous system that's designed to pick up on threat, rejection, or overwhelm at a much lower threshold. This can be adaptive in moments of danger or creativity. But in daily life? It often feels like emotional whiplash.

We'll explore both in more depth later in the book, especially when we unpack the emotional intelligence skills that ADHD students need most. But for now, here's the key idea:

Signal overload isn't a flaw. It's a feature that needs interpretation, support, and structure.

When we begin to track what throws us off—and what helps bring us back—we're not just managing emotions. We're learning how to decode signal patterns that affect everything else: attention, motivation, confidence, and self-trust.

This is more than just a quirky sensitivity—it's a pattern that can derail motivation, decision-making, and self-worth. As Dr. William Dodson points out, RSD is one of the most intense and disruptive emotional experiences for people with ADHD, yet it remains poorly recognized in many clinical settings. At the same time, researchers like Yochman and others have found that problems with sensory processing can explain emotional outbursts and avoiding tasks even better than traditional tests of self-control or organization.

These aren't side notes. They're central signals in the ADHD experience—and they deserve the same attention and structure we give to focus, planning, and behavior.

✎ For Parents, Educators, Clinicians, Coaches, and Curious Minds

Reframing the Chaos: What This Chapter Tells Us About ADHD

This chapter isn't just a collection of quirks or complaints—it's a window into the lived neurocognitive experience of ADHD. Each difference described above—from time distortion to sensory overload to emotional volatility—reveals a key insight: **ADHD is not a disorder of attention. It is a difference in signal regulation.**

What may appear to be inconsistency, avoidance, or over-reaction on the surface is often a **breakdown in signal clarity**, **activation energy**, or **cognitive regulation under pressure**.

The takeaway for parents, clinicians, and educators is this:

"Behavior is communication. And in ADHD, that behavior is often trying to send a signal: I'm stuck. I can't see the future. I've lost the thread. The emotions are louder than the task. The signal isn't getting through."

The goal of intervention isn't to force neurotypical

performance—it's to build environments and relationships that help the signal get through.

That includes:

- o Recognizing that **variability is diagnostic, not defiant**
- o Designing **systems that support time-blind learners**
- o Building structures that **create urgency without crisis**
- o Supporting emotional regulation without shame
- o Paying attention to **what amplifies motivation—and what hijacks it**

This chapter lays the foundation for a more compassionate and accurate approach to supporting individuals with ADHD. In the chapters ahead, we'll dive deeper into system-building, motivational structures, signal-mapping tools, and the emotional scaffolding that allows students and adults with ADHD to thrive.

📖 References for Further Reading

o **Barkley, R. A. (1997). *ADHD and the Nature of Self-Control.* Guilford Press.**
A foundational text that reframes ADHD as a disorder of self-regulation and executive function rather than simply attention.

o **Barkley, R. A. (2020). *Taking Charge of ADHD* (Revised ed.). Guilford Press.**
A widely used, practical guide to understanding and managing ADHD, especially in children and adolescents.

o **Boroditsky, L. (2000). "Metaphoric Structuring:**

Understanding Time through Spatial Metaphors."
Cognition, 75(1), 1–28.
Examines how people use spatial metaphors to understand abstract concepts like time—a key idea in understanding ADHD's altered sense of time.

o Csikszentmihályi, M. (1990). *Flow: The Psychology of Optimal Experience.* Harper & Row.
Introduces the concept of "flow"—a deep state of immersion in a task—and explains how it emerges at the balance point between challenge and skill.

o Dodson, W. (2021). "Rejection Sensitivity Dysphoria and ADHD." *ADDitude Magazine.*
Explains the intense emotional reactions to perceived criticism or failure that many people with ADHD experience, often overlooked in clinical models.

o Hengen, K. B., et al. (2024). "Criticality and adaptive learning in cortical networks." *Nature Neuroscience.*
Offers neuroscientific evidence that optimal learning and adaptation happen near the edge of criticality—a concept closely tied to ADHD performance patterns.

o Stevens, E. A., et al. (2022). "Predicting academic success for students with ADHD or learning disabilities." *Journal of Learning Disabilities, 55(3)*, 179–192.
Analyzes predictors of academic outcomes for students with ADHD and LD, highlighting the limitations of traditional assessments and supports.

o Thomas, J. (2019). *Thriving at the Edge of Chaos: Making ADHD a Superpower in College and Career.* ADHD College Success Guidance Press.
Introduces the core metaphor of "thriving at the edge of criticality," framing ADHD not as a disorder but as a high-performance mind in need of the right conditions to thrive—especially in challenging, dynamic environments.

o Tversky, B. (2011). *Mind in Motion: How Action Shapes Thought.* Basic Books.
Explores how movement and physical interaction shape cognition, offering insight into ADHD learning patterns and the role of embodied experience.

o Yochman, A., Alon-Beery, O., & Parush, S. (2022). "Sensory processing and its relation to emotional regulation in children with ADHD." *Research in Developmental Disabilities, 124*, 104196.
Demonstrates that sensory processing challenges often predict emotional dysregulation and task avoidance more strongly than traditional measures of executive function.

Chapter 2

Why We Struggle to Shift

"And the day came when the risk to remain tight in a bud was more painful than the risk it took to blossom."
—Anaïs Nin†

"Human strength lies in the ability to change yourself."
—Saitama, OnePunch Man

🔍 What You'll Get From This Chapter

- Why ADHD is often less about "paying attention" and more about *changing mental channels*
- How your brain runs on two modes—wandering and focused—and what happens when both try to run the show
- The truth about hyperfocus: part superpower, part troublemaker
- Why coffee, nicotine, or even a crisis can feel like magic buttons for getting started
- What "mental bandwidth" really means—and why it can vanish all at once
- Simple tools to spot overload early, reset quickly, and keep your focus where you want it

📜 How to Use This Chapter

This chapter is built for three kinds of readers—and you can jump to the part that fits you best (or read it all, no pressure):

- o 🧠 **For People with ADHD—Students, workers, and curious minds:** What it *really* feels like to get stuck, spin out, or crash—and why none of it means you're broken.
- o 🔬 **For Parents, Educators, Clinicians, and Coaches:** How mode-switching trouble, emotional overload, and bandwidth collapse look in daily life—plus ways to help without cranking up the pressure.
- o 💡 **Key Concepts and Takeaways:** Quick metaphors, simple brain science, and practical tools you can start using right away to recover from overload and protect your focus.

✳️ Introduction: ADHD and the Art of State-Shifting

If you've heard people say, "ADHD means trouble paying attention," they're not wrong—but they're not seeing the whole elephant.

At the heart of ADHD is something we don't talk about enough: **transitions**.

Not just moving from one class to another, but shifting mental gears:

- o From stillness to movement
- o From thinking about it to actually doing it
- o From daydream mode to decision mode
- o From reflecting to performing

For many of us with ADHD, those shifts aren't smooth. We stall. We spin. We get stuck halfway between two modes—not sure how to start... or how to stop.

It's not laziness. It's wiring. The ADHD brain doesn't flip cleanly from idle to drive. It often needs a shove—sometimes from excitement, sometimes from urgency, and sometimes from pure chaos—to get into motion.

In this chapter, we'll look at what's happening in the brain when that "gear shift" won't click—and explore the work-arounds people often discover for themselves (some healthy, some not) to get that shift started and keep it going.

🎓 Student Story: Sofia and the Shifting Self

Sofia, a junior in college, sat across from me with a look I've seen a hundred times—frustrated, teary, and tired of hearing herself say, *"I don't know why I can't just start."*

She had two big papers due. One was already done—written in a single, caffeine-fueled night of unstoppable focus. The other? It had been sitting open on her laptop for six days, untouched except for the blinking cursor.

"I'm not lazy," she said. "I care about both classes. But something just won't... click."

That *click*—the mental gear shift from intention to action—is exactly where so many people with ADHD get stuck. It's not about knowing what to do. It's about bridging the gap between knowing and doing, between "I should" and "I'm in it."

For Sofia, that gap felt like standing on one side of a river with no bridge in sight.

And that's where this chapter begins.

🧠 For People with ADHD—Students, Workers, and Curious Minds

🧠 Meet Your Brain's Two-Mode System

Back in 2001, neuroscientists made a surprising discovery: when people in brain scanners were told to "do nothing," their brains didn't go quiet. Instead, a set of brain regions lit up—areas tied to daydreaming, memory, self-reflection, and imagination.

They called it the **Default Mode Network (DMN)** because it's what your brain does by default when you're not actively focused on a task.

On the flip side is the **Task Positive Network (TPN)**— the "let's actually do the thing" system. It kicks in when you're writing a paper, folding laundry, coding an app, or trying to beat that next game level.

In most brains, these two modes work like a seesaw:

- When the TPN turns on, the DMN turns off.
- When the DMN activates, the TPN steps back.

That smooth back-and-forth is called **anticorrelation**, and it's what lets most neurotypical people focus, reflect, and then slide back into focus again without a fight.

🧠 ADHD: When the Dance Becomes a Wrestling Match

In brains with ADHD, this clean handoff can get messy:

- The DMN keeps running during tasks, flooding attention with inner noise.
- Unless urgency, interest, or novelty is in play, The TPN struggles to stay online.
- Switching modes feels like trying to change lanes in traffic with a blinker that doesn't work and no opening in sight.

It's not just distractibility—it's *dual-processing interference*. Like two radio stations playing at once, the brain gets noisy, unclear, and overwhelmed.

🎭 Theater Metaphor: Welcome to the ADHD Stage

Picture your brain as a small black-box theater:

- The TPN is the director—focused, purposeful, clipboard in hand.
- The DMN is the playwright—dreamy, reflective, wandering the stage in a robe.

In most brains, they take turns under the spotlight.

But in ADHD brains? The playwright never leaves the stage. The director shouts for quiet, but the monologue just keeps going. Cue mental chaos—and a very frustrated crew.

⚖️ The Flip Side of Task Mode

Task Mode is great for getting stuff done—but if you camp out there too long, you miss the gifts of the DMN. That's not "the enemy" you're turning off; it's the part of your brain that lets you:

- o Daydream and connect dots you didn't know were related
- o Replay experiences until the meaning clicks
- o Imagine what's next and see the big picture
- o Process emotions so they don't just pile up in the background

When the DMN gets too little airtime—whether from meds, overwork, or constant stimulation—creativity tanks, big-picture thinking shrinks, and emotional processing gets skipped. You can end up grinding away at the wrong thing or feeling like life is flat and mechanical.

🏷️ How Meds Change the Channel

Everything we've talked about so far—the seesaw, the wrestling match, the theater—is playing out live in your brain all day. Stimulant medication doesn't change *who* is on stage; it changes how easily they trade places.

Think of it like this: your brain has two main "channels":

- o **Channel One (DMN)**—your brain's screensaver. Great for daydreaming, connecting dots, and replaying moments until the meaning clicks.
- o **Channel Two (TPN)**—the "let's do the thing" channel. Perfect for homework, errands, finishing projects, or finally calling the dentist.

In ADHD, Channel One likes to keep playing even when you *want* to watch Channel Two. Stimulant meds like Adderall help by turning down the wandering channel and boosting the "get stuff done" channel. They also smooth the channel change, so you can stay locked on your task without drifting into mental reruns.

In a perfect world, this balance between the two channels would be all we'd ever need. But ADHD brains have a third setting—one that's not quite Task Mode, not quite Default Mode, and far more unpredictable: **hyperfocus**.

🔬 Hyperfocus—A Third State at the Edge

Hyperfocus is one of the most famous—and misunderstood— traits of ADHD. People often describe it as a *superpower*, a hidden gift, or even proof that people with ADHD "can focus when they want to."

But here's the truth: **hyperfocus isn't about wanting**. It's about being pulled—sometimes beyond your control—into a narrow, high-stakes tunnel of attention.

And it may not even be part of the usual two-mode system at all.

🧠 Not Task Mode. Not Default Mode. Something Else.

TPN   DMN

When researchers look at ADHD brains in hyperfocus, they see something unusual:

o   The emotional *salience* of the DMN is high—the task feels personal, urgent, or deeply interesting.
o   The engagement of the TPN is also high—you're locked in and distractions fade away.
o   But executive control is low—so you can lose track of time, meals, and outside priorities.

It's a hybrid state—part emotion, part action—with no easy off-ramp.

⚙ It's Not Flow—It's the Moment Before Flow

You've probably heard of flow—that ideal performance state where everything clicks, and you feel immersed, balanced, and in control.

Psychologist Mihály Csíkszentmihályi defined flow as the sweet spot where skill meets challenge, distractions disappear, and time seems to stand still.

But here's the twist: ADHD hyperfocus isn't flow.

Flow is smooth, expansive, and stable. Hyperfocus is jagged, reactive, and volatile.

ADHD expert Dr. William Dodson explains that hyperfocus isn't something you choose—it usually happens when something feels urgent, exciting, or there's pressure to get it done. It's not like flow, where you're calm, in control, and focused because you're using your skills. Hyperfocus is more like falling into a tunnel—fast, intense, and hard to stop once it starts.

This directly supports the idea that hyperfocus isn't just intense focus—it's an unstable state that often leads to either a breakthrough or a burnout. It's not the calm center of performance. It lives *within* the edge of criticality—that razor-thin zone where urgency and meaning collide and your brain finally locks on. Hyperfocus is one way the edge shows up, but it's the volatile, high-drain version. At other times, that same edge can tip you into more balanced states, like flow, if the conditions are right.

If this feels familiar, it should. In Chapter 1, we explored the **edge of criticality**—that razor-thin zone between chaos and order where ADHD minds often come alive. Hyperfocus is one way the edge can manifest: unstable but potent, capable of launching us into deep engagement when the signal finally cuts through.

And unlike flow, which depends on a steady balance between skill and challenge, criticality can emerge from chaos—from pressure, emotion, novelty, or even boredom that's boiled over into frustration. The edge doesn't care how you got there; it just lights up when meaning and urgency finally collide.

⚠ Why It Matters

Hyperfocus can be a gift—but only if we understand its rules:

- o It can't be turned on at will.
- o It can interfere with relationships, time management, and task-switching.
- o It often emerges when the cost of not acting becomes unbearable.
- o And it usually comes with a **recovery period**—because being in that tunnel burns fuel fast.

But here's the exciting part:

We can learn to **recognize** this state.
We can learn to **approach** it—not just wait for it to strike.

And we can design **systems and supports** that help us use it, rather than be ruled by it.

 Sidebar: The ADHD Underground Pharmacy

Long before most people with ADHD get a diagnosis—or a treatment plan that works—they've already begun to figure out ways to push their own mental "start" and "stop" buttons. Some of these are harmless. Some are risky. But almost all are attempts to manage the brain's mode-switching manually.

Sometimes it's a little trick, tool, or tweak. Other times it's a full-blown behavior, routine, or—in some cases—a pharmaceutical. Put them all together, and you get what I call the **ADHD Underground Pharmacy**—the survival kit of substances, sensations, and situations people turn to when their brain won't shift on its own.

It's not always about escaping. Most of the time, it's about regulating. About finding *something* that turns down the noise, turns up the focus, or changes the channel entirely.

Nicotine: The Hidden Focus Aid

Some long-time smokers with ADHD will tell you they started because it looked cool, helped them fit in, or felt rebellious. But beneath that surface reason, there may have been something else going on—an unconscious search for a substance that could help their brain feel more focused and steadier.

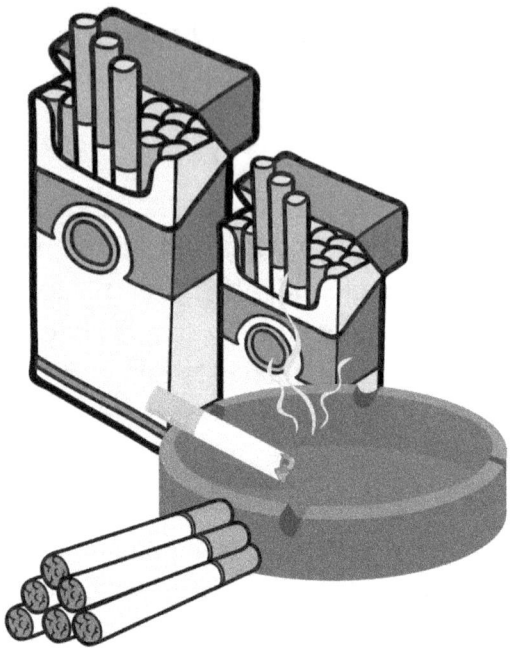

Nicotine is a fast-acting stimulant that:

- ○ Boosts dopamine (attention, motivation)
- ○ Enhances acetylcholine (alertness, memory)
- ○ Suppresses the DMN, quieting the mental chatter
- ○ Activates the TPN, making it easier to lock onto a task

For many, that first cigarette was the first moment their brain felt organized. But it's a costly trick—nicotine is addictive, short-acting, and brutal on long-term health.

☕ Caffeine: The Legal Performance Enhancer

Coffee is the most common ADHD self-medication in the world—and the most socially accepted. Some people drink it for the taste or the ritual, but for many with ADHD, it's an everyday attempt to get the brain into gear.

Caffeine can:

o   Help you cross the "activation threshold" when you're close to getting started
o   Increase coordination in the Task Positive Network (TPN)
o   Decrease Default Mode Network (DMN) activity during tasks, which can reduce mental drift

The difference is that caffeine's effect is less precise, shorter-lasting, and more variable between individuals compared to prescription stimulants. And because it also ramps up other systems (like adenosine blockade), it can cause jitteriness or anxiety even while improving task focus.

It's still a blunt tool. For some, it's a reliable jumpstart. For others, it's a coin toss—focus or jitters. And unlike stimulant medication, it's not tuned for precision or sustained effect.

 Alcohol: The Shut-Off Valve

Not everyone drinks to party. Some drink to *quiet things down*. When the noise in your head won't stop—the replaying of conversations, the self-criticism, the sense that everyone's watching—alcohol can feel like hitting the mute button.

In the brain, alcohol:

- Suppresses Default Mode Network (DMN) activity, easing rumination and self-criticism
- Blunts rejection sensitivity or social anxiety in the moment
- Dampens emotional intensity, sometimes making over-stimulating environments feel manageable

The problem? Alcohol doesn't help the Task Positive Network (TPN) turn on—it numbs without directing. It's like turning off all the lights in the house to get some sleep... only to realize you also shut off the heat. You get quiet, but you also lose the systems that keep you functioning.

And more and more, research is showing that alcohol is not just "hard on the liver"—it's a toxin that can damage brain cells, disrupt gut health, raise cancer risk, and worsen anxiety and depression over time. In the short term, it can feel like relief; in the long term, it quietly takes more than it gives.

🍄 Psychedelics: The Reset Button

For some, psychedelics like psilocybin, LSD, or ketamine feel less like an escape and more like a reboot. When your thoughts are looping and your inner world feels stuck, these substances can act like a hard reset on the mental operating system.

In the brain, psychedelics:

o   Disrupt or "dismantle" the Default Mode Network (DMN), interrupting repetitive thought loops
o   Loosen rigid mental patterns, making it easier to see new perspectives
o   Increase cross-talk between brain regions, sometimes

sparking emotional breakthroughs or a deep sense of connection

But these effects are **highly state- and setting-dependent**. The mindset you bring in—and the environment around you—can shape whether the experience feels healing, confusing, or even destabilizing. Without proper support and caution, psychedelics can amplify anxiety, surface difficult emotions too quickly, or impair judgment in ways that lead to unsafe decisions.

They're not an everyday regulation tool, and they're not a shortcut to lasting change. At best, they can open a window to what's possible—but you still have to build the scaffolding to live there. Used carelessly, they're less like a reset button and more like yanking the power cord mid-download: you might clear the glitch, but you could also corrupt the file.

✧

What Medications Get Right

When prescribed and managed well, ADHD meds do what the underground pharmacy has been trying to do—but with safety, precision, and sustainability.

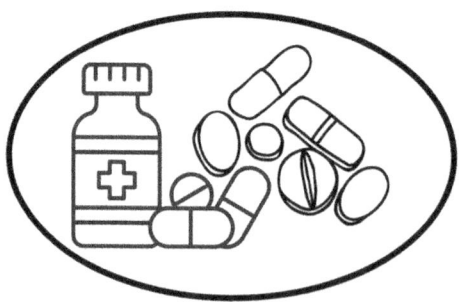

They:

- o Normalize dopamine transmission
- o Support TPN activation and DMN suppression
- o Restore the brain's natural switching rhythm
- o Make it easier to start, sustain, and disengage from tasks

They don't make things effortless—but they remove the friction, so you don't have to rely on crisis, caffeine, or chaos just to get moving.

✸ From Survival to Strategy

If you've been living on coffee, nicotine, adrenaline, or alcohol to get through the day, it doesn't mean you're weak. It might mean you were attempting to solve a real neurobiological problem with the tools you had.

Now you have a map.

And with it, you can build healthier, more reliable ways to shift gears—without having to light your nervous system on fire just to start.

✎ Student Voices—Life in the Underground Pharmacy

"Coffee is my lifeline. I know I overdo it, but without it, I'm a browser with 47 tabs open and no mouse."

—Lena, 21

(Caffeine is Lena's activation threshold booster—quick to help, quick to wear off.)

"I didn't realize why I loved smoking until I quit—and suddenly my brain felt like it had static again."—Devon, 24

(Nicotine was Devon's fast dopamine hit—a mental static clearer, but at a steep cost.)

"Alcohol doesn't make me social—it makes me quiet. Like the voices in my head finally take the night off."—Sofia, 22
  (For Sofia, alcohol is a DMN suppressor, but one that leaves the TPN offline—quiet, but drifting.)

"Mushrooms didn't fix my ADHD, but they showed me a version of myself I'd like to meet more often. Can I find a way to get there without them."—Marcos, 26
  (Psychedelics opened a window—but the work is building a staircase.)

"When I finally got on meds, it felt like someone gave me the manual for a brain I've been hotwiring for years."—Jamie, 20
  (Medication turned trial-and-error survival into strategy.)

As we close this chapter on what makes us neurologically different, we're left with one more puzzle piece: time again—but this time, not just how we experience it, but how much of it we can grasp at once.

⏱ Span of Apprehension: The Other Attention Deficit

Most people think of attention as a spotlight—something you shine on the world.

But cognitive psychology has another definition that's just as important, and often more revealing when it comes to ADHD:

Span of apprehension—how much you can hold in your mind at once while still making sense of it.

Think of it as bandwidth.

Some people can answer emails, field questions from coworkers, keep track of a meeting agenda, and still remember the report deadline. Others can manage two or three before the mental filing cabinet jams. It's not about intelligence—it's about capacity, processing speed, and how quickly you can decide what to handle first.

Everyone has a limit.
The difference is what happens when you hit it.

🎪 The Juggler Metaphor (A Soft Diagnostic)

This is a metaphor I often share with clients and families because it captures something essential—and diagnostic—about ADHD.

Picture yourself juggling three objects. Someone tosses in a fourth.

If you're neurotypical, you probably think, *"Nope, can't do four,"* and instinctively drop one so you can keep the rhythm going. You prioritize, offload, or filter.

But when I ask my ADHD clients the same question, I hear the same answer almost every time:

"They all fall."

For the ADHD brain, hitting capacity isn't just a strain—it's a breaker switch. Once it trips, you don't just drop the new ball. You drop all of them.

📊 What Fills Your Bandwidth?

The answer isn't just "tasks"—it's everything that draws on your mental energy and attention at a given moment: •
Focused thought

- ○ Emotional processing
- ○ Physical sensation
- ○ Stress, anxiety, urgency
- ○ Environmental noise
- ○ Internal dialogue (yes, even that guy)

Every one of these takes up bandwidth. And people with ADHD are often unaware of how full their span is until it's already exceeded.

You might be thinking clearly and feeling fine—but if your emotional bandwidth is already half-occupied by social anxiety, caffeine jitters, or that conversation you had with your mom last night? That fourth "thing" might be the last straw.

✳ When the Bandwidth Breaks

Here's the part that gets missed: when the span of apprehension is exceeded, the collapse doesn't always look like "giving up." It can show up as:

- A panic attack when emotional overload maxes out your system
- A shutdown or dissociation when sensory input overwhelms you
- A freeze response (what some clients call "brain lock") when cognitive load hits critical mass
- A sudden, unexplainable rage burst—not because of the task, but because your brain dropped the thread and couldn't pick it up again

These aren't overreactions. They're what it looks like when the brain's juggling act ends not with a choice, but with a crash.

✳ What This Reveals About ADHD

That moment—when everything collapses—tells us three key things about ADHD:

1. It's not just about attention allocation—it's about overload response.
2. We don't always have a graceful fallback system—no internal buffer kicks in.
3. Recovery is harder when we're flooded, especially

without tools like bookmarks, external scaffolds, or signal-driven resets.

This is why people with ADHD:

- Abandon tasks midstream when overwhelmed
- Forget what they were doing or why
- Panic under pressure, even when stakes are low
- Have difficulty returning to an interrupted task—the "entry point" is lost

That's the executive function system saying: "I lost the thread. I can't get back in."

⊛ The Importance of Monitoring Bandwidth

Because our span of apprehension is so vulnerable to collapse, one of the most important skills people with ADHD can learn is:

Monitor your mental bandwidth—and respect it.
This means:

- Recognizing the early signs of overload (fatigue, irritation, "spinning" thoughts)
- Practicing externalization—lists, notes, timers, whiteboards, mind maps
- Using "bookmarks"—quick cues or signals to help us return to where we left off

This isn't about limitation. It's about preservation—maintaining clarity long enough to complete the loop.

In future chapters, we'll introduce the SDSS—Signal-Driven Support System—which helps students and adults build exactly this kind of scaffolding, customized to their own signal thresholds.

🌱 Looking Ahead: Recovery, Not Perfection

Eventually, this ties directly into something deeper—our ability to recover from overload.

In a later chapter, we'll explore the *Antifragile ADHD Model*—the idea that our brains don't just break under stress. They can grow stronger when we learn how to navigate overload, rebuild trust in our systems, and create pathways for bounce-back.

But it starts here, by acknowledging that span of apprehension is real, measurable, and different in ADHD brains. And by realizing that when the fourth ball hits... we don't need to juggle faster. We need to pause, reset, and take a moment to bookmark it so that we can find our way back.

🌀 Summing Up: From Difference to Design

What if everything we've explored in this chapter—from time blindness and emotional sensitivity to hyperfocus and the span of apprehension—wasn't just a list of challenges, but a map of traits that evolved for a reason?

What if these weren't flaws to be corrected, but clues to an effectively different kind of functioning?

A signal-based brain. A high-salience nervous system. A mind that learns on the edge, connects across dimensions, and sometimes overloads under pressure—not because it's weak, but because it's wired for more.

In the next chapter, we'll follow that trail further. We'll look at how these traits—when named, supported, and understood—can give rise to the kind of thinking the world badly needs: whole-picture thinkers, lateral problem-solvers, emotional translators, social cartographers.

You might even call it a polymath mind.

But for now, let's pause and hold this: difference is not deficit. It's design. And design—when honored—becomes strength.

This chapter has mapped the terrain of how we

differ—neurologically, emotionally, and systemically. The next chapter begins to ask: What does this make possible?

And what if our differences—our sensitivity, urgency, complexity, volatility—are the raw materials of creative intelligence the world is only beginning to understand?

🔬 For Parents, Educators, Clinicians, Coaches, and Curious Minds

Understanding ADHD as a *state-shifting disorder*—rather than simply a problem with focus or attention—changes everything about how we respond to it.

Beneath the surface of missed homework, delayed assignments, meltdowns, or emotional shutdowns are neurological systems struggling to switch modes, manage bandwidth, and recover from overload. These breakdowns are not willful. They're structural. And they're often invisible until they're overwhelming.

Here's what to look for—and how to help:

🧠 1. Difficulty with Mental Mode Switching (DMN ↔ TPN Interference)

What it looks like: A student who can't start tasks, stalls out, or zones out during lessons—even if they know what to do.

What helps: Use clear transitions and "rituals of entry" to activate task mode (e.g., 3-2-1 countdowns, movement breaks, sensory signals like music). For exit, give time and space to decompress—the switch goes both ways.

⚡ 2. Hyperfocus as a Reactive State

What it looks like: A student who loses track of time while working or gaming, misses meals, and gets agitated when interrupted.

What helps: Don't punish hyperfocus—structure it. Use timers, visual alerts, and gentle exit cues. Encourage reflection afterward: "What pulled you in? What helped you stay there? What's the recovery plan?"

◑ 3. Self-Medication as State Regulation

What it looks like: Heavy use of caffeine, nicotine, energy drinks, or risky behaviors to jumpstart motivation.

What helps: Normalize the need for regulation. Discuss what the student is trying to feel when they self-medicate, and then build healthier, signal-based systems to meet that need.

🧩 4. Span of Apprehension Collapse

What it looks like: A student who suddenly shuts down, lashes out, forgets everything, or "goes blank" after juggling too many demands.

What helps: Teach them to monitor their bandwidth in real time. Use mind maps, visual timers, "bookmarks" (e.g., sticky notes or audio memos), and task chunking to preserve cognitive thread. If collapse happens, help them *find the entry point back in*—don't just tell them to try harder.

Span of apprehension is an under-recognized but clinically

significant cognitive trait in ADHD. It intersects with executive function, working memory, and emotional regulation—and its collapse often masquerades as oppositionality, avoidance, or mood disorder.

Clinically, teaching students to track their own bandwidth through tools like journaling, signal mapping, or real-time scaffolds can offer profound improvements in reliability and self-trust.

✳ 5. Emotional Overload and Recovery Lag

What it looks like: Emotional outbursts, intense mood swings, or mysterious resistance to "simple" tasks—often following high-stimulation events.

What helps: Co-regulate first. Support nervous system recovery before expecting performance. Consider using post-event processing tools (body scans, feelings maps, reflection prompts) to rebuild emotional tracking.

✕ 6. Executive Dysfunction as Re-Entry Failure

What it looks like: A student who abandons work mid-task, avoids restarting, or says "I don't even remember what I was doing."

What helps: Focus less on willpower and more on re-entry tools. Use checklists, labels, verbal cues, and even visual placeholders, such as an open notebook or paused video. Reinforce that recovery is a skill, not a sign of failure.

📖 References for Further Reading

o **Anticevic, A., Cole, M. W., Murray, J. D., et al. (2012).** *The role of default network deactivation in cognition and disease. Trends in Cognitive Sciences, 16*(12), 584–592.
Highlights the importance of DMN deactivation during task performance and how disruptions in this pattern, common in ADHD, contribute to cognitive interference and poor task control.

o **Arnsten, A. F. T. (2009).** *The emerging neurobiology of attention deficit hyperactivity disorder: The key role of the prefrontal association cortex. Journal of Pediatrics, 154*(5), I–S43.
Explains how stress, emotion, and under-stimulation impair prefrontal functioning in ADHD, reinforcing the concept of executive breakdown during emotional or cognitive overload.

o **Barkley, R. A. (2012).** *Executive Functions: What They Are, How They Work, and Why They Evolved.* Guilford Press.
Offers a comprehensive model of executive function, including how inhibition, shifting, and emotional regulation are impaired in ADHD—and how this impacts real-world functioning.

o **Brown, T. E. (2013).** *A New Understanding of ADHD in Children and Adults: Executive Function Impairments.* Routledge.
Provides a clinical framework for understanding ADHD as an impairment in activation, focus, effort, emotion, memory, and action—key themes that support the chapter's focus on shifting and regulation.

o **Csikszentmihályi, M. (1990).** *Flow: The Psychology of Optimal Experience.* Harper & Row.
Defines the concept of flow and explains how it differs from ADHD hyperfocus. Flow is skill-aligned and balanced, while hyperfocus is reactive and often unsustainable.

o **Dodson, W. (2019).** *ADHD and Hyperfocus: The Other Side of the Coin.* ADDitude Magazine.
One of the few clinicians to directly contrast hyperfocus with flow, Dodson explains how hyperfocus emerges from urgency and emotional intensity—not the controlled, balanced conditions that define flow. His framing supports the view of hyperfocus as a reactive brain state that lives near the edge of criticality.

o **Furukawa, T. A., et al. (2020).** *Psychiatric comorbidity and self-medication in adult ADHD: A meta-analytic review. Journal of Affective Disorders, 276,* 658–670.
Explores the prevalence of self-medication in adults with ADHD, including use of substances like nicotine, caffeine, and alcohol to manage attention and mood.

o **Menon, V. (2011).** *Large-scale brain networks and psychopathology: A unifying triple network model. Trends in Cognitive Sciences, 15*(10), 483–506.
Introduces a network-based understanding of cognition, including the DMN, TPN, and salience network—a framework that helps explain state-switching difficulties in ADHD.

o **Porges, S. W. (2011).** *The Polyvagal Theory: Neurophysiological Foundations of Emotions, Attachment, Communication, and Self-Regulation.* Norton.
Introduces a model of nervous system state regulation that adds depth to the emotional overload and recovery mechanisms seen in ADHD, including shutdowns and reactivity.

o **Raichle, M. E., et al. (2001).** *A default mode of brain function. Proceedings of the National Academy of Sciences, 98*(2), 676–682.
The landmark study that identified the Default Mode

Network—foundational for understanding ADHD-related inter-ference during task performance.

o **Seli, P., et al. (2015).** *Mind wandering in ADHD: An exami-nation of executive control and the default-mode network. Journal of Attention Disorders, 19*(8), 627–638.
Directly links increased DMN activity during task engagement to the mind-wandering and executive function failures com-mon in ADHD

o **Thomas, J. (2019).** *Thriving at the Edge of Chaos: Making ADHD a Superpower in College and Career.* ADHD College Success Guidance Press.
Introduces the metaphor of thriving at the edge of criticality and reframes ADHD hyperfocus and volatility as edge-state intelligence, with implications for learning and productivity.

o **Yochman, A., Alon-Beery, O., & Parush, S. (2022).** *Sensory processing and its relation to emotional regulation in chil-dren with ADHD. Research in Developmental Disabilities, 124,* 104196.

Demonstrates how sensory modulation differences predict task avoidance and emotional reactivity, supporting the idea that bandwidth overload, not just distractibility, drives behavior.

o **Zentall, S. S. (2005).** *Theory- and evidence-based strate-gies for children with attentional problems. Psychology in the Schools, 42*(8), 821–836.

Offers classroom-tested strategies for managing distractibility, hyperfocus, and self-regulation in ADHD learners, reinforcing practical applications of the chapter's concepts.

Chapter 3

A New Perspective—Why the Way You See ADHD Changes Everything

"The real voyage of discovery consists not in seeking new landscapes, but in having new eyes."
—Marcel Proust

"No problem can be solved from the same level of consciousness that created it."
—Albert Einstein

🧠 Quick Preview: What You'll Learn in This Chapter

o ADHD isn't just what you *do*—it's how you see, sort, and feel the world
o How shifting your lens can change your whole relationship with ADHD
o Why signal detection, emotional intensity, and gear-shifting attention are core to the experience
o How metaphors like "fish in the pond" and "hands of the clock" reveal what most models miss
o How signal-based thinking can turn confusion into clarity—and struggle into strategy

▨ How to Use This Chapter

This chapter is built to shift your perspective—not just to add knowledge, but to change how you *see*. ADHD isn't just a list of symptoms—it's a different relationship to time, attention, emotion, and meaning.

- o 🧠 **For People with ADHD—Students, workers, and curious minds:** This section helps reframe ADHD as a system difference rather than a deficit. It explores how your experiences, strengths, and struggles may come from a different kind of signal logic.
- o 🔖 **For Parents, Educators, Clinicians, and Coaches:** This section offers a framework for understanding ADHD through systems theory, criticality, and the salience network. It shifts away from a "compliance model" and toward adaptive design.
- o ♀ **Key Concepts and Takeaways:** Includes metaphors like the "lens," the "fish in the pond," and the "hands of the clock," along with visual tools and reframing prompts.

> 💡 Read it straight through—or use the visuals and metaphors as thinking tools when supporting ADHD minds.

Introduction: A Shift in Lens Before a Shift in Life

Before we dive into tools, systems, or strategies, we need to talk about something that changes everything else: perspective.

If we bring the wrong lens—if we keep seeing ADHD through the filters of laziness, lack of willpower, or poor time management—we'll keep reaching for tools that miss the mark. We'll chase strategies that don't stick, blame ourselves when they fail, and misread the root of what's actually going on.

But when we change the way we view the problem, everything changes—including the solutions that occur to us.

This chapter is about making that shift.

Whether it's how we define a breakdown, how we frame our own behavior, or how we interpret failure, the perspective we hold shapes everything that follows. It's not just about mindset—it's about possibility. Because perspective determines which options we even notice, and which ones we believe might work.

In the world of ADHD—where struggles are so often misinterpreted as resistance or apathy—the stories we tell ourselves matter. They can reinforce shame or open the door to clarity, compassion, and lasting change.

That's why we'll begin with five powerful metaphors—not just for understanding ADHD, but for shifting the way we engage with it. These aren't just illustrations. They're tools. Tools to help you pause, shift your view, and ask better questions—about your brain, your needs, and what might help in this moment.

For ADHD thinkers, metaphors don't just explain concepts—they offer shortcuts to insight.

Because if we want to support ADHD minds—our own or someone else's—it's essential to learn to see the whole elephant. We must get outside the car, become a pond, and bring a beginner's mind.

That's where real understanding begins—and where all sustainable systems start.

Section 1: Six Blind Men and the Elephant
One person says ADHD is a lack of discipline.

Another blames trauma.

A third swears it's screen addiction, while a fourth insists it's bad parenting.

But what if they're all describing just *one piece* of a much larger picture?

We begin with a classic parable.

In 13th-century India, a fable was told of six blind men who encountered an elephant for the first time. Each man touched a different part of the animal and drew wildly different conclusions:

- One touched the side and said, "An elephant is like a wall."
- Another touched the tusk and said, "No, it is like a spear."
- A third felt the trunk: "Clearly, it's like a snake."
- The fourth touched a leg and said, "It's like a tree."
- The fifth felt the ear and said, "It is like a fan."

- o And the sixth grabbed the tail and said, "An elephant is like a rope."

Each was right in their limited way. However, each was also profoundly wrong in assuming that their partial truth explained what an elephant truly looked like.

This tale is especially relevant when considering how people with ADHD are often viewed. Teachers, clinicians, and even parents often say things like:

- o "He'd do better if he just tried harder."
- o "She could succeed if she just got organized."
- o "He'd be fine if he could just pay attention."

Each of these statements may reflect something real. But each is only one piece of the elephant. And none of them, on their own, reflect the complexity of what's going on.

They lose sight of the whole person and the complexity of the impact of ADHD. They're each grasping at one dimension of the individual's behavior—and mistaking it for the whole elephant.

Only when we can take in the entire view—understanding the interplay of motivation, attention, emotional regulation, executive function, and context—can we truly offer support that is empowering rather than reductionist. ADHD isn't one behavior to fix: it's a complex system of internal experiences, responses to environment, and deeply individual perspectives.

However, when we reduce it to a single issue—"He just can't focus"—we end up solving the wrong problem with the wrong tools.

In school, this narrow lens leads to detention for daydreaming, missed diagnoses for gifted children who zone out in math, and behavior plans that reward compliance but stifle curiosity. A kid who hyperfocuses on building a fantasy world in Minecraft instead of outlining their social studies paper doesn't need punishment—they need translation.

At home, when a teenager forgets to take out the trash for the fifth time, it's easy to call it defiance. But what if it's time blindness, weak working memory, and the existential black hole known as "just a sec"? You can't discipline executive function into existence—though many have tried.

At work, an employee might be seen as unreliable for missing deadlines or switching projects midstream. No one sees the four hours of spiraling self-talk before they even open the file. When you measure output without understanding mental friction, you're only grading the symptom.

And in relationships? Forgetfulness gets mistaken for apathy. Emotional intensity gets read as overreaction. Being late becomes a moral failing, rather than what it usually is: a tragic comedy of misplaced keys, poorly timed shower epiphanies, and one more thing they thought they could squeeze in.

Every time we treat one behavior as the whole elephant, we miss the point—and miss the person. But when we widen the lens, when we see ADHD not as a flaw to fix but a pattern to understand, everything shifts. Compassion becomes possible. So does change.

Section 2: The Hands of the Clock

If the elephant showed us the danger of limited perspective, the clock reminds us that where we stand shapes what we see.

Ask a group: "Which direction do the hands of a clock turn?" Most say, "Clockwise."

But what if you're the clock? Then the hands appear to turn counterclockwise. And if you're perched on top, looking down, they may seem to go up and down.

It's the same clock. But your position changes everything.

This shift in perspective is significant for individuals with ADHD. A teacher might see a student "not trying." A parent might see procrastination. The student might be struggling with task initiation, executive function, or internalized shame—all of which are invisible from the outside.

Perspective isn't just about where you're looking. It's also about where you're standing.

This metaphor also hints at something more profound: Our default setting, as noted by author David Foster Wallace in his commencement speech, "This Is Water," at Kenyon College, is self-referential. We tend to assume that the way we experience the world is universal—that everyone else sees the hands of the clock the same way we do. But they don't.

Developing empathy—especially for neurodiverse

minds—requires an extra step. We must move consciously around the clock. Stand in someone else's shoes. Peer through someone else's lens. Only then do we begin to see the emotional friction, invisible effort, and daily recalibration that ADHD can involve.

Empathy, like perspective, isn't passive. It's an act of intentional imagination.

And for those of us with ADHD, learning to offer that same imaginative grace to ourselves can be just as transformative.

Section 3: Inside and Outside the Car

Now that we've acknowledged how position influences meaning, let's move to an experiential tool—one that helps students practice one of the most essential executive skills ADHD minds often struggle with: **perspective-shifting**.

This isn't just a metaphor. It's a teachable skill—the foundation of **metacognition** or thinking about your own thinking. And for people with ADHD, who often experience intense emotional reactivity and mental clutter, it can be life changing.

I often guide students through a reflection: "Go back to the first time you drove a car. Feel the steering wheel. See the dashboard. Look through the windshield. Notice what you feel in your body. What thoughts run through your mind?"

This immersive exercise brings up strong, first-person memories and emotions—often a mix of excitement, fear, and pressure. Then I shift the frame: "Now imagine you're outside the car—watching yourself preparing to drive. What do you feel and think now? Is this different? The same?"

Most students report a very different experience. From the outside, they're more compassionate, more insightful, and less overwhelmed.

That's perspective-shifting in action.

Here's another example:

Imagine freezing during a class presentation. Inside the car, your mind is racing—*"Everyone's judging me. I sound stupid."* But from outside the car? You see someone who's scared, not failing. You notice how hard they're trying. You want to help them, not punish them.

Learning to move between these two vantage points—between the driver's seat and outside the car—allows students to shift from emotional reactivity to executive reflection. And just like the TPN/DMN network described in Chapter 2, this is a kind of **mental mode-switching**. It allows students to downshift from internal noise and emotional overload, and step into a calmer, more strategic mindset.

Sometimes we need to be in the driver's seat and fully experience the situation. At other times, we need to become the observer—to reduce overwhelm, gain context, and reclaim our perspective.

And when we observe without judgment, we create space to pause—to *bookmark* the moment—so we can return to it later with clearer insight and less shame.

ADHD makes these shifts harder, but not impossible. With tools like this—and a growing awareness of how our brain toggles between different internal states—we can learn to navigate more flexibly.

🐟 Section 4: The Pond and the Fish

Once students can shift between perspective modes, we go deeper—into emotional identity.

When helping young people gain insight into their internal experience—their emotions, thoughts, and conflicting motivations—I often invite them into a simple but powerful metaphor:

Imagine you are a pond.

Still. Deep. Containing everything that moves inside you.

Let that image settle. Then we shift the frame:

Now become one of the fish that swims in your pond.

Each fish represents a part of your emotional experience—a feeling, a voice, a state of mind. As you become each fish, notice how it moves through your body, how it colors your thinking, how it shifts your posture or breath.

o Become the **anger fish**. Swim with it. What does it feel like in your muscles, your jaw, your chest? What's it pushing you toward?

- Let that go and become the **sad fish**. What's the weight in your body? What does it want you to remember or release?
- Try the **curious fish**. How does it move? What does it notice?
- Now the **tired fish**, or the **"I-don't-care" fish**. Where does it live in your body? What's it asking for?

Let each one have their moment—not to take over, but to be seen, heard, and felt.

And then, return.

Become the pond again.

Still. Steady. Watching your fish swim without chasing them. Holding space for them but not being any one of them.

This metaphor offers more than insight—it teaches **emotional posture**. You are not your emotions. You are the one who holds them. You are not the fish—you are the pond.

And when that truth lands, something powerful shifts. There's room to breathe. To notice. To choose.

This approach helps students with ADHD recognize that

their intense emotional states—their frustration, anxiety, excitement, boredom—are not the whole story. They are temporary. They are parts. And they don't have to take the wheel.

Because when you remember that you're the pond?

You can let the fish swim—and still steer your own course.

◯ Student Voice

"When I became the fish, I noticed how I hold anger in my shoulders and stomach. I was clenching without even knowing it. But when I went back to being the pond, I felt... calm. Like I was bigger than the feeling."
—Jamal, 18, gap year student with
ADHD and mood sensitivity

Section 5: Beginner's Mind

There's an old story about a truck that got stuck under a low bridge. No one could figure out how to free it. Engineers gathered with tape measures, blueprints, and growing frustration. Some even considered lifting the bridge, piece by piece.

Then a child watching nearby asked,

"Why don't you just let the air out of the tires?"

That's **Beginner's Mind**—the ability to see the whole, not just the part. It asks simple questions. It bypasses the ruts of expertise and drills into insight. It's not just "thinking outside the box"—it's seeing that the box was optional.

Beginner's Mind means approaching a problem as if you're seeing it for the first time—without assumptions, without ego, and without the weight of what "should" work. And for ADHD students, this can be a hidden superpower.

While others rely on familiar routines, many individuals with ADHD are natural pattern-breakers—not because they want to be difficult, but because their minds are wired to notice what others miss: the outliers, the edge cases, the paths no one else has considered. They don't always follow the map. Sometimes, they redraw it.

Beginner's Mind is what allows ADHD thinkers to see new connections that others may miss. It's also what makes them frustrating to some teachers—they may not remember the formula, but they'll invent their own solution. When nurtured and supported, this mindset becomes a lifelong advantage: the ability to adapt, rethink, and simplify when complexity gets stuck.

But there's a catch: when those insights are dismissed, punished, or misunderstood, students often stop offering them. They learn to mask their creativity behind "the right answer"— or to stop trying at all. Insight dries up when curiosity feels dangerous. **Judgment and shame don't just hurt—they shut the door to fresh thinking.**

In workshops, I invite students to explore Beginner's Mind with simple prompts:

- "If you were solving this for a friend, what would you try first?"
- "What's a playful or ridiculous idea that might actually work?"

o "What's something you'd try if you believed it wasn't too late to start?"

o "What would you do if you weren't afraid of failing?"

The responses are often surprising and brilliant. These questions lower the stakes and open the door to something ADHD brains crave but rarely feel permission to access: **curiosity.**

Beginner's Mind isn't just about solving problems—it's about remembering that insight doesn't always come from the top down. Sometimes it shows up sideways, barefoot, and unexpected.

As you move through the rest of this book, try keeping that spirit close by. What happens when you read not as a critic or a student, but as a curious beginner, open to noticing what others might overlook?

Beginner's mind doesn't mean ignorance. It means presence. It's not about forgetting what you know—it's about loosening the grip of past patterns long enough to see something new.

It's also a powerful emotional reset. When individuals with ADHD feel stuck, judged, or boxed in by
failure, a beginner's mind offers a moment of freedom. It says: You don't have to get it perfect. You just need to begin.

And when we start from wonder—instead of fear—even the stickiest problems begin to move.

🎒 Student Voice

"I used to freeze any time I got behind—like it was too late, so why bother. But beginner's mind helped

me reset. Now I ask myself: 'What if this were day one?' And suddenly, I don't feel stuck. I feel curious."
—Maya, age 21, community college student

Summary: Perspective Is the Tool That Makes the Tools Work

You've just explored five metaphors—five different ways of seeing.

- The **Elephant** showed us how easy it is to mistake one part of ADHD for the whole.
- The **Clock** revealed that where we stand—physically, emotionally, relationally—shapes what we see.
- The **Car** taught us how shifting between first-person and observer mode changes how we process experience.
- The **Pond and the Fish** offered a way to experience emotions without becoming them.
- And **Beginner's Mind** reminded us that innovation often begins where assumptions end.

Each of these is more than a parable—it's a shift. A move away from automatic thinking and toward intentional seeing.

And for those with ADHD, that shift matters.

Because most tools, systems, strategies, and structures only work if you're using them from the *right state of mind—* and the *right point of view.*

You can't organize what you haven't understood.

You can't build support systems around a self you haven't met.

And you can't stay motivated if the only story you've heard about yourself is that you're broken.

That's why this chapter matters.

Perspective is what allows us to personalize everything that follows—to recognize the tools that fit, to name the signals that move us, and to reclaim agency in the face of overwhelm, shame, or confusion.

Now that you have those lenses in hand, we can move forward—

Not just with tools, but with valuable insights.

Not just with strategies, but with self-understanding.

Not just trying harder, but trying differently.

Because the path ahead isn't one-size-fits-all.

It's a path designed around *you*.

🎒 Try This: A Quick Perspective Shift

Take 5 minutes and try one of the following. Pick whichever speaks to you:

🔁 The Clock Exercise

Think about a moment this week when something felt confusing, frustrating, or unfair.

Now ask:

"What might this moment have looked like from someone else's angle—a teacher, a friend, even me on a different day?"

You don't have to *agree* with their view—just try it on. What do you notice?

🐠 The Pond and the Fish

Pause. Name the fish you're swimming with right now—maybe it's stress-fish, tired-fish, or not-good-enough-fish.

Now breathe.

Become the pond again.

What changes?

🧠 Beginner's Mind

Pick a problem that's been bugging you. Big or small.

Ask yourself:

"If I didn't *already know* how this was supposed to go, what would I try first?"

Or even:

"If I were helping a friend, what would I say?"

Sometimes your wisest answers come when you stop trying to be right, and start being curious.

✏️ For Parents, Educators, Clinicians, Coaches, and Curious Minds

Why Perspective Is Foundational to Effective ADHD Support

Perspective work isn't a soft skill. It's a prerequisite for successful intervention.

Too often, we view ADHD through the narrow lens of observable behavior—missed assignments, impulsive comments, disorganization, and resistance to structure—and then reach for behavioral solutions that never quite take hold.

What gets missed is the inner landscape:

- What state was the student in when they tried to start that task?
- How do they *interpret* a late grade, a failed attempt, a blank page?
- What emotions or signals were they managing beneath the surface?

This chapter's metaphors—the Elephant, the Clock, the Car, the Pond, and Beginner's Mind—offer more than insight. They provide **shared vocabulary** for reframing what we see in our students and clients. They allow adults and learners to speak the same language when unpacking breakdowns and designing support.

Clinical and educational implications:

- **Perspective-taking** builds executive function by fostering metacognition—the ability to think about one's thinking.
- **Emotional distancing tools** like the pond-and-fish metaphor reduce anxiety and shame spirals and allow students to stay in problem-solving mode.
- **Beginner's mind** invites collaboration and student-led innovation in designing accommodations, supports, or workarounds.
- **Observer mode** (inside vs. outside the car) builds resilience by helping students reflect without over-identifying with setbacks.

For many students, this is the first time they've been offered *meaning-making* rather than moral judgment.

And for professionals, perspective tools offer a way to step outside the urgency of behavior management and begin building trust, collaboration, and insight—the foundation for sustainable change.

📖 References for Further Reading

- **Barkley, R. A. (2012).** *Executive Functions: What They Are, How They Work, and Why They Evolved.* Guilford Press. Outlines how executive function develops and breaks down, and how perspective-taking and metacognition are critical for self-regulation in ADHD.

o **Brown, T. E. (2013).** *A New Understanding of ADHD in Children and Adults: Executive Function Impairments.* Routledge.
Explores ADHD not as an attention disorder but as a broader challenge of activation, emotion, and insight—all of which are reframed through the metaphors in this chapter.

o **Dweck, C. S. (2006).** *Mindset: The New Psychology of Success.* Random House.
Presents the growth vs. fixed mindset model—a crucial perspective shift for individuals with ADHD and those who support them. Aligns strongly with the "Beginner's Mind" metaphor.

o **Gilbert, P., & Choden. (2013).** *Mindful Compassion: How the Science of Compassion Can Help You Understand Your Emotions, Live in the Present, and Connect Deeply with Others.* New Harbinger.
Blends neuroscience with mindfulness-based techniques to help individuals develop self-compassion and nonjudgmental awareness, foundational to the pond-and-fish exercise.

o **Kross, E., & Ayduk, O. (2011).** *Making meaning out of negative experiences by self-distancing. Current Directions in Psychological Science, 20*(3), 187–191.
Presents research showing how adopting an observer's perspective helps people process emotions more effectively and reduces rumination, directly relevant to the "outside the car" reflection.

o **Siegel, D. J. (2010).** *The Mindful Therapist: A Clinician's Guide to Mindsight and Neural Integration.* W. W. Norton & Company. Introduces the concept of mindsight—the ability to observe one's inner world with clarity and compassion. This model aligns with multiple metaphors in the chapter, especially the pond.

✺ Part II: Diagnosing Executive Function—From the Elephant to Execution

Diagnosing Executive Function – From the Elephant to Execution

A Guide to Understanding ADHD Breakdowns Before Reaching for Solutions

In the last chapter, we explored how perspective—the angle from which we view a challenge—can profoundly shape what we understand about it.

Now, we're shifting from understanding **ADHD identity** to decoding **ADHD execution**. What moves us, what stops us, and how we can work with our system—not against it.

This is the territory of **executive function**—the brain's system for organizing behavior over time. It governs the ability to start tasks, sustain attention, remember goals, manage time, regulate emotions, shift between activities, and follow through on plans.

People with ADHD struggle not because they lack intelligence or insight—but because executive function breaks down in unpredictable ways. The plan makes sense in your head, but your brain can't seem to carry it out. You know what you want, but can't make yourself get started. You start strong and then stall out halfway through. Sound familiar?

We call this the **execution gap**—the frustrating space between intention and action. And it's one of the most misunderstood aspects of ADHD. Because it's invisible. It doesn't look like hard work or exhaustion. It looks like avoidance, laziness, or apathy—to others, and sometimes even to ourselves.

That's why this section of the book is so important. It introduces a practical, diagnostic way to **sort through executive function challenges** using a simple but powerful framework.

Let's borrow a trick from the FBI.

🕵 The MMO Framework: Method, Motive, Opportunity

In criminal profiling, investigators often use a triad to understand behavior:

Method, Motive, and Opportunity.

To solve a case, they ask three questions:

o   Did the person **know how** to do it? (Method)
o   Did they have a **reason** to act? (Motive)
o   Did they have the **chance** and the right conditions? (Opportunity)

Surprisingly, this same lens helps us understand ADHD execution problems.

Because ADHD is not just a disorder of attention—it's a disorder of **action**. Of follow-through. Of momentum. And when someone with ADHD struggles to take action, it's not because they're lazy, broken, or undisciplined. It's usually because one of these three components is missing or mismatched.

Let's break it down:

🛠 Method: Do you know how to do the thing?

This includes both **knowledge and process**. A student might be told to study for a test—but do they know how to study in a way that works for their brain? A client might be told to break down a project into steps—but can they actually do that without feeling overwhelmed or confused?

Many executive function breakdowns happen here—not because the person isn't capable, but because no one ever taught them *how* in a way their brain could actually use.

💧 Motive: Do you feel moved to act?

This is about **ignition**—not just any reason, but the right kind of reason.

People with ADHD often don't respond well to external expectations or delayed rewards. Motivation must be **felt**, not forced. It often comes from signals: meaning, urgency, emotion, novelty, or personal interest. Without that inner fire, even the best method won't start the engine.

This is where emotional logic kicks in: "I can't do it unless I feel it."

And that feeling—the **signal**—is the heartbeat of ADHD motivation.

Opportunity: Do your surroundings support success?

Even if you know what to do and want to do it, you still need the **right conditions**.

That means time, space, tools, structure, and support. It means the task is visible, the steps are clear, and the distractions are managed. ADHD minds are highly sensitive to **context**—and without the right opportunity, execution stalls.

Concrete supports that create opportunity include:

- A quiet place to work or study
- Accommodations like extended time or flexible deadlines
- A formal diagnosis that opens access to services
- The right medication, if part of your plan
- Support from coaches, mentors, or therapists
- Tools that make tasks visible and manageable

Pulling It Together: Diagnosing the Real Breakdown

In the chapters ahead, you'll find powerful tools—from motivational frameworks to attention strategies to signal-based scheduling systems.

But before we start handing you tools, we want to make sure you know **how to choose the right one**. The Method–Motive–Opportunity (MMO) heuristic is your compass.

A few quick examples:

- o A schedule offers **opportunity** (when and where), but without motive, it's just ink on a calendar.
- o A motivational quote might spark **motive**—but without method, that energy goes nowhere.
- o A skill-building video provides **method**—but if your environment is chaotic, there's no opportunity to apply it.

So, whenever something isn't working, ask yourself:

? *What am I missing here?*
Is this a problem of **method**, **motive**, or **opportunity**?

While the MMO framework helps us decode any executive function breakdown, this section focuses most deeply on the **Motive** layer—what sparks the engine and keeps it running.

Because for most ADHD learners, the real struggle isn't knowing what to do. It's **feeling moved to do it**—and building systems that work with that kind of motivation, not against it.

This section of the book—beginning with **Signal Mapping**—is about learning to work *with* your unique ADHD operating system.

We'll help you recognize your signals, build your systems around what moves you, and finally close the execution gap that so many students (and adults) with ADHD struggle to cross.

Let's open the toolbox.

Chapter 4

Starting with Why

Why Purpose Is More Than Motivation— It's Your ADHD Ignition Switch

"ADHD isn't a failure of discipline—it's a feedback system waiting for a signal. And nothing signals the brain like purpose."
—Jon Thomas

🔍 What You'll Get From This Chapter

- Why ADHD motivation fizzles without a clear, personal "why"
- How identity-based goals supercharge focus, memory, and follow-through
- Why "shoulds" fall flat—and what actually sparks action
- How to find your "crystal"—the values you can't afford to drop
- How to fuel motivation by asking sharper questions about meaning and self

📑 How to Use This Chapter

This chapter is designed with *three perspectives in mind.* You don't have to read it all at once—and you're free to skip to what's most relevant for you.

- o 🧠 **For People with ADHD**—Students, workers, and curious minds: This section shares real stories, strategies, and internal language that reconnects purpose to action.
- o ✏️ **For Parents, Educators, Clinicians, and Coaches**— If you support someone with ADHD, this section offers research-backed tools for uncovering and honoring what truly motivates them.
- o 💡 **Key Concepts and Takeaways**—Throughout the chapter, you'll find metaphors (like the Crystal–Steel–Plastic model), reflection prompts, and practical examples to guide real-world application.

> 💡 *You can read this chapter straight through—or use it like a compass, returning to the parts that point you toward what matters most.*

Introduction

If you've ever struggled to get started on something—not because you're lazy or incapable, but because your brain just didn't care—you're not alone. And you're not broken.

For a lot of us with ADHD, the hardest part isn't the work itself. It's the why. The reason to begin. The sense that what we're doing matters. Without that inner spark, tasks feel meaningless. Deadlines feel hollow. And even the most important goals can fall apart under the weight of... nothing.

That's not defiance. It's design. Your brain is wired to move when it *feels* the reason, not just when someone says you "should." And that's what this chapter is about. It's not just about motivation—it's about purpose and how finding your own *why* can change everything.

Long before Simon Sinek made "Start with Why" a TED Talk sensation, ADHD minds were already wired that way. If there's no internal signal of meaning, no connection to who we are or what we value, the brain doesn't engage. It doesn't drift because it's lazy—it drifts because the signal hasn't landed.

✧

For People with ADHD—Students, Workers, and Curious Minds

Purpose as a Neurochemical Event

You've probably heard that ADHD has something to do with dopamine, the brain chemical linked to reward and motivation. But here's the thing: it's not just about chasing rewards. It's about whether your brain feels that something *matters*. That sense of relevance? That's what turns the lights on.

When you know *why* you're doing something—and it means something to you—your brain starts firing on all cylinders. Memory works better. Focus gets easier. Motivation clicks in. And if that "why" connects to something personal, something *real*? That's when everything starts to move.

That's why we're going to talk about Signal Mapping later in the book. Because for most of us with ADHD, motivation doesn't come from pressure—it comes from *signals*. And the most powerful signals don't come from to-do lists or grades—they come from purpose. From identity. From the kind of meaning that makes you want to show up, even on the hard days.

✧

The Empty Fuel Tank of "Should"

Now let's talk about what *doesn't* work—the "shoulds."

You should do this. You should finish that. It's due Friday. It counts for your grade.

For some students, that stuff lights a fire. But for a lot of us with ADHD? It just... doesn't. In fact, it often backfires.

Why? Because there's no *real* signal behind it. "Do it because it's due" isn't the same as "Do it because it means something to me." Deadlines might kick in a wave of panic the night before—but that's not the same thing as being *engaged*.

A lot of us with ADHD will tell you: if we don't know why we're doing something, it's like the brain just refuses to turn on. It's not because we don't care. It's not about attitude. It's about wiring. If the signal isn't there, the system doesn't start. Period.

Identity-Driven Motivation

One of the most significant shifts you can make as an ADHD learner is this:

Don't just think about *what* you're doing.

Think about *who you're becoming* by doing it.

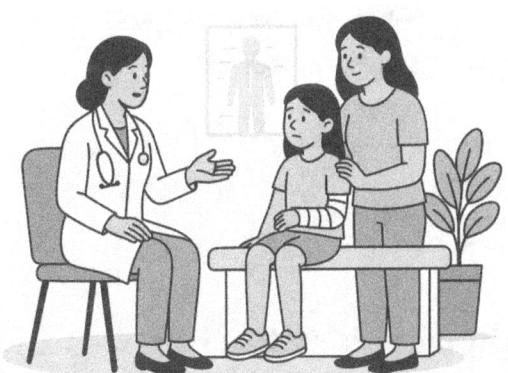

For example, instead of thinking, "I need to pass biology," imagine saying, "I want to understand how the body works, because I want to help people one day." That's not about the grade. That's about *you*.

That kind of thinking is what we refer to as **identity-driven motivation**. When your goals align with who you are—your story, your values, and your future—it creates a much stronger signal. Suddenly, the work isn't just about finishing something. It's about *becoming someone.*

Coaching the Why

Here's the truth: if your "why" is shallow—like "because I'm supposed to"—it's tough to stay with the work.

But when you find a deeper why, the whole game changes.

That's when your brain starts to *care.*

Try asking yourself questions like:

- What first made me care about this?
- Who do I want to help with what I'm learning?
- What makes this feel like *my* goal, not someone else's?

You don't need a perfect planner or a bulletproof to-do list.

You need a signal—something tangible to hold onto.

When the *why* is strong, your brain can begin to build the *how.*

But if there's no why? No signal? Then all the strategies in the world won't make it stick.

The Emotional Logic of Action

If you've ever thought, "I just can't *start,*" you're not alone.

That's emotional logic—a kind of inner signal that says, "I have to *feel* this before I can *do* it."

It's not laziness. It's just how some of our brains work.

The trick is learning how to create that feeling intentionally.

Not by faking urgency or waiting for a last-minute panic—but by connecting to something real. When the reason is strong enough, the energy follows.

So next time you catch yourself saying, "I just can't get going," try this:

Don't force it—*revisit your why.*

That might be precisely what your brain is waiting for.

What Moves You

The real question isn't "What do I want?"

It's "What *moves* me?"

That's the signal that matters.

And that signal can change over time—so don't be afraid to keep checking in.

Your purpose can evolve as *you* do.

This is especially important during college or early adulthood—when you're figuring out who you are, what you stand for, and what kind of life you want to build.

Your purpose doesn't have to be a grand plan.

It just needs to be *a compass.*

Something to guide you when everything else feels foggy.

From Why to What Matters Most: The Crystal Concept

Now that you have a better sense of your why, let's discuss how to *keep it close.*

Purpose can't just float around in the background—it must show up where you live:

In your room, your planner, your playlists, your notes.
Somewhere your brain can *see* it.

One of the metaphors we use is the **Crystal, Steel, and Plastic** model.

Think of your life like juggling a bunch of balls.
Some are plastic—you can drop them, and they'll bounce.
Some are steel—they'll dent, but they survive.
But some are *crystal*—drop them, and they'll break.

Your "why"? That's usually crystal. That's the part you don't want to lose.

Keeping your crystal visible helps your brain know what's important.
It catches your attention: *Hey—this matters.*
This isn't just another assignment—this is *me* in motion.

So, here's the question: What's crystal for *you?*
What's so important to your story that it should never get lost in the mess?
Once you know that it becomes a whole lot easier to stay steady—even when things get chaotic.

Informing the Crystal

And what's underneath your crystal?
Your values.
What matters to you, not just emotionally, but at your core.

That's where values sorting comes in. (Yep—we're going to help you figure that out.)

Your values are like the GPS settings in your brain.

They shape what you care about, what gets your attention, and what you stand by even when no one's looking.

For an ADHD brain, *making your values visible* helps your attention system tune in to what truly matters.

Later in the book, we'll walk you through a simple values sort to help you find your top five.

These are your non-negotiables—the stuff that helps you make decisions, stay focused, and come back to yourself when you feel lost.

And when you know your values?

That's how you *spot the crystal.*

That's how you start designing a life that moves with your brain, instead of against it.

Chapter Reflection
Try this exercise:
Think of a task you've been avoiding.
Now ask yourself:

1. Why does this matter to me?
2. What would change when I completed it?
3. Who might benefit from me doing this well, including my future self?
4. Is this task connected to a crystal in my life?

If your answer feels shallow or forced, dig deeper.

Find the signal.

The real *why* is in there, and once you find it, the task might just start pulling you instead of pushing back.

For Parents, Educators, Clinicians, Coaches and Curious Readers

What Moves You—And How to Help Students Name It

The question is rarely "What does this student want?" It's "What moves them?"

Helping students identify meaningful internal motivators—not just external obligations—is the foundation of identity-driven coaching. And for ADHD learners, this isn't just preferable. It's necessary.

The ADHD brain often fails to respond to abstract rewards or social expectations. However, it can lock in when the task aligns with purpose, especially when that purpose reflects a personal story, a future vision, or a core value.

Interventions grounded in this lens often begin not with schedules, but with values clarification, future self-visualization, and strengths-based storytelling. Tools such as values sort cards, Crystal–Steel–Plastic metaphors, and Signal Mapping are designed to make these internal drivers visible.

When a student has a name for their *why,* the *how* often becomes clear.

This chapter's focus on identity-driven motivation draws from the intersection of:

- o   Self-determination theory (Deci & Ryan)
- o   Purpose research in adolescence and emerging adulthood (Damon, Oyserman)
- o   The salience network and meaning-based attention models (Menon)

o   Neurochemical underpinnings of relevance and action readiness (Volkow, Damasio)

📑 References for Further Reading

Bechara, A., Damasio, H., & Damasio, A. R. (2000). Emotion, decision making and the orbitofrontal cortex. *Cerebral Cortex,* *10*(3), 295–307.
➤ A foundational neuroscience paper exploring how emotions and decision-making are linked, relevant to understanding why emotion-based relevance is critical for ADHD action readiness.

Menon, V. (2011). Large-scale brain networks and psychopathology: A unifying triple network model. *Trends in Cognitive Sciences, 15*(10), 483–506.
➤ Introduces the salience network—a key attentional switching system that underlies why personally meaningful stimuli trigger ADHD engagement more reliably than abstract rewards.

Oyserman, D., & Destin, M. (2010). Identity-based motivation: Implications for intervention. *The Counseling Psychologist, 38*(7), 1001–1043.
➤ Offers a research-grounded view of how motivation is strengthened when tied to identity, directly supporting the concept of purpose-driven academic strategies.

Sinek, S. (2009). *Start with Why: How Great Leaders Inspire Everyone to Take Action*. Portfolio.
➤ Though not ADHD-specific, this popular book outlines the power of leading with purpose—a useful parallel for coaching students to begin with meaning rather than just tasks.

Volkow, N. D., Wang, G. J., Kollins, S. H., et al. (2009). Evaluating dopamine reward pathway in ADHD: Clinical implications. *JAMA, 302*(10), 1084–1091.
➤ Examines the neurochemical basis of motivation and reward in ADHD, helping explain why "meaning" acts as a signal more than a schedule for many ADHD brains.

Chapter 5

Mapping Your Signals—A User's Guide to the ADHD Operating System

*"The world is full of signals. We just
have to learn how to listen."*
—Henry David Thoreau

"There is a voice that doesn't use words. Listen."
—Rumi

🔍 What You'll Get From This Chapter:

- What a *signal* is—and why it matters more than motivation alone
- The difference between cues, signals, amplifiers, and noise
- How ADHD motivation actually works (and why it often doesn't)
- How to start noticing your personal signal patterns in daily life
- How to build a system that listens back—not just pushes forward

▨ How to Use This Chapter

This chapter is designed with *three perspectives in mind*. You don't have to read it all at once—and you're free to skip to what's most relevant for you.

- ○ 🧠 **For People with ADHD**—Students, workers, and curious minds: This section shares lived experiences, motivational strategies, and signal-based tools written from the inside out.
- ○ ✎ **For Parents, Educators, Clinicians, and Coaches**— If you support someone with ADHD, this section offers research-aligned insight and practical guidance based on neuroscience and lived experience.
- ○ ♀ **Key Concepts and Takeaways**—Throughout the chapter, you'll find reference charts, exercises, and reflection tools to revisit or print.

> 💡 *Feel free to read straight through—or dip in and out, using each section like a different window into the same system.*

🧠 For People with ADHD—Students, Workers, and Curious Minds

🔄 Rethinking the Operating Manual

Most ADHD strategies start with structure. Reminders. Alarms. Color-coded calendars. Reward charts. Habit stacks.

All of which are great—*if* your brain is already ready to go.

But if you've lived with ADHD, you know that most of the time... it's not.

You don't need another to-do list.

You need a reason to move—a spark, a pull, a thread to follow. Something that cuts through the fog and says: **now**.

That's what we call a **signal**.

If you've ever noticed that a certain playlist makes you clean the house, or a song lyric pushes you to start writing, you already understand this:
some signals **bypass resistance entirely**.

Music moves us before we understand why.
It bypasses logic and lands directly in the body.
A single chord progression can shift our mood.
A rhythm can get us up and moving when no to-do list could.
A melody can carry motivation where words fail.

For people with ADHD, this is more than poetic—it's **practical**.
We are not primarily moved by obligation or sequence.
We are moved by signals: emotional resonance, sensory cues, meaningful patterns.

And music is one of the purest forms of this.

It isn't time based.
It isn't effort based.
It's **signal based.**

🎧 Sound as Signal—Why Music Works So Well

Music engages multiple brain systems at once—auditory processing, emotional centers, memory recall, and even motor planning.

Unlike a calendar ding (which relies on frontal-lobe prioritization), music cuts straight to the **limbic system**—the part of the brain responsible for emotion, motivation, and movement.

In other words:
Music doesn't ask for permission—it moves you.

For many ADHD brains, this makes music the perfect **amplifier**. It turns a faint inner impulse into something full-bodied.

If you've ever cleaned your room with a speaker blasting, studied better to the hum of ambient sound, or written a paper to the same song on repeat, you've already discovered this:

Music is a signal. And sometimes, it's the only one loud enough to break through.

This chapter will help you find those signals, name them, and use them with intention.

You're not lazy. You're not broken.
You're just tuned differently.

And like any good song, the key is to find the **signal that moves you.**

Signals aren't the same as cues.
Cues are external: a ding, a deadline, a Post-it note on your bathroom mirror. Signals are internal: a shift in energy, emotion, urgency, or meaning that actually gets you moving.

Cues are what the world gives you. Signals are what your body and mind give back—if you're listening.

And here's the twist: ADHD doesn't ignore signals—it's often hyper-attuned to them. It's just not tuned into the ones most systems expect.

That's why so many well-intentioned tools fall flat. They assume if you just remind someone enough, they'll follow through. But ADHD brains don't run on reminders. They run on activation—and activation starts with a signal that feels real.

In other words, your brain isn't disobedient. It's responsive. It just responds to a different kind of language—one made of interest, emotion, urgency, or meaning. And if that language isn't being spoken? The system stays offline.

This isn't a failure of discipline. It's a mismatch in translation. Your brain isn't broken. The manual you were handed just wasn't written for the way you're wired.

In the last section, we introduced the Method–Motive–Opportunity model as a way to diagnose why things break down. This chapter starts where breakdowns often begin—with motive. And motive begins with signal. That's what we're about to explore.

📖 Signal, Cue, Motivation, Action— What's the Difference?

If you're going to build a system that actually works for your brain, you need to know what you're working with.

One of the biggest mistakes people make with ADHD—including well-meaning professionals—is confusing cues, signals, motivation, and action as if they're all part of the same thing. They're not.

Let's break it all down:

◇ **Cue**

What it is: An external reminder or trigger.

What it does: Gets your attention.

Think: alarm, calendar, Post-it, person tapping you on the shoulder.

Cues are useful, but they only work if your system is already open to responding. For most ADHD brains, cues alone often fall flat—especially if there's no emotional engagement, urgency, or reward on the other side.

◇ **Signal**

What it is: An internal shift—a spark, urge, emotion, or sense of meaning.

What it does: Moves you toward action.

Signals are how your brain actually gets going. It might be a surge of interest, a rise in adrenaline, a flash of insight, or even a burst of frustration.

Signals don't ask politely. They pull you. They bypass logic and speak in the language of urgency, relevance, or emotion. They're not always loud—but they're personal. And for ADHD, they're everything.

◇ **Motivation**

What it is: The state of being ready to act.

What it does: Translates signal into intention.

Motivation is what happens when the signal gets through clearly—when you feel ready to do something, not just supposed to. It's the tipping point between noticing and doing.

For ADHD, motivation is less like a fuel tank and more like a match—it flares when the right conditions strike.

◇ **Action**

What it is: The thing you actually do.

What it does: Turns intention into behavior.

This is what the world sees. But behind every action is a chain:

If something breaks earlier in the chain, action doesn't happen—no matter how many reminders you've set.

Signal Mapping helps you see the whole picture—not just the foot (cue), the tail (reminder), or the tusk (pressure), but the entire system. It gives you a map of how your ADHD brain actually works—so you can work with it instead of against it.

And it starts by asking the simplest question:

What moves me?

⚡ A Quick Word About Amplifiers— and the Bigger Picture

Some signals are obvious. Others? Not so much. That's where amplifiers come in.

Amplifiers are forces that make a weak signal louder— or sometimes distort a helpful one. Urgency, emotion, risk, novelty, even pressure—these can all amplify the system in different ways.

If a cue doesn't move you, and a signal feels fuzzy, the right amplifier can make all the difference.

And if you're wondering how all of this fits together—cue, signal, motivation, action—there's a broader pattern behind the scenes.

Let's come back to Method, Motive, and Opportunity:

- o **Method** is how to do something—the plan, process, or strategy.
- o **Motive** is why you'd do it—the signal that moves you, the meaning that matters.
- o **Opportunity** is the window—the space, time, tools, or cue that makes it possible.

Think of it this way:

- o A cue creates **opportunity**—it tells you something needs to happen.
- o A signal gives you **motive**—it's the internal pull to act.
- o A method gives you the **how**—the steps or strategy to get it done.

When all three line up, action becomes possible—even effort-less. When one is missing? That's when things fall apart.

You don't need more discipline.

You need better alignment.

Here's another way this all fits together—a useful ADHD-specific sequence:

Let's break that down briefly:

- o **Signal**—A moment of spark or inner resonance
- o **Amplifier**—Something that intensifies or clarifies that signal
- o **Reinforced Signal**—A stronger internal "go" based on that amplified input

- o **Motivation**—The felt readiness to act
- o **Action**—The behavior that follows

Signals don't always start out strong. But when they're noticed—and amplified—they gain clarity. That's what creates motivation. And that's what leads to action.

Case Example— *Riding the Success Roller Coaster*

One of my clients is a high-ticket salesperson. Every time he closes a deal, it's an emotional high water mark event. His body and mind are in overdrive. But just as predictably, he then experiences a crash. A missed sale, or even just a quiet stretch without activity, plunges him into a low that feels equally intense.

Over time, he began to anticipate the low whenever he hit a high —almost bracing himself for the crash. This left him exhausted and suspicious of his own success.

Through the lens of **Signal Mapping**, we reframed the experience. Instead of seeing the "low" as failure or weakness, we named it as a *signal* —the natural drop after an intense burst. Just as your muscles feel shaky after a sprint, your nervous system feels depleted after a surge of reward.

But there was another factor: **amplifiers.** The way he thought about sales turned the volume up on both ends of the curve. A single success wasn't just a win—it became proof of worth. A single miss wasn't just a setback—it became catastrophe. These amplifiers magnified the natural signals, making the roller coaster steeper and harder to manage.

For him, the work became not just about riding the signals, but about **dialing down the amplifiers** and managing the signals on both ends of the curve:

- o **During the high**: Celebrate the rush, but ground yourself. Don't let "I'm unstoppable" amplify into overcommitment.
- o **As the drop arrives**: Reframe it as recovery, not failure. Don't let "I'm doomed" amplify into despair. Journal, walk in nature, connect with purpose.
- o **In the low**: Ask, "What is this state giving me?" Often, it was space to rest, reflect, and refocus.

This pattern illustrates a broader truth: **people with ADHD often experience emotional intensity that mimics bipolar swings, but doesn't meet the criteria for bipolar disorder.** It's part of the signal system being turned up too high. Mapping and managing signals—while noticing what amplifies them—can turn the roller coaster into a cycle of growth.

 Takeaway: *How to Ride the Roller Coaster*

- o **Name the pattern**: Highs and lows are signals, not failures.
- o **Dial down the amplifiers**: Notice when thoughts or meanings are intensifying the swing.
- o **Ground the highs**: Celebrate wins without overcommitting in the rush.
- o **Reframe the lows**: Treat them as recovery periods, not collapses.

- ○ **Use the drop**: Journal, walk, reflect—the low has purpose.

⚠ Common Signal Pitfalls—Why We Miss What Moves Us

Even once you start noticing signals, it's easy to misread them—or miss them entirely. Here are a few common ways that signals get scrambled, distorted, or ignored in the ADHD brain:

1. **🚨 False Urgency**
   That rush of panic? That flood of adrenaline? It might feel like a signal—but it's often a last-ditch amplifier, not true motivation.
   Try this: Ask, "What would this look like if I caught the signal earlier—before the fire drill started?"

2. **🔮 Emotional Echoes**
   Sometimes we confuse emotional noise (like anxiety or shame) with a valid internal signal.
   Pause and ask: Is this signal coming from within me... or from a story I'm afraid of?

3. **🔁 Looping on One Signal Type**
   We all have go-to activation styles. But when you over-rely on just one, it can lead to burnout or boredom.
   Upgrade the map: What other signal types could work for you—if you started noticing them?

4. **✒ Mistaking Cues for Signals**
   Just because something shows up on your calendar doesn't mean it has motivational weight.
   Ask: What would it take to feel like starting this task—not just know I'm supposed to?

5. 🔕 **Missing the Quiet Signals**
    Not every signal comes with a fire alarm. Some are soft: a twinge of curiosity, a flicker of inspiration, a moment of wanting to help.
    Tip: Keep a notepad or voice memo app handy. When a small idea sparks... honor it.

✧

Case Study: Tommy Cleans His Room—A Signal Mapping Breakdown

> *"I get messages from the universe sometimes*
> *that clearly motivate me. But if someone*
> *tells me what to do, it all goes fuzzy."*
> **—Tommy, 18, on ADHD, autonomy, and motivation**

Tommy is an expressive, self-aware young man with ADHD who's learning to decode how motivation works for him. Like many students with ADHD, he struggles with follow-through on tasks that don't feel urgent or emotionally relevant—especially when they're externally assigned.

One of Tommy's long-standing challenges is keeping his room clean. But when we broke it down using Signal Mapping, we found a surprisingly rich and insightful pattern that reveals exactly how ADHD motivation gets activated, distorted, and rerouted.

Tommy's SASMA Breakdown

SASMA Step	Real-Life Example
Cue	He can't find something because it's buried in the clutter on his floor.
Signal	He blurts out, "Oh no, it's really bad." This spontaneous reaction is the true internal signal.
Amplifier (Positive)	When Tommy listens to his own signal, he starts by moving his speakers into the room and turning on music. This becomes a voluntary amplifier—it transforms cleaning from a chore into a personally meaningful act.
Amplifier (Distorted)	If a parent steps in, it scrambles the signal. External pressure short-circuits his process. He's "uneasy in the harness"—deeply motivated by freedom and autonomy.
Motivation (Plan A)	In ideal moments, Tommy reclaims the signal as his own. He's moved by a desire to reset his energy and space. This is values-aligned motivation.
Motivation (Plan B)	Sometimes he lies to his dad—says he's already cleaned the room. Fear of being discovered creates an urgency loop. He cleans in a panic, driven by fear-based motivation.
Action	Either way, the room gets cleaned. But in the second version, the act feels reactive and disconnected from pride or ownership.

Rewiring the Map—What Could Help Tommy?

Problem	Reframe or Intervention
Signal distortion by external pressure	Give Tommy space to respond to his own signal. Invite, don't command. Ask: "Want to cue up your reset playlist?"
Overreliance on urgency/fear-based triggers	Help him notice when he's creating panic just to get started. Ask: "What would it feel like to start without lying to protect your space?"
Motivation doesn't feel values-aligned	Reconnect to his freedom value: "Cleaning is something I choose—a way to make space for music, ideas, and breathing room."
No safe amplifier to activate positive signal	Lean into his music ritual. Encourage him to treat speakers + playlist as a signal amplifier. Add a visual cue: "When the speakers go in, I'm in motion."

⊛ Takeaway for Readers

Tommy's story shows how ADHD motivation isn't random—it's patterned.

When we decode the sequence—**Cue → Signal → Amplifier → Motivation → Action**—we see opportunities to redesign it.

He doesn't need better willpower.

He needs better signal clarity, values-based amplifiers, and non-threatening commitment tools that preserve autonomy.

> ### 🔛 Sidebar: From Spark to System—10 ADHD Signal Types
>
> Use this reference to identify what kinds of signals most often activate you:

Signal Type	Example Activation Triggers
Urgency	Deadline, timer, last-minute crunch
Novelty	New topic, unexpected twist, surprise task
Emotion	Anger, joy, guilt, care
Curiosity	Open question, mystery, unanswered puzzle
Meaning	Personal values, relevance, "why it matters"
Challenge	Game, competition, high stakes
Recognition	Praise, social feedback, being seen
Structure	External order, schedule, countdown
Movement	Walking, pacing, kinetic activity
Sensory Input	Music, lighting, textures, ambiance

📝 *Tip: Use this chart to spot patterns after completing your first Signal Map. Everyone has a different mix of activation languages.*

✹ Signal Mapping Exercise: Find What Moves You

Your ADHD brain already knows what works—it's time to start noticing. Use this simple reflection tool to begin building your own Signal Map:

Step 1: Recall a recent task you actually completed. Then ask:

- o   What helped me get started?
- o   What kept me going?
- o   What emotional or sensory support was present?
- o   What gave it meaning?
- o   How did I know I was done?

Step 2: Sort your answers into these five zones:

1. **Starting Signals** – Music, movement, timers, social pressure
2. **Sustaining Signals** – Lo-fi sound, visuals, breaks, body doubling
3. **Emotional Signals** – Lighting, pets, humor, calming textures
4. **Meaning Signals** – Identity links, story frames, curiosity paths
5. **Completion Signals** – Crossed-off list, small reward, exhale

Step 3: Make a map for just one task this week using these zones. Then experiment.

See what happens when you intentionally activate the signals that already work. Because motivation isn't random—it's responsive.

Sometimes, the biggest challenge isn't identifying a signal—it's believing we're allowed to follow it. Elijah's story shows what it looks like to rediscover your own compass—not all at once, but one faint signal
at a time.

✧

Signal Story: Elijah—Reclaiming Internal Signals After a Lifetime of External Tuning

Elijah was a bright, sensitive young man in his early twenties who had learned to read a room better than he could read himself. By the time we met, he could predict when someone else was frustrated, uncomfortable, or proud with near-perfect accuracy—but when asked how he was feeling, he'd pause, tilt his head thoughtfully, and answer like someone trying to read a weather forecast for a city he no longer lived in.

It wasn't always like that. As a kid, Elijah had emotions with full sound and color. But those signals were often met with discomfort, dismissal, or directives. When he was sad, he was told to focus on someone else who had it worse. When he was overwhelmed, he was told he was overreacting. And when he struggled to find joy, he was handed this quiet, insidious message:

"If you can't make yourself happy, try making someone else happy."

That sentence became a script. A survival strategy. A morality. He began tuning in to the people around him—their needs, their tones, their unspoken expectations—and turning down the volume on his own.

Somewhere along the way, his own signals—the ones that told him what mattered, what hurt, what moved him—faded into the background. And in their place, these limiting beliefs took root:

Limiting Belief:

- My needs aren't urgent.
- I'm better at helping others than figuring myself out.
- If I get it wrong, I'll disappoint people.
- Wanting something too much is dangerous.

Neutralizing Reframe:

- My needs are signals too—not emergencies, but navigational tools.
- Helping others works best when I'm grounded in myself.
- If I lose myself, I'll disappoint the most important person—me.
- Desire is a compass—not a guarantee, but a direction worth exploring.

These weren't just thoughts—they were filters that muted Elijah's internal signal system and distorted feedback. When a real desire showed up, it was wrapped in guilt or hesitation. When a boundary formed, it felt like selfishness. He'd learned to second-guess his own compass.

So we began with a question:
"What are the faintest signals you still notice?"

At first, there was silence. Then a slow smile.

"Music. I still get something from music. And animals. And I get this itch—not a real itch, more like a pull—when I'm near water or mountains. It's like something in me leans forward."

That was the beginning of signal reclamation.

We started tracking those faint but trustworthy moments using a Signal Map—not just what he should do, but what stirred his system, what gave him a flicker of motion or emotion. And then we layered in amplifiers—tools to help those signals get louder:

- A morning playlist that anchored him in his own energy
- A journal prompt asking not what the world needed, but what he wanted to move toward
- A daily pause to check: Am I reading myself, or just reading the room?

It wasn't quick. It wasn't easy. But it was real. Elijah began to reclaim what ADHD often hides beneath layers of distraction or duty: a powerful, emotion-linked motivational compass.

Key Insight:

When someone has spent years listening to everyone but themselves, their signal system isn't broken—it's buried under belief scripts. Reframing those scripts and using small amplifiers to spotlight internal cues can reconnect them to the signals that move them.

✧

 Signal Awareness is ADHD Intelligence

You're not "finally being responsible." You're becoming fluent in your own operating system.

Signal Mapping doesn't fix everything. But it gives you a map—and the compass to follow it.

From here, we're not building control.

We're building partnership.

Let's design systems that don't just manage ADHD—but move with it.

✧

🔬 For Parents, Educators, Clinicians, Coaches, and Curious Readers

Signal Mapping offers a reframed approach to ADHD motivation grounded in both neuroscience and lived experience. While traditional interventions often emphasize external structure (e.g., reminders, routines, behavioral incentives), Signal Mapping begins one layer deeper—at the source of internal activation.

The model distinguishes among **cues, signals, amplifiers, motivation,** and **action**, using the SASMA sequence (Signal → Amplifier → Signal → Motivation → Action) as a tool to decode and reconstruct motivational chains. Unlike top-down strategies that assume willpower can be summoned on demand, Signal Mapping aligns with findings from Barkley, Brown, and Porges that highlight the emotional, interoceptive, and context-sensitive nature of activation.

Notable theoretical influences include:

- **Russell Barkley's** framing of ADHD as a disorder of self-regulation (vs. attention alone)
- **Thomas Brown's** emphasis on activation as a distinct executive function domain
- **Antonio Damasio's** somatic marker hypothesis, linking emotion to decision-making
- **Stephen Porges'** polyvagal theory and neuroception
- **BJ Fogg's** behavioral model, in which motivation is responsive, not constant
- **Daniel Kahneman's** System 1–System 2 model, reframed for signal-based cognition

In this chapter, you'll find language and structure suitable for psychoeducation, therapeutic coaching, classroom support, or student-guided exploration. The Signal Map worksheet and reflective practice tools can be used in 1:1 or group formats to help ADHD individuals identify patterns of activation, learn to amplify adaptive signals, and reduce overreliance on urgency- or shame-based motivators.

In short, Signal Mapping shifts the question from "Why can't they just start?" to "What moves this person—and how can we listen for that?"

Modern neuroscience tells us that attention is not a fixed spotlight, but a dynamic network process. For people with ADHD, that spotlight is often drawn not by rules or plans, but by emotionally charged, personally meaningful signals. These signals activate brain systems that orient us to what matters right now—even when that differs from what's scheduled on a planner.

🧠 DMN, TPN, and the Tug-of-War for Attention

Two major brain networks help explain this:

- The Default Mode Network (DMN) is associated with mind-wandering, internal thought, and memory.
- The Task Positive Network (TPN) governs focused, goal-directed activity.

In neurotypical brains, there's a clean switch: when one turns on, the other turns off. But in ADHD, these systems often fail to toggle smoothly, leaving individuals stuck in a tug-of-war—distracted, restless, or flooded with competing inputs.

🔍 Enter the Salience Network

The salience network acts as the brain's signal triage system—deciding what deserves attention. For people with ADHD, this system prioritizes emotionally meaningful, novel, or urgent stimuli, even when those are unrelated to the task at hand.

In other words: the ADHD brain doesn't respond well to neutral cues—like a calendar alert or a vague instruction. It responds to signals that feel real.

⊛ Why Signal Mapping Works

Signal Mapping builds on this neuroscience. Instead of forcing the ADHD brain to conform to a linear model of time and willpower, it asks:

- What actually activates your attention?
- What patterns light up your system and pull you toward action?
- What kinds of tasks, environments, and emotional tones move you forward—or shut you down?

✒ Origins and Authorship

The language and framework introduced in this chapter—including the terms *signal*, *signal mapping*, *signal types*, *amplifiers*, and the **SASMA** sequence—were developed over the course of my work with ADHD students and professionals across multiple disciplines and over many decades.

While the individual concepts draw from well-established theories in psychology and neuroscience, this particular integration—the idea of *signal as the unit of activation*, and the *mapping* of individual motivational pathways—is original to this book and the ADHD College Success Guidance Program.

My goal in naming and structuring this system is not to replace the wisdom of researchers or clinicians, but to offer a **unifying language**—one that honors the lived experience of people with ADHD and helps practitioners, educators, and families translate insight into action.

In clinical training, we often say, "If you can name it, you can work with it." Signal Mapping gives us a way to name what has long gone unnamed—the felt sense that drives or derails behavior—and to build collaborative systems around what actually moves each individual.

This model is still growing. And like any good map, it's meant to be used, tested, and adapted.

Thank you for walking this path with us.

📖 References for Further Reading

Barkley, R. A. (2011). *Executive functions: What they are, how they work, and why they evolved.* New York: Guilford Press.
➤ Barkley's model of executive function lays the groundwork for understanding ADHD as a disorder of self-regulation, offering context for how signal mapping tools compensate for internal timing, planning, and feedback disruptions.

Brown, T. E. (2005). *Attention deficit disorder: The unfocused mind in children and adults.* Yale University Press.
➤ Brown introduces a cluster-based model of ADHD that aligns with the concept of attentional signals being scrambled, delayed, or misprioritized—key themes in the chapter's discussion of signal clarity and responsiveness.

Damasio, A. R. (1994). *Descartes' error: Emotion, reason, and the human brain.* New York: Putnam.
➤ Damasio's work on somatic markers supports the idea that internal emotional signals guide decision-making and motivation—a foundational argument for using signal mapping as a navigation tool for ADHD minds.

Fogg, B. J. (2019). *Tiny habits: The small changes that change everything.* Houghton Mifflin Harcourt.
➤ Fogg's habit formation strategies reinforce the idea of working with micro-signals and small shifts, which mirrors the chapter's approach to signal stacking and chaining as methods for behavior change.

Hallowell, E. M., & Ratey, J. J. (2011). *Driven to distraction: Recognizing and coping with attention deficit disorder from childhood through adulthood* (Revised ed.). Anchor Books.
➤ This classic text offers personal stories and clinical insight into the lived ADHD experience, grounding the chapter's signal-mapping exercises in emotional reality and common challenges faced by ADHD learners.

Kahneman, D. (2011). *Thinking, fast and slow.* Farrar, Straus and Giroux.
➤ Kahneman's distinction between fast, intuitive thinking (System 1) and slower, deliberate reasoning (System 2) parallels the chapter's exploration of signal reactivity, impulsivity, and attentional shifts.

Porges, S. W. (2011). *The polyvagal theory: Neurophysiological foundations of emotions, attachment, communication, and self-regulation.* W.W. Norton & Company.

➤ Porges' theory explains how physiological state affects signal processing and attention—supporting the chapter's emphasis on bodily cues, environmental tuning, and the emotional underpinnings of signal interpretation.

Chapter 6

What Moves Us – A Signal-Based Guide to ADHD Motivation

"You can lead a horse to water, but if you can get him to swim on his back, you're really doing something."
—An old cowboy in my Texas hometown

"What finally got me moving? It wasn't the planner, the checklist, or the deadline. It was hearing my own voice say, 'I can't not do this anymore.' That was the signal."
—College student in ADHD coaching

🄰🄱🄲🄳 Quick Guide to Chapter 6

- Learn how signals evolve into complete motivational systems (SDSS).
- Explore 10 key motivation styles common in ADHD.
- Discover how to activate motivation without relying on panic or shame.
- Use the Motivation Compass to identify your strongest signal paths.
- Download the worksheet to build your own personalized system.

▨ How to Use This Chapter

This chapter speaks to three types of readers—and three ways of seeing motivation.

- ○ 🧠 **For People with ADHD—Students, Workers, and Curious Minds**
  Explore how motivation actually works in an ADHD brain—from signal-driven action to emotional momentum. This section unpacks why pressure backfires, what truly moves you, and how to harness that signal in real time.

- ○ 🔬 **For Parents, Educators, Clinicians, and Coaches**
  Learn why traditional motivation models often fall short for ADHD learners—and what signal-based strategies can do instead. Grounded in neuroscience and real-life case studies, this section offers tools for scaffolding sustainable motivation.

- ○ 💡 **Key Concepts and Takeaways**
  Watch for signal types, motivational engines (like fear vs. desire), and tools like the SASMA Pathway and Motivation Signal Map. These aren't just theories—they're designed to help you spot what moves you and build systems that match.

> 💡 Feel free to read it straight through—or jump into the section that best fits your role. ADHD motivation isn't one-size-fits-all. This chapter gives you lenses, language, and tools to find your own fuel.

🧠 For People with ADHD—Students, Workers, and Curious Minds

It's easy to do the things we like. Interesting classes, late-night gaming sessions, passionate conversations with friends—all of these have a kind of gravitational pull that requires minimal conscious effort. They draw us in, almost as if our brain has been waiting for something to feel like this before fully engaging.

But what about the things that don't come preloaded with interest or urgency? What about the essay due in a week, the laundry piling up, or the slow, unglamorous work of applying for internships or planning next semester's schedule?

This is where the trouble starts—not with ability or knowledge, but with movement.

ADHD isn't so much a disorder of knowing what to do as it is a disorder of getting going. What moves us, especially when the task feels boring, ambiguous, or distant?

That question launched a thousand psychology books and motivational speeches. But for those of us who are wired with ADHD, many of those answers miss the mark—because they're based on an assumption that motivation is something you can summon on command. Like flipping a switch. Like reading a to-do list and suddenly feeling inspired to do the dishes.

But here's the truth: clocks don't move us—signals do.

✧

A Brief Review: Time Doesn't Motivate—Signals Do

Let's take a moment and review some important concepts from Chapter 5 and how they connect the dots to motivation.

If you've ever promised to start at 2 p.m. and looked up to find it's now 3:45 and you're still scrolling, you already know this. Time alone doesn't carry the same urgency for brains with ADHD. It floats. It drifts. And we drift with it.

What does move us are cues—specific sights, sounds, emotions, or inner sensations that activate a chain reaction. But not every cue is enough. Some are ignored. Others fade into the background.

The ones that move us?

Those are what I call **signals**.

Cues, Signals, and the ADHD Operating System

A **cue** is a trigger—raw information from our environment or body: A ringing phone, a blinking cursor, the sound of your name, a hungry stomach. Cues are everywhere. But ADHD minds are selective. We don't respond to just any cue.

A **signal** is a cue with emotional meaning—something that carries weight, urgency, importance, or desire. Signals make us act. They don't just knock on the door of attention—they kick it open. Signals are how ADHD brains decide what matters.

A cue says, "Hey, just FYI..."
A signal says, "Move. Now."

This is why a looming deadline often succeeds where a carefully planned schedule fails. It's why students with ADHD frequently procrastinate until the panic hits—because panic is a powerful signal. It creates the feeling of necessity, and suddenly, focus arrives.

The problem is that most of our systems—in school, at work, and even in therapy—are built around time, not signals.

They ask, "What time will you do it?"

When the better question is:

"What will tell you it's time to start?"

That's the shift we make with the Signal-Driven Support System (SDSS). It's not just a different way of planning—it's a different way of living. One built around meaning, emotion, and context, not clocks.

✕ Signals and the Myth of Motivation

Let's start by clearing something up: people with ADHD are not unmotivated. We are dynamically, sometimes explosively motivated—just not always at the right time, in the right direction, or toward the things we're "supposed" to care about.

If anything, the problem isn't a lack of motivation. It's a **mismatch** between what's motivating and what's meaningful in the moment.

Think about it this way: motivation is a powerful engine. But engines don't run without fuel or a starter. In ADHD brains, that starter isn't a time, a plan, or a carefully organized list. It's a **signal**. Something must happen—emotionally, sensorily, viscerally—for that ignition to fire.

For a toddler, it might have been as simple as a parent's command or a bowl of M&M's. Back then, the external structure was the signal.

But now? Now you're the one holding the reins.

And that's where things get complicated.

Internal vs. External Motivation: The Shift That Trips Us

In early life, external motivation reigns. Authority figures, structure, routines—they're everywhere, and we usually just follow along. You go to school because you're told to. You do your homework because someone's checking.

But something happens during that tricky transition to college and adulthood. The scaffolding falls away. Parents aren't waking you up. Teachers aren't reminding you. Coaches aren't yelling from the sidelines.

And here's the kicker: You're suddenly expected to run on internal motivation, like flipping a switch you didn't even know was there.

"You're sailing your own ship now. And like it or not, you're holding the rudder."

That's a line I used in my first book, and I still stand by it. The problem is, nobody gives you sailing lessons. You're told, "Be more responsible." "Try harder." "Just do it."

But if you've got ADHD, those words fall flat. You want to sail. You just can't feel the wind.

SDSS: Building a System That Moves You

This is where the **Signal-Driven Support System (SDSS)** comes in. SDSS isn't about motivation as an abstract force—it's about learning what gets your attention to fire, your emotions to engage, and your body to act.

It's about translating everyday cues into personally meaningful **signals**—and doing it intentionally.

Instead of waiting for the panic of a last-minute deadline to light you up, you learn to create **micro-signals** ahead of time— nudges, visuals, rituals, body doubles, music, context shifts— anything that flips the switch without the cortisol surge.

You create a world that cooperates with your brain, instead of scolding it.

This is not a one-size-fits-all recipe. Your signals will be different from mine. But they're there—waiting to be discovered, shaped, and strengthened.

In the next section, we'll unpack some of the most effective forms of motivation I've seen in my practice, many of which are nuanced by the ADHD experience and often misunderstood or dismissed in traditional models.

But first, here's the key takeaway:

Don't wait to feel motivated. Learn what moves you. Then design for that.

Lighting the Fire: Fear and Desire as Motivational Fuel

"If you dream the dream, it will pull you into it."
—Carl Jung

For people with ADHD, motivation doesn't start with logic—it starts with emotion. Whether it's excitement or dread, curiosity or shame—emotion gets your body involved. It makes the cue matter. It turns it into
a signal.

In the most basic sense, humans tend to move for two reasons:

- o   We desire something good.
- o   We fear something bad.

You've felt both. The desire to get an "A". The fear of failing. The dream of a better future. The anxiety of disappointing someone. These are powerful engines, and you already use them—even if you don't realize it.

But here's the catch: ADHD minds often favor one over the other. And when you use the wrong type of fuel for your engine, everything sputters.

◇ **Fear Motivation** You imagine what will go wrong if you don't act—and that imagined outcome becomes a strategy for kickstarting action, especially when other motivators fail to spark.—a failing grade, a disappointed parent, a missed opportunity. It creates urgency. That anxious edge often brings clarity, even focus. For many people with ADHD, this is why procrastination "works"—panic is a powerful signal.

But here's the problem: if you overuse fear, it turns from mobilizing to paralyzing. The same panic that starts a task one day might shut you down the next, especially if you have a low fear threshold.

◇ **Desire Motivation** This is when you're pulled toward something—the dream, the outcome, the reward. You imagine what it would feel like to succeed, what you'll get, what it means to win.

But desire isn't always loud. It whispers. And if the signal isn't strong enough—if the task feels too far off, or the reward too abstract—it won't move you.

The key isn't choosing one over the other—it's knowing which one gets your motor running in a given situation.

Here's a simple cue-to-signal strategy I give clients:

- Feeling stuck? Ask a fear question: "What's the worst that could happen if I don't do this?"
- Feeling unmotivated? Ask a desire question: "What would this help me move toward that I really want?"

Then listen. Whichever one creates a spark, follow that. That spark is your flame, and in the brain with ADHD, learning to strike it yourself is the beginning of building a sustainable fire.

Spontaneous vs. Intentional Motivation

There's a reason video games don't need a calendar invite.

When you're immersed in something that *truly inspires you, motivation becomes* spontaneous. It rises out of the moment. Your focus locks in. Your attention sustains. You don't need a timer. You don't need a pep talk.

This is what I call **Spontaneous Motivation**—and it's one of the secret superpowers of ADHD when the conditions are right.

But it's also unpredictable. You can't rely on spontaneous motivation to write your term paper or show up for a lab at 8 a.m. That's where **Intentional Motivation** comes in.

Intentional motivation is **structured**. It's built. It's crafted out of awareness.

You know what works for you, and you put it in place *before* you need it.

Let's say you know you get focused when you hear a particular playlist. Or when you sit next to a study partner. Or when you use a certain scent or light or location. That's not magic—that's **you creating the signal**.

🔧 **SDSS is the systemization of intentional motivation.**
It turns lucky sparks into lanterns. Instead of waiting for
motivation to strike, you build supports that catch the spark
and hold it. And when that support stops working? You don't
blame the fire—you go back to the matchbox.

Next up, we'll explore the most ADHD-specific motivational
forms—ones that aren't often talked about in traditional psychology but may already be showing up in your life:

- Novelty
- Curiosity
- Possibility
- Belonging
- Entrepreneurial Drive
- Developmental Milestones
- Efficacy
- Mindful Motivation

Each one is a **signal path** waiting to be activated.

The Pull of Novelty and Curiosity

*"He sure doesn't seem to have ADHD when
he's playing that video game..."*
—Every parent, ever

That's novelty striking—fast, bright, and gone before you can grab it.

In the ADHD brain, novelty acts like a lightning strike. It lights up attention networks and floods the brain with dopamine. It feels good. It *is* good—at least at first.

But novelty is fickle. What's interesting today might be boring tomorrow. It fades fast, which is why so many people with ADHD jump from one task, relationship, hobby, or career to another—always chasing that first spark.

◇ **Novelty as a Signal**
In an SDSS framework, **novelty is one of the strongest signal types**—but also one of the least stable.

You can't make boring things inherently novel. But you *can* layer in novelty to *how* you do them.

- o   Change the environment.
- o   Use a different tool or app.
- o   Add a competitive or time-based twist.
- o   Work in bursts with varying challenges.
- o   Rotate tasks or alternate subjects.

You're not tricking your brain—you're **respecting how it works**. You're saying, *"If I'm wired to respond to what's new, I can design work that always feels slightly new."*

The ADHD need for novelty isn't a flaw—it's a navigational

tool. The key is to **consciously harness it before it takes control of you**.

Without direction, novelty leads to distraction.

With direction, novelty becomes strategy. It's not chaos—it's kindling.

Curiosity: The Motivation of Not Knowing

*"The intellect has little to do on the road
to discovery... and solutions come to you,
and you don't know why or how."*
—Albert Einstein

Curiosity is different from novelty. Novelty is about what's **new**.

Curiosity is about what's **not yet known**—and wanting to know.

Curiosity is quieter than novelty, but deeper. It fuels exploration, learning, and even creativity. It's what makes us pull at a loose thread until the whole thing unravels—or reveals something important underneath.

And like novelty, curiosity is *an emotionally charged experience*. It becomes a signal when the unknown becomes compelling.

But there's a catch: most people with ADHD have been **socialized out of curiosity.**

We were taught from early on that *not knowing* is bad—that if we don't have the answer, we've failed. Shame enters the picture. We fake it. We shut down. We stop asking questions.

And with that, the motivation to explore—to engage—quietly dies.

◇ **Rekindling Curiosity with SDSS**
To reactivate curiosity as a motivational force, we must create a sense of **safety around not knowing**. This means:

- Embracing questions without demanding answers.
- Using blank space in journals or workbooks to spark "wondering."
- Building rituals that track moments of curiosity ("I don't know yet, but I want to...").
- Encouraging curiosity as a **process**, not a performance.

In my workshops, I often have participants open their workbook to a blank first page and write "CURIOSITY" in big letters. On the last page? "EPIPHANY." That simple framing creates a structure where *not knowing* becomes the entry point for discovery—and a **signal** to lean in rather than shut down.

Curiosity turns the unknown into an invitation—a whisper

that says, "Come closer." An invitation is one of the most elegant motivational signals we have.

The Motivation of Possibility: Seeing What's Within Reach

"The motivation of possibility is generated when we commit to goals that are realistically within our reach but also challenging."

Possibility is one of those quiet motivators that doesn't make a big entrance—but when it lands, it sticks. It's the motivational force that wakes up when you see just enough progress to believe *maybe, just maybe, this could work.*

Not too easy. Not too hard. Just right.

There's research behind this: in a dental hygiene study you may remember from my first book, the group most motivated to change their brushing habits wasn't the one shown perfect teeth or completely ruined ones. It was the group shown **salvageable teeth**—pictures that said, "This could be you—if you take the next small step."

That's **possibility**—not perfection, not catastrophe.
A signal that says: There's still time. This can still be done.

◇ **Possibility as a Signal**

The ADHD brain often struggles with *long-term* goals. That's not because we don't care about it, it's because the reward is too far away to feel real. The signal gets weaker the further out it goes.

So, how do you make possibility *feel now?*

You break it down. You chain it. You turn it into **visible progress**. Each step becomes a micro-signal reinforcing the larger arc.

- ○ Break your goal into smaller, meaningful checkpoints.
- ○ Celebrate progress publicly or socially.
- ○ Use visual cues (like charts, puzzles, even literal chains) to show how far you've come.

In SDSS terms, possibility becomes motivation **when it becomes tangible.** Not just *what's out there*, but *what's next.*

The Motivation of Belonging: We Move Together

> *"The structure of a nearby intentional presence has the power to encourage action."*

Let's talk about Nelson.

He was my best friend growing up—and, looking back, my very first "body double." Nelson was the kind of student that teachers trusted. I think they sat me next to him, hoping his calm would rub off. When I lost focus or bombed a test, he'd grab me by the ankles and walk me upside-down around the playground, demanding, "Are ya gonna pay attention?!"

Strange? Absolutely. Effective? Strangely yes.

Many years later, I found myself in front of a mountain of paperwork in my counseling practice—paralyzed. On a whim, I asked my partner to just sit in the room with me while I worked. Not to help. Just to *be there*. Fifteen minutes later, I was humming along.

That's the **Motivation of Belonging**—the drive to be connected, mirrored, and supported.

◇ **Belonging as a Signal**

We are social creatures. Mirror neurons fire when we're in sync with others. Just seeing someone else focused can trigger your own focus. Even strangers in a coffee shop can become silent co-regulators of your attention.

For ADHD students, this signal is often underused—or used in the wrong direction. Partying all night, oversharing in new relationships, joining groups that substitute chaos for connection. Belonging without structure can hijack motivation and send it off course.

But when used intentionally, this motivator is gold:

- Study groups with the right people
- "Body doubling" with a quiet peer
- Working in public or shared spaces
- Social accountability (text check-ins, shared goals)
- Choosing environments where people are *doing the thing you want to be doing*

Belonging turns motivation into **movement with others**.

And sometimes, *it's not the task that gets us going—it's the person sitting next to us while we do it.*

Entrepreneurial Motivation: Uneasy in the Harness

"Boys, you just can't do that with this kinda
horse... they're uneasy in the harness."

I grew up around ranchers and horses, including a special breed called cutting horses—fast, smart, and independent. One day, in a flash of youthful brilliance, a friend and I thought we'd hitch two of these sharp, twitchy animals to a wagon for a joyride. Fortunately, a rancher intervened before disaster struck. His warning stuck with me.

That phrase—**uneasy in the harness**—might as well be a personality type, especially for people with ADHD.

We chafe at micromanagement. We question authority. We resist rigid systems, especially when they don't make sense to us. And while this can look like defiance or disorganization, underneath it lies something important:

A deep drive for autonomy, vision, and self-directed impact. With proper shaping, **uneasy in the harness** can evolve into **entrepreneurial motivation.**

🗣 Language Matters—Especially When It's Yours

The ADHD mind often resists pressure, not just from others, but even from within. Phrases like "I have to," "I should," or "I can't fail" trigger what we call the *uneasy-in-the-harness* response—a recoil against anything that feels like someone else's agenda.

That's why the **language of self-motivation** matters. Some words create pressure. Others restore permission. When we learn to spot these moments and shift our internal script—using what we call **Signal Words**—we can align with our own motivation instead of pushing against it.

For a deeper dive into how internal language shapes action, identity, and emotional tone, see Chapter 13: *Nested Selves—Internal Voices, Roles, and Self-Compassion.*

◇ Entrepreneurial Drive as a Signal

People with ADHD are **overrepresented among entrepreneurs**—and it's not hard to see why. When the goal is personal, when the structure is chosen, when the work feels aligned with identity and freedom—we come alive.

That drive, that urgency to build something of your own—that's **Entrepreneurial Motivation**. It emerges early as resistance to imposed systems and matures into leadership when paired with relevant skills.

In SDSS terms, this motivator works best when:

- o   Tasks are linked to personal vision or values
- o   Systems are self-chosen or co-created
- o   There's visible ownership and freedom in execution

The challenge? Without adequate structure, entrepreneurial minds spin out. We jump from vision to vision without scaffolding. That's why we pair this motivator with **executive function tools**—to harness the horse, without killing its spirit.

Uneasy in the harness isn't a flaw—it's the signature of a future leader.

You just need to build a better saddle.

Developmental Motivation: The Drive to Become

"You are sailing your own ship now. And like it or not, you are holding the rudder."

There's a quieter force working in the background of every young adult's life—especially those in transition. It's not about achievement. It's not about pressure. It's about *becoming*.

I call it **Developmental Motivation**—the sense that you are supposed to be growing, evolving, becoming more fully yourself.

You won't find it on a to-do list. It doesn't shout. But it's there—in the questions people ask:

o   "What are you going to do after school?"

- o "Are you seeing anyone?"
- o "What do you want to be?"

And more subtly, in the stories, media, and social expectations around you. Culture whispers that it's time to move forward—to separate from home, to find a path, to do something *adult.*

◇ Developmental Signals in SDSS

Here's where ADHD makes this tricky.

Research shows that students with ADHD often lag in developmental milestones—executive function, emotional regulation, and life skills. But society doesn't delay its expectations. You're still supposed to apply for school, find work, and make decisions.

The result? Shame. Anxiety. That hollow "I should be further along" feeling.

But what if we honored this motivator instead of fearing it?

Developmental signals are subtle but sacred—compass points for who you're becoming.

They say, *"It's time."* Not perfectly. Not all at once. But forward.

In SDSS, we listen for these cues and design supports that help them become actionable:

- o Mentorship or coaching for life transitions
- o Rituals that mark "growing up" moments
- o Journaling or reflection tools that connect small actions to long-term growth
- o Honest dialogue about what feels "next," not just what feels "urgent"

You're not behind. You're on a different developmental rhythm.

The goal isn't to catch up—it's to keep moving with intention.

The Motivation of Efficacy: The Confidence Loop

"The more you do something well, the more you want to do it. The more you do it, the better you get. The better you get, the more confident you become. And the more confident you become... well, now we're getting somewhere."

This is the **motivation of efficacy**—and it's one of the most empowering forces we can activate, especially in ADHD learners who've been repeatedly told they're inconsistent, unreliable, or "not living up to potential."

Efficacy doesn't come from abstract encouragement. It comes from evidence.

You did something. It worked. You felt good about it. So you want to do it again. That's the loop. That's *recursion*—a self-reinforcing cycle of skill → confidence → action → more skill.

I stumbled onto this unexpectedly after scoring 100% on a written driver's test at the DMV. It was such a small thing—a booklet, a few questions, and a quick win—but it gave me a surge of belief. A sense that maybe, just maybe, I could go back to school. And I did. All the way through doctoral studies.

◇ **Efficacy Signals in SDSS**
This motivator often starts small—but it grows fast if nurtured

well. The key is to notice success early and often. And then use that success to create momentum.

- ○ Start with tasks that *can* be done well
- ○ Track success visually (small wins board, sticker charts, gamified apps)
- ○ Celebrate competence, not just completion
- ○ Reflect on *why* something went well to reinforce the recursive loop

For people with ADHD, the motivation of efficacy can be life-changing—especially after years of feeling like effort rarely leads to results.

The signal here is success—no matter how small.

Once your brain sees itself winning, it wants more.

Mindful Motivation: Doing the Thing Because It's Time to Do the Thing

> *"Well now, I'm desire motivated... someone else will need to take out the trash."*
> **—My son, Morgan**

Let's face it: not every task will spark desire or dread. Some things in life just need to be done—not because they're inspiring or terrifying, but because **they keep your life functional**.

This is the realm of **Mindful Motivation**—the quiet power that gets you to clean the bathroom, pay your bills, or reply to that email you've been dodging.

It's not flashy. It doesn't chase novelty or rewards. It just shows up.

And sometimes, that's the bravest thing a person with ADHD can do.

◇ **Mindful Signals in SDSS**

Mindful motivation requires a shift in mindset: from emotional urgency to intentional presence. It's a kind of internal agreement that says:

"This needs doing. I choose to do it. Let's go."

The practice is simple, but powerful:

- ○ Create a calm cue (deep breath, bell, candle, visual token)
- ○ Ask: *Why does this matter?*
- ○ Then gently *set the emotion aside* and begin
- ○ Focus not on results, but on the ritual of action

This is closely related to practices in mindfulness and even

Karma Yoga—action for the sake of harmony, rather than the outcome.

Mindful motivation is the antidote to chaos.

It's what gets the trash taken out. And sometimes, that's everything.

⊛ Bringing It All Together

Each of these motivation types—fear, desire, novelty, curiosity, possibility, belonging, entrepreneurial spirit, developmental drive, efficacy, and mindful presence—can be seen as **unique signal systems** within the ADHD mind. While you might not need all ten all the time, knowing which few drive you is where the compass starts to point."

When we stop expecting clocks and calendars to do the work of moving us, and instead begin identifying **what *actually* activates us**, motivation becomes a tool, not a mystery.

With SDSS, you don't wait for motivation.

You design for it.

🖋 For Parents, Educators, Clinicians, Coaches, and Curious Readers

Why This Chapter Matters Clinically

Motivation is often misunderstood as a character trait—a matter of "will"—rather than a dynamic, neurobiological process. This misconception is especially damaging for students and adults with ADHD, who may show extraordinary motivation in one area and total inertia in another.

Chapter 6 reframes motivation through the lens of **signal activation** rather than compliance. The SDSS (Signal-Driven Support System) model draws on research from Self-Determination Theory (Deci & Ryan, 2000), Expectancy–Value

Theory (Wigfield & Eccles, 2000), and affective neuroscience (Panksepp, 1998; Immordino-Yang & Damasio, 2007), all contextualized for the unique needs of ADHD learners (Barkley, 2012; Brown, 2009).

This chapter makes a clinical and coaching case for seeing motivation not as missing or fixed—but as something that can be uncovered, reinforced, and intentionally designed.

Signal-Based Systems vs. Time-Based Interventions

Most time-based strategies—such as schedules, timers, and point systems—assume that time is inherently meaningful. But for many ADHD brains, time is emotionally flat. It doesn't spark urgency, clarity, or engagement (Barkley, 2012). That's why reinforcement models and compliance frameworks often fall short. They speak in clocks, but the ADHD mind moves in signals.

The SDSS model shifts the question from "What time will you do it?" to "What signal will tell you it's time?" This reframe aligns with advances in affective neuroscience and polyvagal theory (Porges, 2011), which demonstrates that motivation is biologically linked to emotional salience, safety, and context, rather than abstract planning.

This approach is also deeply congruent with the foundations of ADHD coaching. Jodi Sleeper-Triplett's work emphasizes co-created structure, emotional presence, and developmentally appropriate scaffolding. Her "Designed Alliance" model and focus on student-led goals map naturally onto SDSS—especially in activating motivational styles like belonging, autonomy, and developmental drive.

Coaches and clinicians who adopt a signal-based lens move away from a deficit framing ("Why aren't they trying?") and toward a systems question:

"What signal is missing—and how can we help them find it, shape it, or co-regulate with it?"

Motivation Types and Intervention Opportunities

Each motivational style explored in this chapter opens a door for targeted intervention. These signal paths are not hypothetical—they represent real, observable leverage points in ADHD support with a solid basis in the literature. Below are examples of how signal-awareness informs practice:

- **Fear:** Help students identify early anxiety cues and convert urgency into forward momentum using pacing tools, interoceptive tracking, or emotion-labeling strategies (Brown, 2009).
- **Desire:** Use narrative-based future pacing and visual goal-mapping to bring rewards into the now (Wigfield & Eccles, 2000).
- **Novelty:** Offer rotating content delivery (Zentall, 2005), task gamification, or modularized lesson formats to keep engagement fresh.
- **Curiosity:** Design open-ended inquiry projects, "epiphany journals," or safe uncertainty rituals to reclaim exploratory learning (Engel, 2011).
- **Possibility:** Show visible markers of progress—chains, checklists, maps—and highlight "just within reach" wins (Dweck, 2006).
- **Belonging:** Create co-working spaces, structured peer study, or intentional co-regulation (Porges, 2011). Use "body doubling" to anchor focus in connection.
- **Entrepreneurial & Developmental:** Link tasks to personal meaning and allow co-design. ADHD students

often thrive when they feel ownership and agency. Offer mentorship, transitional coaching, and identity-based goal planning. Honor lagging milestones without shame (Deci & Ryan, 2000; Sleeper-Triplett, 2010; Barkley, 2012).

o **Efficacy:** Build confidence ladders, small wins boards, or recursive feedback loops that reward skill progression (Bandura, 1997).

o **Mindful Motivation:** Incorporate grounding cues, breathwork, and non-outcome-oriented rituals to build task presence (Kabat-Zinn, 2005; Hayes et al., 2011). *(See Chapter 13 for more on mindfulness tools.)*

🧩 Summary—Designing for What Moves Us

At the heart of signal-based support lies a deceptively simple truth:

ADHD motivation is not summoned—it is sparked.

When we identify the specific signal types that activate a student and then build supports that reinforce them, we shift from managing behavior to building momentum.

The clinician's role is not to provide motivation—
but to help students **map their own**. That process includes signal detection, strategic scaffolding,
emotional alignment, and—in the coaching models aligned with SDSS—a relationship of safety and shared ownership.

When students discover what moves them, they gain more than momentum.

They gain the tools to move themselves.

📚 References for Further Reading

The following are foundational sources cited or referenced in this chapter. Each is briefly annotated for relevance and use in applied settings.

Bandura, A. (1997). *Self-Efficacy: The Exercise of Control.* New York: Freeman.
→ Introduces the concept of efficacy as a self-reinforcing loop; essential to understanding ADHD motivation through competence and confidence building.

o **Barkley, R. A. (2012).** *Executive Functions: What They Are, How They Work, and Why They Evolved.* New York: Guilford Press.
→ Defines ADHD as a disorder of executive function and self-regulation; highlights why time-based systems fail for ADHD learners.

o **Brown, T. E. (2009).** *A New Understanding of ADHD: Unlocking the Potential of the ADHD Brain.* San Francisco: Jossey-Bass.
→ Provides a nuanced model of ADHD as a constellation of impairments in activation, emotion, and memory; foundational to SDSS signal identification.

o **Deci, E. L., & Ryan, R. M. (2000).** *Self-Determination Theory: Intrinsic Motivation and Self-Determination in Human Behavior.* New York: Plenum.
→ Core theory behind autonomy, competence, and related-ness; central to understanding the motivational structure of SDSS.

o **Dweck, C. S. (2006).** *Mindset: The New Psychology of Success.* New York: Random House.
→ Emphasizes the role of belief systems in motivation and growth; aligns closely with the motivation of possibility.

o **Engel, S. (2011).** Children's need to know: Curiosity in schools. *Harvard Educational Review, 81*(4), 625–645.
→ Explores the motivational power of curiosity and how traditional schooling can suppress it—a major theme in this chapter.

o **Hayes, S. C., Strosahl, K. D., & Wilson, K. G. (2011).** *Acceptance and Commitment Therapy (2nd ed.): The Process and Practice of Mindful Change.* New York: Guilford Press.
→ Describes values-aligned action and mindfulness as motivation strategies; basis for mindful motivation interventions.

o **Immordino-Yang, M. H., & Damasio, A. (2007).** We feel, therefore we learn: The relevance of affective and social neuroscience to education. *Mind, Brain, and Education, 1*(1), 3–10.
→ Demonstrates the neurobiological roots of emotion-driven learning, reinforcing SDSS as a neurologically valid model.

o **Kabat-Zinn, J. (2005).** *Wherever You Go, There You Are: Mindfulness Meditation in Everyday Life.* New York: Hyperion.
→ Offers practical tools for presence-based task engagement; relevant to mindful motivation and task initiation.

o **Panksepp, J. (1998).** *Affective Neuroscience: The Foundations of Human and Animal Emotions.* New York: Oxford University Press.
→ Foundational text connecting emotion, motivation, and brain circuitry—a key underpinning of signal theory.

o **Porges, S. W. (2011).** *The Polyvagal Theory:*

Neurophysiological Foundations of Emotions, Attachment, Communication, and Self-Regulation. New York: Norton.
→ Critical to understanding how safety, social context, and co-regulation influence motivation and executive functioning in ADHD.

o **Sleeper-Triplett, J. (2010).** *Empowering Youth with ADHD: Your Guide to Coaching Adolescents and Young Adults.* Plantation, FL: Specialty Press.
→ A practical ADHD coaching framework that aligns directly with SDSS's collaborative, developmental, and emotionally safe approach.

o **Wigfield, A., & Eccles, J. S. (2000).** Expectancy–value theory of achievement motivation. *Contemporary Educational Psychology, 25*(1), 68–81.
→ Offers a framework for how expectations and task value determine motivation—echoed in SDSS's use of desire, efficacy, and possibility.

o **Zentall, S. S. (2005).** Theory- and evidence-based strategies for children with attentional problems. *Psychology in the Schools, 42*(8), 821–836.
→ Research-backed strategies for keeping ADHD learners engaged; highlights how novelty can sustain motivation.

Chapter 7

Signal-Driven Support Systems—Designing Your Inner World Around What Moves You

"Sow a thought, reap an action; sow an action, reap a habit; sow a habit, reap a character; sow a character, reap a destiny."
—Ralph Waldo Emerson and William James fight over authorship of this one

🧠 Quick Preview: What You'll Learn in This Chapter

- Why most ADHD support systems fail—and how signal-based systems succeed
- How to design systems that feel *right* instead of just *right-sized*
- What it means to "follow the signal" in your space, schedule, and social life
- How internal and external signals work together to drive sustained momentum
- Tools like Signal Stacking, Signal Stabilizers, and Signal-Responsive Scaffolding
- How to build ADHD-friendly environments that cue action and reduce friction

🪨 How to Use This Chapter

This chapter is your blueprint for designing systems that *fit your signal*—not just your schedule.

- 🌐 **For People with ADHD—Students, Workers, and Curious Minds**
  If you've ever built a to-do list and ignored it the next day, you're not alone. This section helps you create support systems that actually *work with* your brain—using cues, context, and emotional signals to build habits that stick.
- 🖊 **For Parents, Educators, Clinicians, and Coaches**
  Understand how to help ADHD learners build external structures that act as *signal amplifiers*—not just reminders or pressure. Learn why executive function support must be signal-responsive, emotionally grounded, and identity-aligned.
- 🔎 **Key Concepts and Takeaways**
  Look for tools like Signal Stacking, SASMA integration, and the Express-Contain-Channel model of emotional scaffolding. These tools will help you map signal-responsive environments that support motivation, focus, and follow-through.

💡 Don't try to build the perfect system overnight. Start with what already gives you a signal—and build out from there. This chapter shows you how.

🧠 For People with ADHD—Students, Workers, and Curious Minds

In Chapter 6, we uncovered what truly motivates us. Not pressure, deadlines, or grit—but signals: the emotional, sensory, and meaningful sparks that tell the ADHD brain, *"This matters."* We explored ten different motivational styles, each revealing that ADHD doesn't lack motivation—it follows a different kind of compass.

But insight alone won't get you to the finish line. This chapter is where motivation meets design, where signals get translated into structure. Where you start building an **inner world** that actually supports the way your brain works.

ADHD motivation runs hot, but it also burns out fast. What kind of internal systems can help keep your fire burning? Let's find out.

🔄 From Motivation to Structure

Most time management systems are built around priorities and time. But Signal-Driven Support Systems (SDSS) are built around energy and meaning.

They don't ask, "What should I do?"
They ask, "What will move me?"
And then they build around that answer.

If your signal is Novelty, an SDSS might rotate tasks every 30 minutes or introduce themed workdays. If your signal is Belonging, it might involve body-doubling, friend check-ins, or study groups. If your signal is Efficacy, your system might start with a "starter task"—something you know you can complete successfully to activate momentum.

These are not hacks. They're personalized structures built to keep your motivational circuits online.

🖌 Signal Decay: Why Good Intentions Fade

Even strong signals don't last forever.

That burst of motivation you felt at 9 a.m.? It might be gone by 10:15—not because you don't care, but because the signal decayed.

For people with ADHD, this is one of the most frustrating experiences:

You meant to start. You wanted to do it. You felt the pull...

But then the moment passed—and it didn't come back.

Signal decay refers to the natural fading of urgency, emotion, or salience that once sparked engagement.

For neurotypical brains, motivation often lingers long enough

to translate into action. However, ADHD brains operate within a tighter window—a shorter span of
activation.

 Think of signal decay like the cooling of a spark plug.

If the engine doesn't turn over quickly, the heat dissipates, and you're back to stillness.

This is why it's critical not just to notice a signal, but to act on it quickly or design a stabilizer that catches and holds the signal long enough to convert it into momentum.

✦

▦ Sidebar: TikTok Brain—When the Algorithm Hijacks Your Signal

Short-form content is built to hijack salience. One swipe, one hit. Dopamine. Surprise. Repeat.

For ADHD minds, it's catnip. But for everyone—even neurotypical students—it's reshaping attention.

What used to be a *signal* ("this matters") is now re-placed by a flood of micro-signals. The brain can't sort what's important from what's just stimulating. It's not that people can't focus—it's that the world is asking them to focus on *too much, too fast, too often.*

Psychologists are now observing ADHD-like symptoms in kids *without* ADHD:

- ○ Shorter attention spans
- ○ Emotional dysregulation
- ○ Low boredom tolerance
- ○ Constant novelty-seeking

This isn't ADHD. It's an **adaptive neural response to an overstimulating environment.**

But ADHD minds already start closer to the edge. When the world speeds up, we go over first.

That means we're also the first to *notice the problem—* and the first to build new tools for living well in a distracted world. The systems you'll find in this book are made for ADHD minds... but they may be just what the modern mind needs.

📋 Signal Stabilizers: Keeping the Spark Alive

A good signal gets us moving. But when distractions hit, anxiety rises, or the dopamine drops off, even the strongest motivation can fade.

That's where signal stabilizers come in.

If a signal is a spark, stabilizers are what keep the fire going. They help the ADHD brain hold onto momentum long enough to bridge the gap between wanting to act and following through.

Signal Stabilizers are:

- o Routines that create rhythm
- o Environmental cues that re-trigger intention
- o Tools that reduce friction and decision fatigue
- o Social scaffolding that keeps you in motion
- o Emotional regulation techniques that quiet interference

For example:

- o If your signal is Curiosity, a stabilizer might be a designated "Rabbit Hole Hour" with clear exit points.
- o If your signal is Possibility, a whiteboard full of ideas with a visible "Next Step" column can keep motion going.

- o If your signal is Fear, a countdown timer paired with a calming playlist can hold the tension while still creating safety.

We don't need to force stability through shame. We need to design it through stabilization.

🎗 **Sidebar: Signal Words—Internal Language That Stabilizes (or Scrambles) the Signal**

When we think about signal-driven systems, we usually focus on the *external world*—alarms, checklists, tools, and environments that prompt action. But one of the most powerful stabilizers (or saboteurs) is invisible: **our internal language**.

Some phrases help preserve a signal's strength, even after urgency fades:

"I'm doing this now—and that matters."

"This is the point I'm starting from."

"I'll take a step and see what's next."

These are **Signal Words**—short internal phrases that reinforce permission, momentum, or progress. They act like scaffolding, helping the original impulse stay upright even when motivation dips.

Other phrases, though, trigger decay:

"I should have already done this."

"If I don't finish, I'll fail."

"I can't mess this up."

These words often stem from feelings of guilt, fear, or perfectionism. They don't reinforce the signal—they distort or scramble it. What starts as motivation becomes a burden.

😵 ADHD minds are susceptible to emotionally charged language. That's why **Signal Words** matter. They operate as internal **amplifiers**—either boosting a signal or short-circuiting it, depending on how they're phrased and felt.

🔄 For a full breakdown of Signal Words and how to reframe your inner dialogue, see Chapter 13: *Nested Selves—Internal Voices, Roles, and Self-Compassion.*

🎲 Signal Stackers: Layering What Works

When one signal isn't enough, we stack them.

Signal stacking involves combining multiple small signals into a single, cohesive experience that boosts momentum. Like layering music + movement + time constraint to create flow.

Example stacks:

- o **Urgency + Social + Novelty** = 20-minute co-working sprint with a friend and a new challenge

- o **Beauty + Clarity + Identity** = aesthetic workspace, post-it plan, and a visible "Future Me" affirmation

Stacking gives you more than one chance to catch fire. It's redundancy, but on purpose.

🕵️ The MMO Diagnostic: Decoding Where Motivation Breaks Down

Sometimes, you know what moves you. You even build a system around it. And then… it still doesn't happen.

That's not failure. That's feedback.

The MMO Diagnostic helps you figure out where your support system broke down. MMO stands for:

- o **Method**—Do I have a strategy that fits?
- o **Motive**—Am I using the right signal for this task?
- o **Opportunity**—Is my environment or timing blocking me?

Each of these can be a choke point. The key is knowing which one you're stuck on.

Let's break it down:

🔢 Method: The Tool Doesn't Fit

Sometimes the method we try doesn't match the task, or the brain we're bringing to it. Trying to force a rigid planner onto a highly variable attention profile just won't hold.

Check for Method problems when:

- o You start the task but hit friction immediately
- o You avoid the system you built
- o You feel like the structure is too tight or too loose

Fix it by:

- o Matching structure to signal (e.g., more novelty, more flow, more containment)
- o Asking: What's the minimum viable structure I need to begin?

🔢 Motive: The Fuel Isn't There

If the signal doesn't land, the system won't start. Motivation without Signal is like a engine with no ignition.

Check for Motive problems when:

- o You know the plan, but feel zero emotional pull
- o You feel disconnected or numb about the task
- o You're relying entirely on pressure or shame

Fix it by:

- o Reconnecting to purpose: Why this, now?
- o Using signal stacking (adding music, light, body movement)
- o Swapping to a different signal type that's active today

🔢 Opportunity: The Environment Blocks You

Even with the right signal and strategy, some tasks won't start if the external context is off. ADHD doesn't just require internal motivation—it needs an environment that doesn't sabotage it.

Check for Opportunity problems when:

- You feel constantly interrupted or overstimulated
- The tools or space you need aren't ready
- The time window is unrealistic

Fix it by:

- Designing a "Ready State" before you try to begin
- Creating micro-routines to prepare the space or body
- Shrinking the task window to 5–15 minutes to start

🔖 Case Vignettes and Adaptive Strategies Using MMO
Let's examine how the MMO model unfolds in real-life situations and how learners with ADHD and their supporters can adjust their approach when motivation wanes.

Case 1: Alex—The Method Misfit

Alex loves brainstorming but freezes at follow-through. He tries using rigid daily planners but avoids them after two days. He feels ashamed. In truth? His planner method is choking his novelty-driven brain.

MMO Fix: Alex replaces the planner with sticky-note walls and daily reflection cards. His strategy shifts from "plan it all" to "capture what worked." This matches his signal for insight and variety.

Clinician's View: A coach or clinician might recognize Alex's avoidance not as laziness, but as a mismatch between system and signal. Instead of pushing executive function strategies that rely on rigid structure, they'd guide him to explore pattern-based planning, flexibility, and novelty integration—building methods that match his unique motivational profile.

Case 2: Kiara—The Motive Disconnect
Kiara sets study goals but can't make herself start. Her tasks feel distant and lifeless, even though they matter in the long term. She's stuck in a flat emotional zone.

MMO Fix: She starts creating short visual mood boards before big assignments, watches one inspiring TED Talk before writing, and changes her workspace lighting to reset the emotional climate.

Case 3: Eli—The Opportunity Trap
Eli has a to-do list, a timer, and a playlist—but interruptions surround him. Notifications ping every 3 minutes. His workspace is a mess. He's trying to drive with the brakes on.

MMO Fix: He creates a "power hour" ritual: his phone is silenced, headphones are on, and his desk is pre-cleared the night before. Just 45 minutes, but in a tuned environment.

The most effective systems aren't built alone. Whether at home, in school, or therapy, ADHD-friendly design becomes truly powerful when others understand and support the signals that drive us.

🔗 Chaining—Bridging the Gap from Insight to Action

"Hard work pays off in the future.
Laziness pays off now."
—Steven Wright

For ADHD brains, this isn't just a joke—it's a neurological reality.

Even the best motivational systems face one persistent enemy: **time**. In college and adult life, goals stretch far into the distance—weeks, months, sometimes even years away. For many people with ADHD, that **temporal gap** between present effort and future reward becomes a motivational black hole. No matter how meaningful the outcome, it's just too far off to light a fire *now*.

That's where **Chaining** comes in.

It's a strategy for designing your **inner world** around how your brain works. It links present action to future meaning—one emotionally relevant step at a time. It builds **mental bridges** where gaps in executive function used to be.

⚗ Let's Start with a Classic

You might remember one of those old **DIRECTV ads** that hilariously spirals from mild annoyance to total catastrophe. Like this one:

"When your cable company keeps you on hold, you get angry.
When you get angry, you blow off steam.
When you blow off steam, accidents happen.
When accidents happen, you get an eye patch.
When you get an eye patch, people think you're tough.
When people think you're tough, they want to see how tough.
And when people want to see how tough...
you wake up in a roadside ditch.
Don't wake up in a roadside ditch. Get rid of cable and upgrade to DIRECTV."

It's funny because it's ridiculous—and also **eerily familiar.**

🔁 In Real Life, It Might Look Like This:
If you don't study for your test, you fail.

    If you fail your test, you fail the course.

    If you fail the course, you lose your scholarship.

    If you lose your scholarship, you drop out of school.

    If you drop out of school, your plans fall apart.

    If your plans fall apart, you feel like a failure.

    If you feel like a failure...

you wake up in a roadside ditch. (Not literally. But you get the point.)

    This kind of **negative chaining** happens automatically.

    ADHD minds are experts at worst-case scenario prediction. But here's a twist...

🔄 What If We Flip the Script?
Now imagine the chain running in the opposite direction—one step toward possibility.

    If you open your laptop now, you can write the first paragraph.

    If you write the first paragraph, the rest feels doable.

    If it feels doable, you keep going.

    If you keep going, you finish on time.

    If you finish on time, you feel proud.

    If you feel proud, your confidence grows.

    If your confidence grows...

you start building the life you actually want.

This is **positive chaining**—a signal-based bridge from now to why.

🧩 Case Study: The Puzzle Poster

Some years back, I sat with the parents of a young man who had failed a nine-month computer training program for the third time. He was capable, smart, and even enthusiastic at the start—but midway through, his motivation would always vanish.

The parents had a theory: *maybe he just needed the right incentive*. He had been negotiating with them for months about a specific car he desperately wanted. "If we offer him this car for completing the course, would that motivate him?" they asked.

"Yes," I said. "But not all at once."

The problem wasn't the reward—it was the **distance**. Like many students with ADHD, he struggled to maintain long-term motivation. The car at the end of nine months wasn't close enough to create a signal now. So, I said something that sounded ridiculous at first:

"You'd have to take the car apart and give him a different piece each week—the wheels this week, the engine next week, the transmission after that. And then at the end, you reassemble the car."

It got a laugh, but it also made the point. A whole reward at the finish line doesn't mean much if the finish line never *feels real*. So, we brainstormed a tangible version of that idea.

The solution? A **chained reward**. The parents bought a poster of the car and turned it into a puzzle. Each week he completed successfully, he earned one piece. Every piece brought him visually and emotionally closer to his goal—and served as a **present-tense reminder** of what was at stake. When he had the full poster, he got the car.

This simple visual system flattened time. It transformed one giant, abstract goal into a series of small, visible, motivating wins—and it worked.

Why Chaining Works

Chaining is a form of **cognitive scaffolding** that supports internal motivation.

It's not about tricking your brain—it's about working with its unique wiring. ADHD minds often struggle to hold distant rewards in emotional memory. Even if something matters *deeply*, it can feel irrelevant in the moment if the signal isn't strong.

Negative chains happen automatically, but positive chains can be designed intentionally. When you show your brain how the smallest action now connects to the bigger "why," you flatten time, reduce overwhelm, and create momentum.

Chaining connects the dots your brain can't hold all at once—linking now, to next, to meaning.

🕐 **Sidebar: Why the Future Feels Fuzzy— and the Present Takes Over**

If you've read Chapter 1: *What Makes Us Uniquely Different*, you might remember this:

For many with ADHD, **time doesn't unfold in a straight line**. Instead, the future shows up as a chaotic stack of

---

overlapping moments—none of them clearly outlined, all of them shouting at once.

It's like trying to watch ten shows on the same screen.

Long-term goals often get flattened and drowned out by the emotional intensity of the moment. And when the present is overwhelming, the future gets filtered out.

Neurologically, this is often tied to differences in the **salience network**—the part of the brain that determines what matters most at any given moment. When the future isn't emotionally relevant or signal-rich, it gets ignored.

Chaining helps flatten that stack into a story.

It reconnects the present moment to the future self—not through pressure, but through emotional relevance. One link at a time.

Try This: Build Your Own Chain

Pick something you're avoiding—studying, finishing a project, or showing up to class.

Now ask yourself:

- *What's in it for me to do this today?*
- *If I do this, what will happen next?*
- *And what would that make possible?*

This becomes your **motivational map**.

Some students write it out. Others draw it. One made a vision board. And some—like Matt—record messages to their future selves.

🎥 Case Example: Matt's Motivation Signal

Matt, a college student with ADHD, wanted to train for a 5K but kept stalling. "I hate running," he said. "But I like how I feel after."

One day, after a run, he pulled out his phone and recorded a short video to his future self:

> "Right now you don't want to run. But look—I'm sweaty, I'm hot, and I'm really happy. You're gonna be glad you came."

That video became a **signal**—not a command or a threat, just a **reminder** of what mattered to him. And it worked better than any planner or app. Because it wasn't pressure—it was permission.

The next time he felt resistance, he hit the play button. The signal landed. The run happened. The chain held.

🛠️ Take Chaining a Step Further

Try this structure:

1. **Pick one small action** you need to take today.
2. **Link it to a short-term reward** ("If I do this, I'll feel relieved tonight").
3. **Link that to a longer-term outcome** ("If I keep this up, I'll pass the class").
4. **Link it to something that deeply matters** ("If I pass, I move closer to becoming a teacher").

The goal is not guilt—it's grounding.

You're not forcing action. You're **designing alignment—** one link at a time.

So where does all of this take us?

If mapping signals helps us manage motivation and build support systems, what happens when we take a step back and look at the whole picture?

We usually talk about two kinds of intelligence.

The first is **book smarts**—the kind of intelligence schools test for: memorizing facts, solving structured problems, proving you know the "right answer." Book smarts can help you ace an exam or impress people with trivia, but when life gets messy, book smarts often run out of road.

The second is **street smarts**—the kind of intelligence that grows from experience: reading the room, sensing when something's off, adapting on the fly. Street smarts help you survive in unpredictable environments. If book smarts get you through the classroom, street smarts get you through the parking lot after dark.

Both are valuable. But neither is enough.

There's a third kind of intelligence—one that doesn't usually get named, but that every one of us can develop. You can see it in the world around you through a principle called **emergence**.

Watch a flock of starlings wheel across the sky in a giant murmuration. No bird sees the whole shape. Each one is just following a few simple rules—don't crash into your neighbor, match their speed, stay close. From these local signals, something breathtaking emerges: a coherent, dynamic pattern.

Or consider traffic jams. No driver intends to create one. Each car just brakes a little, changes lanes, slows for a curve. But when those small signals interact, they ripple into stop-and-go waves of congestion that no single driver chose, yet everyone experiences.

This is how emergence works: simple signals, when integrated, create something larger than the sum of their parts.

And that's where these skills—noticing, mapping, and integrating signals—really point. They don't just help us manage a single task, or even a single support system. **On the product side**, they lead to better outcomes: goals accomplished, systems stabilized, problems solved. But **on the process side**, something deeper is happening. Simply practicing signal awareness—noticing, making meaning, integrating, and acting—*forms a higher order of intelligence in us as we go.*

Where book smarts help us pass tests, and street smarts help us adapt, this emerging form of intelligence helps us thrive—not just by giving us better results, but by reshaping the way our minds work. The process itself is the training ground for something bigger.

We'll name it more fully in the chapters to come. For now, it's enough to recognize that every signal you track and every pattern you integrate is doing two things at once: helping you right now, and also building in you the foundation of a new kind of intelligence.

✏️ For Parents, Educators, Clinicians, Coaches, and Curious Readers

Understanding the principles of signal-based motivation is powerful, but applying them in real-world settings is where the real change happens. This section provides tailored guidance for individuals supporting learners and workers with ADHD at home, in school, or therapeutic settings.

👨‍👩‍👧 For Parents:

- Observe and reflect on what consistently sparks your child's engagement—is it collaboration, curiosity, humor?
- Help build micro-routines at home that align with those motivational signals, like starting homework with a silly warm-up or using visual checklists with emoji reactions.
- Provide autonomy when possible—offer choices instead of commands.

🏫 For Educators:

- Integrate SDSS-aligned practices in your classroom: movement breaks, rotating partner work, or time-limited "sprints."
- Identify patterns of motivation across students and design "menu" options for tasks (write a paragraph, record a voice memo, draw a diagram).
- Normalize tools like noise-canceling

headphones, sensory fidgets, and visual timers.

🧠 For Clinicians and Coaches:

- Use the MMO diagnostic during sessions to help students and clients troubleshoot their own patterns.
- Introduce signal-mapping worksheets to identify and track motivation triggers.
- Consider incorporating Motivational Interviewing techniques to help clients clarify values, amplify intrinsic motivations, and reduce ambivalence.
- Help clients identify not just what moves them, but what derails them emotionally, and design stabilizers that protect signal strength in those moments.
- Model co-regulation in sessions: pacing, tone, and attuned presence are tools that help transfer safety and rhythm into real-world applications.

🗡️ Sidebar: Helping Students Enter a Ready State

- For parents, teachers, and counselors supporting someone with ADHD, here's how to help create an environment that fosters readiness—the zone where signals have a chance to convert into action:
- Minimize friction: Have materials pre-staged and visible—notebooks open, chargers plugged in, apps queued up.
- Set an emotional tone: Music, lighting, or familiar sensory inputs can help reduce overwhelm and create psychological safety.

- o Offer visual cues: Whiteboards, sticky notes, or visual task outlines can reinforce intent.
- o Build transitional rituals: Use a 5-minute setup routine (e.g., water, breathwork, noise-canceling headphones) to signal a shift into focus.
- o Limit decision fatigue: Use default choices—"Start with math," "Use your blue folder," "Today is body-doubling day." Creating micro-routines to prepare the space or body, shrinking the task window to 5–15 minutes to start.
- o These steps don't just prepare the body or space. They stabilize the signal window—and that's where sustainable motivation begins.

📚 References for Further Reading

o **Barkley, R. A. (2012).** *Executive functions: What they are, how they work, and why they evolved.* Guilford Press.
A foundational text explaining the neurological basis of executive function and how it applies to ADHD behavior and motivation systems.

o **Dawson, P., & Guare, R. (2018).** *Executive skills in children and adolescents: A practical guide to assessment and intervention* (3rd ed.). Guilford Press.
Offers practical strategies for identifying and supporting executive skill development—a helpful framework for understanding SDSS challenges in school-aged learners.

o **Deci, E. L., & Ryan, R. M. (2000).** The "what" and "why" of goal pursuits: Human needs and the self-determination of behavior. *Psychological Inquiry, 11*(4), 227–268.
Introduces Self-Determination Theory—a key foundation for understanding intrinsic motivation and emotional engagement, both central to signal-based support.

o **Miller, W. R., & Rollnick, S. (2013).** *Motivational interviewing: Helping people change* (3rd ed.). Guilford Press.
Explores techniques for eliciting internal motivation, widely used in counseling and coaching to help clients identify meaningful signals and reduce resistance.

o **Nadeau, K. G. (2005).** *Survival guide for college students with ADHD or LD.* Magination Press.
Offers direct, student-facing tools and strategies tailored to the college experience of individuals with ADHD, many of which align naturally with SDSS principles.

o **Sleeper-Triplett, J. (2010).** *Empowering youth with ADHD: Your guide to coaching adolescents and young adults for coaches, parents, and professionals.* Specialty Press.
Focuses on strengths-based coaching and signal-sensitive support approaches for teens and young adults navigating school, motivation, and independence.

o **Tomchek, S. D., & Dunn, W. (2007).** Sensory processing in children with and without autism: A comparative study using the Short Sensory Profile. *American Journal of Occupational Therapy, 61*(2), 190–200.
Provides evidence for sensory sensitivity differences—a crucial layer in understanding how environmental signals impact ADHD engagement and regulation.

o **Tuckman, A. R. (2009).** *More attention, less deficit: Success strategies for adults with ADHD.* Specialty Press.
An engaging and practical guide that supports adults with ADHD in managing work, tasks, and motivation through real-world strategies aligned with signal logic.

o **Willis, J. (2007).** *Brain-friendly strategies for the inclusion classroom.* ASCD.
Shares classroom strategies based on brain science—highly relevant for teachers aiming to align learning environments with students' signal-based needs.

o **Zentall, S. S. (2005).** Theory- and evidence-based strategies for children with attentional problems. *Psychology in the Schools, 42*(8), 821–836.
Connects classroom behaviors to neurological and motivational dynamics, emphasizing signal alignment in academic success for students with ADHD.

Chapter 8

Signal-Driven Environments— Redesigning the World Around the ADHD Brain

"You can't change the wind, but
you can adjust the sails."
—Proverb

 Quick Preview: What You'll Learn in This Chapter

- Why "just try harder" fails—and "change the system" works
- How environments shape focus, energy, motivation, and follow-through in ADHD minds
- Why ADHD brains need **visible**, **emotionally resonant**, and **action-ready** cues
- How to build environments that *speak in signals*—not just systems
- Tools like **Visual Anchors**, **Emotional Zoning**, and **Supportive Friction**
- Real-world redesigns—from dorm rooms to digital dashboards—that help ADHD students thrive
- How to create an ecosystem that supports the *brain you have*, not the one the world expects

✧

📰 How to Use This Chapter

This chapter is structured to meet the needs of multiple readers—whether you're living with ADHD, supporting someone who is, or simply curious. You can read it straight through or jump to the section that fits your role right now.

- ○ 🧠 **For People with ADHD—Students, Workers, and Curious Minds:**
  This section offers practical strategies for redesigning your space, schedule, and systems to better match your brain. It focuses on tools that create clarity, reduce resistance, and help motivation flow more naturally.
- ○ 🖊️ **For Parents, Educators, Clinicians, and Coaches:**
  This section explores how environmental scaffolding supports executive function in ADHD learners. It includes design principles, case examples, and evidence-based practices that show how small changes can produce big outcomes.
- ○ 💡 **Key Tools and Takeaways:**
  Throughout the chapter, you'll find exercises, models, and redesign prompts—including the Visual Anchor Grid, Emotional Zoning Map, and the Signal-Based Environment Checklist.

💡 You don't need to read every word. Let the signals guide you—skip around, pause where it clicks, and come back when you need it.

🧠 For People with ADHD—Students, Workers, and Curious Minds

Introduction

In the previous chapter, we examined how motivation can break down, even when we are aware of what motivates us. We looked at how Method, Motive, and Opportunity work together in the MMO Diagnostic, and we saw how mismatches in any of these can cause frustration and false starts. Now we zoom in on one key element that often goes overlooked: opportunity—or more precisely, context.

The world around us matters more than most productivity tools acknowledge. For people with ADHD, environments aren't neutral—they are active participants in success or failure. They can amplify signals or squash them, stabilize momentum or scatter it.

This chapter is about redesigning our world—our homes, schools, and workplaces—to work with our brains, not against them.

📝 Designing for Opportunity: ADHD and the Built Environment

Opportunity doesn't just mean time. It means access to the tools, emotions, clarity, and space that allow a signal to become action.

Too often, students are blamed for a lack of follow-through when the truth is that their environment never provided the necessary support for ignition. The book was buried. The charger was missing. The lights were too bright. The table was noisy. The brain didn't fail—the world wasn't ready.

For the ADHD mind, the setup matters more than the plan.

Let's explore what it means to design environments that are:

- **Low-friction** (tasks are easy to start)
- **Signal-congruent** (aligned with motivational style)
- **Sensory-regulated** (not under- or over-stimulating)
- **Emotionally safe** (especially in trauma-impacted learners)

Amplifiers start the fire. Stabilizers keep it burning.

So what does it look like to create a world that supports you instead of subtly working against you? A signal-driven environment isn't about perfection—it's about alignment.

Let's walk through four real-world contexts where ADHD brains often get stuck—and where small environmental tweaks can unlock big momentum.

☞ Let's explore how small shifts can create a big difference:

1. Classrooms: Focus Without Shame

- Use flexible seating: movement helps memory
- Light filters or natural light for sensory regulation
- Allow headphones or quiet corners to reduce auditory overload
- Normalize fidget tools without spotlighting the user
- Structure transitions with visual timers or routines

When the environment aligns with the nervous system, students spend less time masking and more time learning.

2. Home: Stabilizing Transitions

- Anchor routines with sensory cues: music, scent, tactile objects
- Create visual "launch pads" for keys, backpacks, or supplies
- Use lighting to cue different brain states: warm for winding down, bright for action
- Keep task spaces distinct from rest zones—even a curtain can make a difference

Think of your home as a signal station: everything you see or touch is a potential cue for action—or
overwhelm.

3. Workplaces: Reduce Switching Costs

- Chunk tasks and match them with specific zones (email at the standing desk, creative writing on the couch)
- Reduce decision friction: pre-decide your top 3 priorities and post them
- Use "Done for Now" trays to contain open loops visually
- Lightly script your re-entry rituals: what gets you back on task after a break?

Environmental clarity = cognitive clarity. Structure isn't about control—it's about making room for flow.

4. Tech: Guardrails Against Digital Hijack

- Use app timers and browser extensions to filter distractions
- Make your phone less shiny: grayscale mode, rearranged icons

- o Create a single homebase app or dashboard where your essential tools live
- o Design "offramps" for scrolling: something easy and meaningful to transition into

Your tech environment is one of the most potent signal amplifiers—and one of the most easily hijacked.

🎨 Sidebar: A Note for the Scroll-Weary

You don't need an ADHD diagnosis to feel like your attention span is shrinking.

If you've ever closed TikTok or Instagram and felt foggier than before you opened it...

If you've struggled to finish a paragraph without checking your phone...

If you've caught yourself needing *more stimulation* just to stay motivated...

You're not alone. And you're not broken.

You're living in a world that's speeding up faster than your brain was built for.

ADHD may be a clinical diagnosis—but it's also a mirror. A preview of what happens when motivation systems, emotional regulation, and focus get pushed past their limits.

In this book, we're exploring tools to live well with ADHD—but many of these tools may help *anyone* trying to think clearly, feel deeply, and act with intention in a world that increasingly fragments all three.

So whether you live with ADHD, love someone who does, or simply want to reclaim your attention from the digital tide—you're in the right place.

☞ *So, how do we translate these design ideas into something practical—a space audit you can actually use?*

📋 ADHD Environmental Checklists—Signal-Supportive Design in Action

ADHD-friendly environments aren't just cleaner or quieter—they're designed for ignition. Here are some key signal-shaping elements across five key domains:

1. Space

- Clear surfaces for focused tasks
- Distinct zones for different activities (study, rest, create)
- Movement-friendly layout—standing desk, floor seating, or pacing space

2. Light

- Adjustable lighting (natural light, if possible, warm tones when focusing)

- o Dimmable lamps or light filters to prevent overstimulation
- o Light cues that mark transitions (e.g., morning vs. evening setups)

3. Sound

- o Noise-dampening tools: white noise, noise-canceling headphones, music playlists
- o Use of signal sounds to prompt action (e.g., start-of-work chime or nature sounds for transition)

4. Movement

- o Chairs that allow rocking, fidget stools, or resistance bands under desks
- o Scheduled movement breaks with signal cues (e.g., timer that triggers stretch + music)

5. Friction

- o Tasks arranged in order of use (e.g., backpack hook near desk, planner open on workspace)
- o Ready State bins or baskets with all required supplies visible and reachable
- o Fewer steps between thought and action: auto-logins, labeled folders, visual checklists

✦

 Now that you've assessed the environment, let's look at how to prime it for ignition.

🌐 What Is a Ready State?

A Ready State is a preloaded signal environment—a setup that gets your brain halfway to action before you even start. It's not just being organized. It's being primed.

Examples:

- A playlist queued up to your writing flow song
- A yoga mat unrolled and waiting
- A post it note on the door with your 3-step morning launch

A good Ready State reduces the effort to begin and increases the signal strength of what's next. For people with ADHD, that difference can mean everything.

Using the tools from this chapter, you can build your own Ready State Templates by environment, such as morning routine, study zone, and transition time. Start building your own today.

🖊 For Educators, Parents, Clinicians, Coaches, and Curious Readers

Creating supportive environments for people with ADHD is not simply a matter of adding accommodations—it's about shifting the entire lens from compliance to compatibility. This section provides practical strategies, clinical insights, and research-based guidance to help you co-design spaces where attention, motivation, and follow-through can flourish.

1. ADHD Isn't Distraction—It's Signal Vulnerability

Rather than framing ADHD as a disorder of attention, consider reframing it as a disorder of context sensitivity. Signals are hijacked, drowned out, or scattered when the environment doesn't support salience. The intervention isn't just about focusing harder—it's about tuning the space to help the brain detect what matters.

2. Space as Intervention: The MMO Opportunity Lens

If the student or client is motivated (**motive**) and knows how (**method**), then what's often missing is environmental ***opportunity***. Use the MMO Diagnostic to scan for context-based mismatches. Ask: "Does the setting amplify or inhibit the signal they need to act on?"

3. Environmental Cue Coaching

Help students or clients build intentional cue-to-signal chains. Work backward: If brushing teeth fails, is the toothbrush visible? Is the cue buried? Consider proximity, lighting, labeling, and routine sequence.

4. Create "Ready States" Before Performance is Expected

Many individuals with ADHD can perform well once they're started—the challenge is getting started.
Parents and teachers can support this by front-loading routines that stabilize state shifts. Examples:

- In school: soft lighting, noise-canceling headphones, hydration stations, transition playlists.
- At home: visual morning routines, structured task warm-ups, sensory "start zones."

5. Small Shifts, Big Impact: Friction, Flow, and Feedback

- Reduce friction (e.g., preloaded tabs, single-task mode) • Protect flow (e.g., minimize mid-task switches) • Offer feedback loops (e.g., visible progress, affirmations)

6. Case Vignettes

- ○ *Alex (Age 15)*: Once failing algebra due to homework avoidance, Alex now uses a whiteboard calendar, LED "focus light," and phone in a timed lockbox. Signal stabilizers include a "study startup" playlist and a sibling accountability check-in.
- ○ *Kiara (Age 21)*: A college student with RSD and sensory sensitivities, Kiara redesigned her workspace with warm lighting, a standing desk, and noise-dampening panels. A calming scent cue and check-in text with a mentor serve as ignition anchors.
- ○ *Eli (Age 9)*: Diagnosed with ADHD and SPD, Eli now uses a sensory cushion, fidget tools, and personalized task cards in class. A "choose-your-start" approach helped him re-engage with assignments.

7. Integrate with Other Interventions
Environmental design supports, but does not replace, therapeutic, behavioral, or coaching-based strategies. These tools work best in concert with:

- ○ CBT and executive function coaching
- ○ Sensory integration support
- ○ Motivational Interviewing techniques
- ○ Strengths-based self-awareness interventions

✱ Signal-Based Environment Design

Checklist for Clinicians, Educators, Parents, Coaches, and People with ADHD

When ADHD shows up as procrastination, avoidance, or "lack of motivation," the root problem is often environmental—not internal. ADHD brains are signal-sensitive and friction-prone. That means context matters more than most support models account for.

This checklist offers a practical way to audit a space—classroom, workspace, bedroom, or study zone—and identify small changes that can make a big impact. You don't have to implement everything. Start with one or two areas that seem out of sync and build from there.

🪑 SPACE—Structure Without Clutter

- ☐ Clear, uncluttered visual field
- ☐ Task-specific zones (e.g., reading nook, writing desk)
- ☐ Vertical organizers to externalize working memory
- ☐ Proximity to essentials (water, charger, fidget, materials)
- ☐ Adjustable layout (e.g., standing desk, flexible seating)

✦

🔊 SOUND—Calibrate the Noise Floor

- ☐ Noise-canceling headphones or soft ambient sound
- ☐ Sound-dampening materials (rugs, curtains, soft surfaces)
- ☐ Preferred playlists or white noise for different tasks
- ☐ Acoustic privacy or emotional "quiet zones"

💡 LIGHT—Tune the Visual Tempo

- ☐ Access to natural light (from the side if possible)
- ☐ Warm, adjustable lighting (avoid fluorescent flicker)
- ☐ Focused task lighting (e.g., desk lamp, reading spotlight)
- ☐ Light-based transition cues (e.g., sunset lamp for bedtime)

✧

🌀 MOVEMENT—Build in Permission to Shift

- ☐ Room to stretch, stand, or shift positions
- ☐ Subtle-motion seating (wiggle stool, balance ball, rocking chair)
- ☐ Movement breaks integrated into routine
- ☐ Kinetic tools (whiteboards, walk-and-talks, fidget pathways)

✧

⚙️ FRICTION—Reduce Barriers to Entry

- ☐ Materials are visible, accessible, and pre-staged
- ☐ Instructions are clear, brief, and visually chunked
- ☐ Emotional tone is low-stakes and affirming
- ☐ Safe reset options available ("start-over" stations, no-shame retries)

✧

◯ SIGNAL STABILIZERS—Build an Internal Anchor

- ◦ ☐ Anchoring rituals (countdowns, music cues, mantras)
- ◦ ☐ Supportive external accountability (check-ins, study buddy, mentor)
- ◦ ☐ Motivational visuals in view (inspirational quote, post-it map, mission board)
- ◦ ☐ Daily rhythm aligned with energy windows (not just time blocks)

Pro Tip: This isn't a checklist to "fix" ADHD—it's a tool to *support it.* ADHD brains are highly responsive to signals, and that makes the environment a key part of the system. When you shift the context to support salience, effort feels less forced—and action becomes more natural.

✧

📖 References for Further Reading

◦ **Barkley, R. A. (2011). *Executive functions: What they are, how they work, and why they evolved.* New York: Guilford Press.**
A foundational text on the role of executive functions in ADHD, including how motivation and task initiation are impacted by neurological delay—essential for understanding ADHD's challenge with self-regulation in context.

◦ **Boellstorff, T., & Maurer, B. (2015). *Signal traffic: Critical studies of media infrastructures.* Durham: Duke University Press.**
Explores how infrastructure and environmental signals shape

human behavior. While not ADHD-specific, it provides a powerful conceptual backdrop for the idea of "signal-driven environments" presented in this chapter.

○ Dawson, P., & Guare, R. (2018). *Smart but scattered teens: The "executive skills" program for helping teens reach their potential.* New York: Guilford Press.
Offers practical tools for teaching executive functioning through environmental supports and routines. A strong companion to signal-based and MMO-aligned strategies discussed here.

○ Graham, L. (2010). Cognitive load theory and instructional design for ADHD. *Educational Technology Research and Development, 58*(5), 529–548.
Discusses how reducing friction and environmental distractions lowers cognitive load, making initiation and follow-through more manageable for ADHD learners—reinforcing the role of context in success.

○ Koenig, K. P., & Rudney, S. G. (2010). Performance challenges for children and youth with sensory integration disorder: A systematic review. *American Journal of Occupational Therapy, 64*(3), 430–442.
Reviews sensory processing issues that often co-occur with ADHD, emphasizing the importance of physical and sensory environment modifications such as lighting, sound, and movement options.

○ Kuo, F. E., & Taylor, A. F. (2004). A potential natural treatment for Attention-Deficit/Hyperactivity Disorder: Evidence from a national study. *American Journal of Public Health, 94*(9), 1580–1586.
Findings show that time in green, natural outdoor environments reduces ADHD symptoms. Reinforces the "light,

movement, and sensory" environmental redesigns highlighted in this chapter.

o **Levine, M. (2003).** *A mind at a time.* **New York: Simon & Schuster.**
Advocates for individualized learning profiles and environmental fit, emphasizing context-sensitive education that parallels the signal-based approach used here.

o **Peper, E., Harvey, R., Lin, I. M., & Perez, J. (2014). Digital addiction: Increased symptomatology in ADHD.** *NeuroRegulation, 1*(2), 109–120.
Examines the effects of digital environments on attention, stress, and motivation. Provides evidence for the "tech hijack" discussion and supports strategies like app timers, dashboard design, and scroll-offramps.

o **Waber, D. P. (2010).** *Rethinking learning differences: A neuroscientist's perspective on individual learning profiles.* **New York: Basic Books.**
Provides a framework for designing individualized environments that support diverse cognitive styles—aligning with this chapter's theme of building ecosystems that work with the brain you have, not the one the world expects.

-sensitive education that parallels the signal-based approach used here.

✸ Part III Introduction: The Inner Team—Visionary, Producer, and Editor

How ADHD Brains Dream, Do, and Decide

> *"Your brain isn't broken—it's just trying to do the job of three different people at once: the dreamer, the doer, and the editor-in-chief."*

If Part Two helped you build signal awareness and motivation, this section helps you channel that energy through your internal decision-making team.

By now, you've likely started mapping your signals. You've explored how motivation works in an ADHD brain. And maybe—just maybe—you've started to notice something surprising:

Your attention isn't random.
It's responsive.
Intelligent.
Alive.

That means it's not just reacting—it's intuitively following something.

But now comes the big question:
Who's steering this thing?

Inside every ADHD brain is a cast of characters—an internal team that tries to run your life. When they're aligned, it's magic.

When they're at war? Total chaos.

A Note on Origins

This model builds on the idea that we each contain multiple inner roles—a concept first popularized by Robert Dilts in his *Dreamer–Realist–Critic* framework (1994). The **Visionary–Producer–Editor** model expands and adapts this idea through the lens of ADHD, executive function, and signal-based motivation. It introduces a new language, new functions, and role states (*Advanced, Emerging, Dormant*) to help ADHD minds work in sequence—not opposition.

✧

This section introduces the Visionary–Producer–Editor model—a simple but powerful way to understand the three core roles we all carry inside:

- ○ ◉ **The Visionary** dreams, imagines, and feels what could be.

- ○ ⚒ **The Producer** builds the bridge between dream and reality.

- ○ ✺ **The Editor** refines, adjusts, and makes meaning out of the mess.

Each role listens for a different kind of signal—one that reflects its unique job in the system.

And when they're out of sync, they may talk over each other, second-guess decisions, or disappear entirely—leaving confusion in their place.

⚙️ Three States of Inner Roles

These roles aren't fixed personality types—they're states. And just like moods, they shift depending on energy, context, and support.

Each of your inner team members operates in one of three states:

Advanced, Emerging, or Dormant.

You might have a brilliant Visionary but a Dormant Producer.

Or a sharp Editor who only wakes up after failure.

Recognizing which roles are active—and which need support—is part of building your Living Compass.

Here's what each role looks like at different stages of development:

Role	Dormant	Emerging	Advanced
Visionary	Lost in fog, no clear goal	Ideas spark but fade	Inspired, purpose-driven imagination
Producer	Stuck in paralysis	Starting, but inconsistent	Takes action with rhythm and focus
Editor	Harsh inner critic	Sometimes reflective, reactive	Insightful, strategic course-corrector

This inner team is fluid.

Some days, your Producer runs the show.

Other days, your Editor takes over and critiques everything.

But when all three work in sequence—*dream, do, reflect*—your life begins to move with intention and adaptability.

⚠ Common ADHD Role Imbalances

Many people with ADHD tend to over-identify with one role and underuse the others:

- Some chase vision after vision without ever grounding them in action.
- Others stay busy "getting things done"—often in Producer mode—but never connect to purpose or meaning.
- Many struggle with the Editor—turning it into an inner critic instead of a strategic guide.

ADHD doesn't mean you lack direction—it means your internal team may be misaligned.

But when each role is honored in its time, they form a feedback loop of clarity, action, and learning.

✧

Rethinking the Editor: Not a Critic—a Guide

When the Editor is healthy, it's not here to tear you down.

It's here to help you adjust course—not punish yourself for leaving it.

A skilled Editor doesn't judge. It strategizes.

It asks:

- How could this fail—and how might I prevent that?
- How do I recover faster next time?
- What can I learn from this?
- How will that learning guide me in the future?

Used wisely, the Editor becomes your **growth ally**—helping you prepare for setbacks, navigate risk, and extract value from every experience.

It becomes the voice of *course correction*, not criticism.

Meet Your Inner Team—and Learn How to Get Them Working Together

In the next three chapters, you'll:

- o Meet your **Visionary**—and learn how to follow the signal without floating away.
- o Train your **Producer** to show up reliably—even on low-energy days.
- o Reclaim your **Editor** as a strategic guide—and learn how to turn feedback into fuel.

Together, these roles form your **Inner Compass**—a structure that brings clarity to chaos, rhythm to effort, and wisdom to failure.

Let's meet the team.

🖋 **Sidebar: ADHD Isn't Disorganized—It's Misorganized**

Many people with ADHD aren't disorganized—they're trying to run a three-person system on solo energy. Without clear roles:

- o The **Visionary** floods the inbox with big ideas.
- o The **Producer** gets overwhelmed by them.
- o The **Editor** shows up late—and critiques everything, all at once.

What you need isn't more discipline.

It's coordination.

This section is about building that coordination from the inside out.

When your inner team starts working together, every-thing else gets easier—because you're no longer fighting yourself.

Chapter 9

The Visionary—Holding the Dream, Following the Signal

"Everything begins as fiction—until someone believes in it hard enough to build it."
—Visionary Principle, ADHD College Success Guidance Program

📜 How to Use This Chapter

This chapter is built for multiple readers. Whether you're discovering your own internal Visionary or helping someone else learn to trust theirs, each section offers a different lens on how signal-based imagination drives action.

- o 🧠 **For People with ADHD—Students, Workers, and Curious Minds:**
  Explore how visionary thinking works *with* the ADHD brain—not against it. Learn to track inspiration, navigate vision overwhelm, and turn signal-rich ideas into future momentum.
- o ✏️ **For Parents, Clinicians, Educators, Coaches—and Curious Readers:**
  Get research-backed insight into the strengths and struggles of the ADHD Visionary mind. Learn how to support long-term planning by working *with* meaning, identity, and imagination—not just structure.
- o 🔍 **Key Tools and Takeaways:**

This chapter includes the **Visionary Profile Worksheet**, a **Beginner's Mind** sidebar, and visual cues to help students translate insight into direction.

> 💡 You can read this start to finish, or dip in where the signal feels strongest. Like the Visionary mind itself, this chapter works best when explored with curiosity and openness.

🔡 Quick Guide to Chapter 9: The Visionary— Holding the Dream, Following the Signal

🎯 Core Concept:

The Visionary is the part of you that senses meaning before it can be explained. It imagines futures, collects signals of resonance, and directs you toward what matters—before a plan even exists.

🧠 For People with ADHD:

- Learn to recognize the feeling of alignment when something "clicks."
- Discover how visionary thinking works because of ADHD brain wiring—not despite it.
- Explore the difference between inspired direction and vision overwhelm.
- Reclaim the role of your imagination as a source of wisdom, not distraction.

🖊 For Parents, Clinicians, and Educators:

- Support long-range thinking through motivational alignment, not just goal setting.
- Understand how increased default mode network activity supports idea generation.

- o Use the Visionary Profile Worksheet to identify student strengths and barriers.
- o Encourage white space in schedules to allow signal-driven insights to emerge.

✧

For People with ADHD—Students, Workers, and Curious Minds

Inside the ADHD brain, the Visionary is the first voice to speak.

It whispers possibilities. It senses meaning before there's a map. It dreams in signals—flashes of interest, excitement, urgency, or beauty. It doesn't need a reason to imagine something better. It just feels it.

When it's working well, the Visionary helps you:

- o Spot patterns no one else sees
- o Ask questions no one else is asking
- o Imagine futures no one else has considered

But here's the catch: ADHD minds often live in that "what if" space... and sometimes get lost there.

You start the day with a flood of new ideas.

You feel the signal of something exciting—a big project, a new plan, a different future.

But then you stall out, forget the steps, or get overwhelmed by everything it could become.

That's not a failure of intelligence.

That's a signal overload without a container.

And that's where your Producer and Editor come in—to help translate vision into steps, and steps into success.

But before we get to them, we need to spend time with the part of you that holds the dream.

🔭 The Visionary's Job

The Visionary doesn't think in checklists.

It thinks in what-ifs.

In why-nots.

In the emotional resonance of a thing before it's real.

This part of you:

- o Detects emerging possibilities
- o Collects signals of meaning
- o Asks why something matters

🌐 The ADHD brain has extraordinary **functional connectivity**.

That means your mind doesn't just think in a straight line—it thinks like a constellation.

It links ideas from different domains.

It relates the unrelated.

It pulls metaphors from memories, concepts from dreams, and patterns from the air—all in service of meaning.

That's not distraction.

That's visionary pattern recognition.

Beginner's Mind—The Visionary's Hidden Superpower

One of the Visionary's most excellent tools is something we explored earlier in this book: [**Beginner's Mind** (see Chapter 3)]— the ability to see with fresh eyes, free from the weight of what "should" work. It's the part of you that lets go of expertise just long enough to notice what others have overlooked.

ADHD minds, when not shut down by shame or rigidity, often excel at this. They draw from unexpected sources, spot invisible patterns, and propose wild ideas that somehow turn out to be right. It's not just "thinking outside the box"—it's seeing that the box was optional.

Beginner's Mind gives the Visionary room to roam. It creates the internal conditions for signal recognition, spontaneous insight, and creative leaps. And when nurtured, it becomes a lifelong advantage: the ability to adapt, rethink, and simplify when complexity gets stuck.

If the Visionary is the dreamer, then Beginner's Mind is the window they see through—wide open, curious, and ready for surprise.

When your Visionary is strong, your life has direction.

When it's quiet or dismissed, your days can feel hollow—like you're just reacting, not moving toward something.

And for some of us, the Visionary state isn't just about ideas—it's a full-body knowing.

You may not be able to describe it, but you've felt it:

That moment when you glimpse a possible future—and something inside you aligns.

It's not just interest. It's pull.

Like your whole nervous system is pointing north.

You can't always explain it. But you know it's real.

That's the Visionary signal at work—and it's worth listening to.

✧

Visionary Profile Worksheet

Name Your Inner Visionary—How Active Is This Role in Your Life?

Use the sections below to help you recognize how your Visionary shows up—and what kind of support it might need.

🔍 I Know I'm in Visionary Mode When...

- ☑ I get spontaneous ideas that energize or excite me.
- ☑ I feel pulled toward something that resonates deeply—even if I can't explain why.
- ☑ I start to imagine a future version of myself that feels meaningful or aligned.
- ☑ I link together ideas from different areas—like memories, metaphors, or random thoughts—and they click.
- ☑ I feel a quiet sense of focus, like everything around me is pointing toward something important.

✧

⊛ My Visionary Right Now Feels:

- ○ ● **Dormant** – I've lost sight of what excites or matters to me. I feel uninspired or directionless.
- ○ ◐ **Emerging** – I feel sparks of inspiration sometimes, but they come and go quickly. I struggle to act on them.
- ○ ◕ **Advanced** – I regularly notice ideas or signals that energize me, and I've started learning how to follow through on them.

○ Prompt for Reflection:

What's one idea, direction, or future version of yourself that keeps showing up—even if you haven't acted on it yet?

Write a few lines below to explore that vision, even if it feels far away or hard to describe:

⚗ For Parents, Educators, Clinicians, Coaches, and Curious Readers

The Visionary role is often the least supported in educational and clinical environments. We reward task completion (Producer role) and critical analysis (Editor role) but rarely help individuals with ADHD develop and protect their inner sense of direction.

🔍 Key Points to Know:

- ○ Learners with ADHD often have exceptionally high functional connectivity (see Castellanos & Proal, 2012), which supports idea generation and divergent thinking.

- The default mode network (DMN) in ADHD brains is often more active and accessible, which contributes to spontaneous insight, associative thinking, and big-picture imagination.
- The Visionary role is not opposed to structure—it needs a structure to pass ideas into, which is why coordinated inner role development matters.

🛠 Clinical & Educational Applications:

- Help students articulate their long-range vision—even if it feels vague.
- Use motivational interviewing to surface underlying "pulls" toward identity-based goals.
- Protect white space in schedules—downtime often activates the Visionary mode.
- Coach students to recognize the difference between vision overwhelm and productive spark—using body-based awareness cues.

✧

📚 References for Further Reading

◦ Castellanos, F. X., & Proal, E. (2012). Large-scale brain systems in ADHD: Beyond the prefrontal-striatal model. *Trends in Cognitive Sciences, 16*(1), 17–26.
Explores the role of brain networks, including DMN and functional connectivity, in ADHD cognition.

◦ Kaufman, S. B. (2011). Creativity and ADHD: A review of behavioral and neural correlates. *Current Psychiatry Reports, 13*(5), 365–373.

Summarizes evidence for creativity and divergent thinking in individuals with ADHD.

o Vaihinger, H. (1924). *The Philosophy of "As If."*
Introduces the idea of useful fictions—beliefs that shape action, even if not provable.

o White, H. A., & Shah, P. (2006). Uninhibited imaginations: Creativity in adults with ADHD. *Personality and Individual Differences, 40(6), 1121–1131.*
Demonstrates the link between ADHD traits and creative ideation.

🔁 Handoff to Chapter 10: The Producer— Building the Bridge From Vision to Action

The Visionary holds the dream—but dreaming alone won't get you there.

Without a Producer, the spark fades. The plan stays abstract. The vision remains trapped in your head.

In the next chapter, we'll meet your inner Producer—the part of you that takes the raw material of your dreams and begins the slow, steady process of making them real.

Because following a signal is only the beginning.

Now it's time to learn how to build the bridge.

Chapter 10

The Producer—Building the Bridge from Vision to Action

"Men (and women) trip over pebbles; never over mountains."
—H. Emilie Cady

📰 How to Use This Chapter

This chapter is structured with three lenses in mind. Whether you're reading for yourself, supporting someone with ADHD, or looking for practical tools, you'll find what you need in the sections below.

- 🎨 **For People with ADHD—Students, Workers, and Curious Minds**
  Discover how to turn inspiration into action using your brain's unique wiring. Learn how the Producer part of your mind evaluates what matters, builds flexible plans, and keeps momentum alive—even when motivation fades.
- 🔧 **For Parents, Clinicians, Educators, and Coaches**
  Explore the salience network's role in decision-making, tools for priority sorting, and strategies to support ADHD learners in planning, starting, continuing, and finishing. Learn how values, emotions, and structure interact in the planning process.
- 🔎 **Key Concepts and Tools You'll Find Here**
  ✓ The Crystal-Steel-Plastic Prioritization Model

✓ The Three Execution Challenges: Starting, Continuing, Finishing

✓ Commitment Devices for ADHD Minds

✓ Signal-Based Planning and the Producer's Timeline Tool

> 💡 Feel free to read this chapter in order, or skip directly to the section most relevant to your current need. The Producer role isn't about perfection—it's about creating motion where it matters most.

🔡 Quick Guide to Chapter 10: The Producer—Executing the Vision One Step at a Time

🎯 **Core Concept**: The Producer is the Builder—the inner team member who transforms ideas into action. It selects meaningful goals, plans actionable steps, and executes consistently. The Producer bridges vision and reality.

🧠 For People with ADHD:

- o Learn how to choose what to act on when everything feels important
- o Use the Crystal–Steel–Plastic model to sort real priorities from distractions
- o Pattern your goals into time using signal-friendly planning tools that you actually like using
- o Solve the three biggest execution challenges: starting, continuing, and finishing—and use support systems to keep moving forward

🔬 For Parents, Clinicians, Educators, and Curious Minds:

- o Understand the executive functions that impact task initiation, planning, and follow-through

- o Introduce organizational strategies that preserve the original signal behind a goal (e.g., timelines, calendar blocking, scaffolding)
- o Support the use of compensatory tools like micro-deadlines, commitment devices, and motivational anchors
- o Help students clarify what matters most using values exploration and Crystal–Steel–Plastic triage

🧠 For People with ADHD—Students, Workers, and Curious Minds

If the Visionary whispers "What if...?"—the Producer asks, "So what are we actually going to do about it?"

The Producer is the part of you that takes inspiration and turns it into action. It doesn't need to dream up the whole world. It just needs to pick a starting point, map a timeline, and show up—even when your signals flicker, your motivation dips, and your calendar looks like a battlefield.

It's the executive function center of your inner team—the one that actually moves things forward.

But sometimes, ADHD minds get **stuck in the dream**. The Visionary floods you with possibility, but the Producer gets paralyzed by the pressure of choosing, planning, or starting. This can lead to analysis paralysis, avoidance, or overwhelm.

To get unstuck, you may need to:

- Shrink the vision down to a first step
- Use the Crystal–Steel–Plastic model to triage what actually matters
- Change your state before you change your task (move your body, shift your focus)
- Ask yourself: What's one small move I can make right now that honors the dream?

And if you've been told you're a great starter but a terrible finisher—or that you have a million ideas but no follow-through—it's not because you're broken.

It's because your Producer has been trying to do its job without a signal-aligned system.

🔧 The Producer in Action: Select, Plan, Execute

The Producer works in three major phases:

1. Selection—Choosing a goal from among multiple possibilities based on salience, feasibility, and meaning.
2. Planning—Breaking that goal into steps and sequencing those steps across time.
3. Execution—Getting started, staying with it, and finishing it.

We'll walk through each of these phases using the

Crystal–Steel–Plastic model to help clarify what's worth doing, and how to structure it.

⬦ Crystal–Steel–Plastic Breakdown

Crystal—Identity-defining, high-consequence, foundational tasks.

Examples: Paying rent, renewing insurance, attending class, submitting graduation paperwork.

If dropped: Serious harm to future, finances, or core relationships.

Steel—Strong, important tasks that matter but won't break you if delayed.

Examples: Submitting a routine report, making appointments, preparing meals.

If dropped: Minor dents in progress; recoverable with effort.

Plastic—Flexible, low-stakes, avoidant, or time-fillers.

Examples: Organizing socks, deep-diving online, texting mid-task.

If dropped: Nothing breaks. Often better to delegate or ignore.

📄 Producer's Sorting Practice Choose a task on your list and sort it:

- ○ What type is it—Crystal, Steel, or Plastic?
- ○ Why is it on your list—signal, demand, or avoidance?

    ○   What signal would help you act on it?

The Three Core Execution Challenges

1. **Starting**—You know what to do but can't begin.
   Signals: "It's too big," "I'll do it later," "I feel frozen."
   Tools: Commitment devices, body-state changes, activating the "why."
   Examples: Set a 5-minute timer to trick yourself into starting. Text a friend your goal. Break the task into just the first action: "Open the document."
2. **Continuing**—You start but lose momentum.
   Signals: "This is boring now," "Something else feels more urgent."
   Tools: Micro-deadlines, focus environments, checkpoint rewards.
   Examples: Use the Pomodoro technique to break time into sprints. Change your setting or background music to renew attention. Add a reward after a checkpoint.
3. **Finishing**—You're close to done but stall out.
   Signals: "I'm afraid to finish," "The motivation faded," "I'll come back later."
   Tools: Closure rituals, accountability, reconnecting to purpose.
   Examples: Write a post-it note that says "Done is better than perfect." Text a friend your plan to finish by a time. Reread the original reason this task mattered.

🛠 Tools Producers Love

- Calendar blocking with Signal Anchors
- Crystal–Steel–Plastic triage maps
- Goal trackers with feedback
- Commitment devices (e.g., "text me when you start")
- Values-based planning prompts
- Accountability partnerships

📱 Sidebar: Finding the Right Tool to Build Your Timeline

The Producer's greatest need is structure that holds the signal—a way to take steps and put them in order without letting the original motivation fade.

There's no perfect calendar or planner. The best one is the one you'll actually use.

Whether it's:

- A paper planner with stickers and checkboxes
- A visual whiteboard in your room
- Google Calendar color-coded by project
- A digital task board like Trello, Notion, or Sunsama

What matters is this: Can this tool help you see your week, track your steps, and hold the thread of what matters?

If a tool stops working, it's not failure—it's feedback. You're just listening to a new signal.

Integration Note: Values Sorting and Crystal–Steel–Plastic

As part of the Producer's decision-making process, it's not enough to simply ask, "How urgent is this?" The deeper question is, "What matters most—and why?"

That's where the Value Sort Exercise becomes an essential companion to the Crystal–Steel–Plastic model. Values are often just beneath the surface of conscious awareness. When we clarify our values, we strengthen the Producer's ability to recognize what's truly Crystal—not just emotionally charged or externally demanded, but identity-defining and life-sustaining.

The Value Sort + CSP model combination creates a powerful filter, allowing your Producer to see clearly, prioritize wisely, and act with conviction.

✧

For Parents, Educators, Clinicians, Coaches, and Curious Minds

The Producer role is where many executive function difficulties show up—especially in planning, prioritizing, and persistence. Research shows that individuals with ADHD often struggle not because of a lack of intention, but due to impairments in self-directed motivation and temporal organization.

Support strategies include:

- o Scaffolding goal selection using tools like the Crystal–Steel–Plastic model to reduce overwhelm and clarify stakes
- o Breaking down larger goals into micro-steps with visual timelines or student-chosen planners

- o Using commitment devices and accountability structures to support follow-through
- o Embedding values-based planning to help maintain intrinsic motivation

When supporting students or clients, remember: the Producer functions best in an environment that promotes clarity, salience, and emotional safety. Planning isn't just about structure—it's about belief in the path forward.

✧

References for Further Reading

o **Barkley, R. A. (2011).** *Executive Functions: What They Are, How They Work, and Why They Evolved.* New York: Guilford Press.
Clear, foundational explanation of how executive functions operate—and how deficits in initiation, planning, and persistence manifest in ADHD. Supports the chapter's emphasis on the Producer as the "execution center" of the inner team.

o **Duckworth, A. L., & Gross, J. J. (2014).** Self-control and grit: Related but separable determinants of success. *Current Directions in Psychological Science, 23*(5), 319–325.
Explores persistence and follow-through as distinct from intelligence, and how they can be built with structured supports—relevant to overcoming the "continuing" and "finishing" challenges.

o **Gollwitzer, P. M. (1999).** Implementation intentions: Strong effects of simple plans. *American Psychologist, 54*(7), 493–503.
Presents evidence on "if–then" planning as a way to bridge

intention and action—directly linked to the Producer's planning phase and commitment devices.

o **Keller, J., & Bless, H. (2008).** Flow and regulatory compatibility: An experimental approach to the flow model of intrinsic motivation. *Personality and Social Psychology Bulletin, 34*(2), 196–209.
Provides research on maintaining engagement and focus—ties to strategies for sustaining the Producer's momentum in the "continuing" phase.

o **Locke, E. A., & Latham, G. P. (2002).** Building a practically useful theory of goal setting and task motivation. *American Psychologist, 57*(9), 705–717.
Seminal work on goal-setting theory, showing the importance of clarity, challenge, and feedback—all embedded in the Producer's timeline and tracking tools.

o **Sleeper-Triplett, J. (2010).** *Empowering Youth with ADHD: Your Guide to Coaching Adolescents and Young Adults for Coaches, Parents, and Professionals.* Plantation, FL: Specialty Press.
Offers practical coaching strategies for scaffolding, accountability, and persistence—all key support strategies for helping the Producer succeed.

o **Steel, P., & König, C. J. (2006).** Integrating theories of motivation. *Academy of Management Review, 31*(4), 889–913.
Synthesizes multiple motivation theories, providing a framework for understanding why the Producer stalls and how structured supports can reignite progress.

⟳ Handoff to Chapter 11: The Editor—Thinking Clearly Without Turning Against Yourself

The Producer helps you build momentum—but what happens when plans don't go the way you hoped? What do you do when a step fails, or the system breaks down, or a mistake feels like a collapse?

That's when the third role in your Inner Team steps in: the Editor.

The Editor isn't your inner critic—it's your course corrector. In the next chapter, you'll learn how to evaluate outcomes without shame, think clearly without spiraling, and turn setbacks into strategy.

Because thriving isn't about perfection—it's about learning in motion.

Chapter 11

The Editor— Thinking Clearly Without Turning Against Yourself

"Before critical thinking can take root, the Editor must return—not as a critic, but as a compassionate guide. It helps us see clearly, adapt wisely, and rehearse what might go wrong before it ever does. That's how clarity becomes the beginning of insight."

🔡 Quick Guide to Chapter 11

This chapter follows the three-perspective structure used throughout the book. You can read it front to back, or jump into the sections that speak to your current needs.

🎯 Core Concept: The Editor is the adaptive strategist—

the internal role that transforms mistakes into meaning. It evaluates what happened, adjusts plans midstream, and softens the landing when things go wrong.

🧠 For People with ADHD:

- Understand why reflection often feels like rumination—and how to change that
- Learn how the Editor helps you adapt, reframe, and recover from setbacks

- o Recognize the signs of a hijacked Editor (inner critic) vs. a healthy one
- o Begin building resilient thinking habits using signal-aware self-talk

✏️ For Parents, Clinicians, Educators, Coaches—and Curious Readers:

- o Explore the connection between ADHD, shame, and distorted self-reflection
- o Introducing reframing and metacognition strategies to reduce rumination
- o Teach students how to reflect on outcomes without emotional collapse
- o Use tools like failure planning, recovery mapping, and thought-challenge scripts to strengthen insight and resilience

🧠 For People with ADHD—Students, Workers, and Curious Minds

You've dreamed something beautiful. You've started to build. Now what?

You edit. You evaluate. You reflect. You ask the hard questions.

But if you've lived with ADHD long enough, you've probably learned to fear this moment—the moment the project starts to wobble, the moment you make a mistake, the moment your brain says, "You're messing it up again."

That voice? That's the Editor—but it's been hijacked.

The Editor's real job isn't to shame you.

It's to help you see clearly.

✍ What the Editor Really Does

The Editor is your internal strategist and meaning-maker. It looks backward to assess what happened—and forward to anticipate what might go wrong. It's not cruel. It's careful. And when it's healthy, it helps you adapt without spiraling.

Its core functions:

1. Evaluates feedback and patterns
2. Predicts risks and softens failure
3. Makes meaning from mistakes
4. Distinguishes signal from noise
5. Refines goals, beliefs, and strategies

**The Editor isn't the voice of judgment.
It's the voice of adjustment.**

⃠ When the Editor Becomes the Critic

For many people with ADHD, the Editor role has been warped by years of:

- Internalized shame
- Rejection Sensitivity Dysphoria (RSD)
- Black-and-white thinking
- Belief that "if I failed, I must be a failure"

Instead of asking, *What went wrong, and What can I do next time?*

The distorted Editor asks, *What's wrong with me, and why do I always do this?*

This is where reflection turns into rumination.

And insight gets replaced with inner sabotage.

⚔ When the Editor Is Advanced

A healthy Editor:

- Helps you catch faulty thinking patterns before they cause damage
- Pauses long enough to ask, "Is this signal real, or just a fear echo?"
- Plans for likely setbacks and recovery routes
- Updates your beliefs over time, based on actual experience

It's a quiet strength—not flashy but deeply freeing.

📦 Sidebar: The Editor's Job in the Age of AI—How to Keep Your Thinking Yours

The **Editor** in our Visionary-Producer-Editor (VPE) model is your truth-checker—the one who filters ideas, tests assumptions, and decides what's worth acting on. In the age of ChatGPT and other large language models, the Editor's role has never been more important.

AI is fluent, fast, and often right—but sometimes confidently wrong. And for people with ADHD, who tend to favor immediacy, novelty, and clarity over slow verification, that can be a dangerous combination.

ADHD Risk Factors with AI

1. **Immediacy Bias**—Grabbing the first "good enough" answer and moving on.
2. **Salience Over Accuracy**—Favoring what feels important now, even if the facts are shaky.
3. **Cognitive Offloading**—Letting the machine do all the remembering, connecting, and evaluating.
4. **Hyperfocus on Discovery**—Loving the "aha!" moment so much we skip the "is this actually true?" step.

Editor Drills for AI Collaboration

To keep your Editor strong, treat AI like a sparring partner—not a substitute thinker.

- **Double-Source Everything**
  If AI gives you a fact, confirm it in an independent, trusted source.

Ask: "Where else does this show up, and does it match?"

- o **Challenge the Premise**
  Prompt AI to argue against itself: "What might be wrong with this?"
  Ask: "What could make this false or misleading?"

- o **Interrogate the Language**
  Flag overconfident words like "always," "never," or "best."
  Ask: "Is this nuanced enough, or is it oversimplifying?"

- o **Play the Curious Skeptic**
  Respond to every AI answer with a follow-up "Why?" or "How do you know?"
  Ask: "What's the reasoning behind this?"

- o **Own the Words**
  Rewrite AI output in your own voice and structure—not just to avoid plagiarism, but to ensure you've processed and understood it.

Bottom line: The Editor's job isn't to distrust AI—it's to make sure *you* stay the final authority on your own thinking. AI can be a powerful ally, but only if your Editor stays awake at the wheel.

When the Editor Is Emerging

You may begin to notice:

- o "I stopped beating myself up so much when I needed a break."

- o "I caught myself in an all-or-nothing spiral and paused."
- o "I realized I was reacting to shame, not reality."

This is how you know the Editor is waking up—not as a critic, but as a clear-thinking guide.

⬤ When the Editor Is Dormant

When this role is offline, you might:

- o Repeat the same patterns without learning from them
- o Collapse into self-blame with no constructive outcome
- o Avoid feedback entirely
- o Overreact to minor failures as if they erase all progress

🧠 When the Editor Is Advanced, Emerging, or Dormant

State	What It Looks Like	Signal Clues
Advanced	You can reflect without spiraling; course-correct quickly and make meaning	"I know what happened—and I know what to try next."
Emerging	You sometimes pause to reflect, but still fear mistakes or fall into self-doubt	"I caught myself halfway through the spiral."
Dormant	No reflection or highly distorted—cycles of shame, avoidance, and overcorrection	"I avoid thinking about it because it always feels like failure."

The goal isn't to perfect the Editor.

It's to *invite it back*—with clarity, compassion, and curiosity.

💬 From Judgment to Insight—What the Editor Asks Instead

Critic Voice	Healthy Editor Voice
"You always screw this up."	"What part of the plan didn't work?"
"You're just lazy."	"Was the signal missing or hijacked?"
"You should've known better."	"What was the feedback—and what can I adjust?"
"You're too emotional."	"What was the feeling trying to tell me?"
"I'm done. I give up."	"What do I want to carry forward into the next attempt?"

🔄 How the Editor Helps You Recover from Setbacks

The Editor is the one who asks:

- "What might go wrong—and how can we soften the landing?"
- "How could I respond differently next time?"
- "What's the actual signal underneath this feeling?"
- "Where do I need to adjust, rather than abandon the plan?"

A strong Editor helps you fail faster and smarter—not less often, but less painfully, and with more wisdom carried forward.

🧩 Bridge to Thinking Clearly—The Editor & Faulty Thinking

The Editor isn't just about reviewing what happened. It's about how you *think* about what happened—and what you make it *mean.*

This is where many people with ADHD get trapped. Not just in emotional spirals, but in thinking traps that distort perception and sabotage recovery. Patterns like:

o   All-or-nothing reasoning
o   Catastrophizing
o   Mental filtering
o   Personalizing
o   Emotional reasoning

Instead of helping us grow, a hijacked Editor locks us into the wrong story—one where we're the problem, the failure, the flaw. But it doesn't have to be that way.

In the chapters to come, we'll invite the Editor back—not as a judge, but as a partner. You'll learn how to:

o   Catch your own unhelpful thoughts in real time
o   Question those thoughts without attacking yourself
o   Reframe automatic reactions into more adaptive beliefs
o   Build resilient internal logic, not just emotional regulation

And yes—you'll get to play a few rounds of *Cards Against Faulty Thinking*—a practical, brain-friendly toolkit for identifying logical fallacies, rewriting mental scripts, and learning to think more clearly (and kindlier).

Because thinking clearly isn't just about logic.

It's about trusting yourself to handle what comes next—without turning against yourself along the way.

You are not weak because you made a mistake.

You are wise when you learn from it.

And your Editor—when trusted—can be the one who shows you how.

For Parents, Educators, Clinicians, Coaches, and Curious Readers

Many students with ADHD are stuck in cycles of impulsive action and emotional collapse. Reflection becomes punishment. Insight becomes avoidance. This is not a failure of character—it's often a malfunctioning Editor
system.

To support this role in others:

- o Normalize trial and adjustment, not perfection (Tuckman, 2009)
- o Teach the difference between reflection and rumination (Barkley, 2011)
- o Help students label distorted thoughts and reframe them (Ramsay & Rostain, 2015)
- o Build recovery planning into every task (not just success planning)

A student who can't reflect safely can't grow sustainably.

A healthy Editor is one of the strongest predictors of long-term resilience.

📑 References for Further Reading

o Barkley, R. A. (2011). *Executive Functions: What They Are, How They Work, and Why They Evolved.*
Explores how deficits in executive function contribute to difficulties with self-reflection, behavioral regulation, and learning from experience.

o Ramsay, J. R., & Rostain, A. L. (2015). *The Adult ADHD Tool Kit: Using CBT to Facilitate Coping Inside and Out.*
Offers practical cognitive-behavioral tools for challenging distorted thoughts, managing shame, and supporting emotional regulation in ADHD.

o Tuckman, A. (2009). *More Attention, Less Deficit: Success Strategies for Adults with ADHD.*
Focuses on normalizing imperfection, managing setbacks, and using reflection as a tool for growth instead of self-blame.

🔄 Next Chapter: From the Editor to Sprint Thinking

Even when your Editor is steady—wise, compassionate, and clear—that doesn't mean the path forward is easy.

Because knowing what to do is not the same as being able to *do it.*

ADHD minds often struggle not with direction, but with momentum. We start strong... then stall. We get stuck, overwhelmed, or paralyzed by the sheer size of the goal.

That's why before we move into the emotional depth work of the next section, we're adding one more vital piece to your internal toolkit: **Sprint Thinking**.

Adapted from Agile project management—a system built

to move fast, adjust quickly, and recover from failure—Sprint Thinking offers ADHD minds a structure that fits the way we naturally work: in bursts.

Short. Focused. Time-bound. Forgiving.

This next chapter shows you how to harness that burst-based rhythm to take action when motivation falters, energy dips, or clarity slips.

It's not about doing everything.

It's about doing *something*—with enough structure to move forward, and enough flexibility to breathe.

Let's build momentum—one sprint at a time

Chapter 12

Sprint Thinking for ADHD Minds

—Harnessing Momentum One Burst at a Time An ADHD-Adaptive Strategy from Agile Thinking

"ADHD minds don't run on batteries—
they run on lightning."
(Unpredictable. Powerful. And gone if you miss it.)

▨ How to Use This Chapter

Chapter 12: Sprint Thinking for ADHD Minds—Harnessing Momentum One Burst at a Time

This chapter follows the layered structure used throughout the book—with sections tailored for ADHD learners, for those who support them, and with takeaway tools for all readers.

- ○ 🧠 **For People with ADHD—Students, Workers, and Curious Minds**
  Discover why short bursts of focused effort (a.k.a. "sprints") work better than long-haul productivity plans. Learn how to set up your own sprints, recover momentum, and work with—not against—your ADHD rhythms.
- ○ 🧪 **For Parents, Clinicians, Educators, and Coaches**
  Explore the neuroscience and behavioral logic behind sprint-based work. Learn how to support ADHD students using structured bursts of effort, planned recovery, motivational scaffolding, and visible feedback loops.

🏹 In This Chapter: Sprint Thinking for ADHD Minds

- o Discover why short bursts of focused effort work better than long-haul plans for ADHD minds
- o Learn how to structure sprints for motivation, momentum, and recovery
- o Explore real-world sprint examples—from finals week to digital cleanup
- o Understand how sprint cycles support executive function and emotional resilience
- o Get tools for creating your own ADHD-friendly sprints—solo or with a team
- o See how Sprint Thinking integrates with your internal team (Visionary–Producer–Editor)
- o Prepare for the next chapter on Emotional Intelligence by building self-monitoring into action

🧠 For People with ADHD—Students, Workers, and Curious Minds

We surge forward when fueled by interest, urgency, novelty—or sheer panic. But just as often, we stall out. We swirl in indecision. We get halfway up the mountain with no map and no momentum. That's where **sprints** come in.

Originally from Agile project management, a **sprint** is a short, time-boxed burst of focused effort. Usually, 1 to 2 weeks. A goal is clearly defined, steps are outlined just enough to get going, and at the end, the team checks in to review what worked and what didn't. Then... rest. And reset.

Sound familiar?

In many ways, sprint thinking aligns with the way ADHD brains already work—we just rarely structure it. We're often already sprinting—but we're doing it without warmups, without water breaks, and with no finish line in sight.

When you build structure around your bursts, you create something ADHD minds thrive on:

- Urgency, but not panic
- Focus, but with flexibility
- Progress, but with permission to pause

🚀 Why Sprint Thinking Works for ADHD

- It chunks the overwhelming. One semester becomes one 10-day push. One giant paper becomes a "Research Sprint."
- It builds in a natural break. ADHD brains need recovery time—and knowing the sprint ends makes the work more doable.
- It offers real-time feedback. You can reflect and adapt, not just crash and judge.
- It creates intention and containment. You don't have to do everything. Just this. Just now.

🧠 ADHD Tendency → Sprint Advantage

ADHD Tendency	Sprint Feature That Helps
Motivation crashes over time	Sprint sets a short window with a finish line
Struggle with starting tasks	Clear kickoff moment breaks inertia
Get lost in big, vague goals	Sprints clarify just enough to get going
Overcommit and burn out	Sprint scope is limited—by design
Forget to track progress	Sprint reviews create natural reflection points
Avoid rest until collapse	Sprints build in rest and reset time

📇 Types of ADHD-Friendly Sprints

- 📖 Finals Sprint – Knock out missing assignments in the last 10 days of the term
- 🛠️ Starter Sprint – Beginning-of-semester success setup: calendar, supplies, spaces
- 🔍 Research Sprint – No writing. Just 7 days of digging, reading, and idea-mapping
- 📬 Inbox/Task Inbox Sprint – Clear the digital clutter
- 🏃 Motivation Recovery Sprint – Rebuild momentum after burnout or missed deadlines
- 👥 Team Sprint – Coordinate with friends/classmates to support one another's goals

🛠️ How to Build Your Own Sprint
You don't need a coach, a whiteboard, or a project manager to start a sprint. You just need a plan that fits on a sticky note.

Step 1: Pick a Focus. What's one thing that needs a short burst of focused effort? Not everything. Just this.

Step 2: Choose the Length. Most sprints last 5–14 days. Enough time to make progress, not so much that motivation dies.

Step 3: Define the Scope. Keep it tight. What's in the sprint? What's not? Clarity prevents scope creep.

Step 4: Sketch the Plan. List 3–7 steps max. These are guide rails, not shackles. Flexibility is allowed—even encouraged.

Step 5: Set the Start and End. Pick a kickoff time and a clear end date. Add a celebration or rest plan at the finish.

Step 6: Track and Adjust. Check in once mid-sprint. Are you on track? Do you need to adjust the goal or steps?

Step 7: Reflect and Reset. At the end, take 5 minutes. What worked? What didn't? What would you do differently?

🎭 Your Inner Team in Sprint Mode: Visionary, Producer, Editor

What happens when your internal team works *together* on a sprint?

Let's say your ADHD mind wants to launch a bold new project—a podcast, a portfolio, a term paper that doesn't suck. Try assigning sprint duties to your three internal roles.

◎ The Visionary—Sprint Kickoff

What's the idea or dream behind this?
What excites me about it?
What outcome would feel amazing?
Visionaries love naming the sprint and framing the purpose. Let them fire the starting pistol.

▦ The Producer—Sprint Plan

What are the next 3–5 steps?
What materials, schedules, or support do I need?
How do I break this into something doable this week?

The Producer is your project manager. They make the dream operational.

🔍 The Editor—Sprint Review
What did I learn?
What got in the way?
What's one thing I can tweak next time?
The Editor keeps you from repeating mistakes and helps you refine, without spiraling into shame.

🎭 Group Exercise
In a group or workshop setting, assign each person a role (Visionary, Producer, or Editor) and plan a 'Perfect ADHD Sprint Launch.' Use a fun or serious goal like "Launch a T-shirt business in 7 days" or "Win finals week without crying."

- Let the Visionary pitch the dream.
- Have the Producer map the 5 steps and timeline.
- Let the Editor flag risks—without killing the vibe

📄 Sprint Planning Template (Quick Note Format)
🎯 Sprint Name:
(e.g. "Essay Draft Sprint")

🎯 Goal:
(e.g. "Complete full draft of 6-page paper")

🕐 Duration:
(e.g. "July 25 – Aug 1, 7 days")

☐ Steps:

- Gather sources
- Re-read assignment prompt

- o Outline intro/body/conclusion
- o Write messy draft
- o Revise + format

🚧 Out of Scope:
(e.g. "Proofreading for grammar perfection—save for next sprint")

🗓 Midpoint Check-In:
(e.g. "July 29—see what's left")

🎉 Finish + Reflect:
(e.g. "Turn in draft + treat self to iced coffee + write 3 reflection notes")

📑 Case Study: Jordan's Semester Launch Plan

—A 7-Day Sprint to Set Up for Success Jordan had learned the hard way what happened when the semester started without a plan.

Last fall, the first week of classes felt like a blur—syllabi piled up, assignments slipped past unread, and before he even knew it, Jordan was behind. Their ADHD brain wasn't lazy, but it was reactive. And the chaos of the first two weeks had triggered a cascade of missed deadlines, shame spirals, and frantic catch-up attempts.

This time, Jordan wanted a different outcome.

So, he tried something new: a Starter Sprint.

Instead of waiting until the semester "settled in," Jordan created a 7-day sprint—a short, structured burst of intentional effort to launch the term on solid ground.

🎯 Sprint Goal:

"Get ahead of the chaos and build the system before it builds me."

Jordan didn't try to do everything. Just these essentials:

- Set up a semester overview calendar with key dates from each syllabus.
- Organize digital folders and label assignments by course.
- Visit the disability services office to check on accommodations.
- Walk the campus to map out building locations and timing between classes.
- Prep a go-to study space with lighting, headphones, and snacks.
- Draft a basic weekly routine (class, work, meals, and sleep).
- Do a short values check-in: Why am I here? What do I want from this term?

🔄 Structure:

Jordan used a simple 3-step framework:

1. Plan it – A short checklist each morning.
2. Do it – Work in two 90-minute blocks per day.
3. Reflect on it – Each evening, a 5-minute journal check-in: What worked? What's next?

He even texted a friend each night with a one-line update. ("Day 3 done! Office hours scheduled.")

🧠 What Changed: By the end of the sprint, Jordan wasn't just prepared—he was proud.

- o He had a clear calendar and realistic expectations.
- o He knew where they were going—literally and academically.
- o He had fewer surprises and more confidence in week one.
- o And maybe most importantly, he felt agency—the sense that he was guiding the semester, not being dragged by it.

It wasn't perfect. Jordan still missed a couple of things. But instead of spiraling, he saw the gap, adjusted, and moved on. The sprint hadn't just helped him start strong—it gave him a repeatable model for bouncing back.

🏃 Sprint Responsibly—Don't Burn the Engine

It's easy to get excited when you finally find a system that *moves* you. ADHD minds often live with chronic underperformance—not because we don't care, but because nothing quite clicks.

So when you find something like Sprint Thinking—something that finally creates traction—it's tempting to push too far, too fast. You want to make up for lost time. Catch up. Prove something.

But here's the catch: **Sprinting a marathon doesn't work.** Just ask Pheidippides—the original marathoner. Legend says he ran from the battlefield at Marathon to Athens, delivered his message… and died on the spot.

We don't want that.

Sprint Thinking is a strength—but only when paired with rest, recalibration, and boundaries. Otherwise, it becomes just another form of masked burnout

Sprints only work when they're **time-limited, focused**, and followed by **rest or reset**. A good sprint is like a tide: it flows in with power, then recedes to gather strength again.

So, when you design your sprint, ask:

- What's a **reasonable push**, not a punishment?
- Where's the **end point**? (You don't sprint forever.)
- What kind of **recovery** do I need afterward?
- Am I chasing **urgency**—or responding to a real signal?

ADHD minds run hot. That's our superpower. But every engine needs cool-down time. Otherwise, you burn out the system you just got working.

✎ For Parents, Educators, Clinicians, Coaches, and Curious Minds—Understanding Sprint Thinking as a Scaffolding

Tool Sprint Thinking isn't just a productivity hack—it's a robust self-regulation scaffold. It gives ADHD learners structure without rigidity, urgency without panic, and feedback without shame. These are essential ingredients for both academic resilience and emotional development.

For clinicians, educators, and parents supporting ADHD students, sprint-based frameworks can be used to:

- Externalize time and pressure: Rather than saying, "Just work on your paper this weekend," you can co-create a Research Sprint: "From Friday to Tuesday, just gather sources. No writing yet."
- Build trust in the process: Sprint cycles provide short, repeatable windows where effort is rewarded with rest and review. This helps ADHD students recover from burnout and rebuild self-confidence.
- Teach adaptive pacing: Instead of long-term procrastination followed by all-nighters, Sprint Thinking invites a rhythm of "burst and breathe."
- Encourage reflection without shame: Each sprint ends with a review—not to punish what didn't get done, but to gather data for the next sprint. What helped? What got in the way? What needs to shift?

This model is especially helpful for:

- Students with performance variability or executive function fatigue
- Teens and college students who resist traditional planning but thrive with momentum
- Young adults with emotional sensitivity, who need clear wins to re-engage after setbacks

You can also think of Sprint Thinking as a low-barrier on-ramp to broader signal-driven and scaffold-supported systems—helping students gradually build the internal skills needed to thrive independently.

🗐 References for Further Reading:

o Barkley, R. A. (2001). *Executive functions and self-regulation: A clinical perspective.* This foundational model
explains how ADHD disrupts short-term goal planning and why structured scaffolds, such as sprinting, restore
momentum.

o Beck, K. et al. (2001). *Manifesto for Agile Software Development.* The original Agile text introduces sprints as short, adaptive, goal-focused work cycles.

o Dawson, P., & Guare, R. (2009). *Smart but Scattered.* Offers practical strategies for breaking big tasks into manageable parts, echoing core sprint techniques.

o Sleeper-Triplett, J. (2010). *Empowering Youth With ADHD.* Demonstrates how collaborative planning enhances student motivation and ownership—central to successful sprint execution.

🔁 Handoff: From Sprinting to Thinking Clearly

The ability to execute short, focused bursts is powerful—but there's something even more important beneath it: how we think about what we're doing. How we plan, evaluate, reflect, and make choices.

Sprint Thinking works because it introduces structure without rigidity. It provides ADHD minds with a way to organize their energy while honoring their need for flexibility. But to sustain progress beyond the sprint, we need clarity. And that means understanding our thoughts, beliefs, and blind spots.

In the next chapter, we'll shift from action to reflection. We'll explore how ADHD minds process information, where thinking can become tangled or distorted, and how emotional reasoning often interferes with clarity. It's time to think clearly—not perfectly, but powerfully. Let's go.

✴ Part III Wrap-Up—The Inner Team in Motion

By now, you've built something powerful—not a rigid system, but a living, breathing internal team.

You've met the **Visionary**, who senses what matters and follows the signal.

You've trained the **Producer**, who builds structure around momentum and transforms ideas into real-world progress.

You've empowered the **Editor**, who learns from mistakes, recalibrates direction, and helps you think clearly without turning against yourself.

And you've begun working in **sprints**—short bursts of focused energy that align with how ADHD minds naturally move.

Together, these roles form a new kind of architecture—not just for productivity, but for purpose.

This isn't about grinding harder. It's about working with your brain instead of against it.

But even the most well-aligned internal team can lose its way without a compass.

That compass is *emotional intelligence*.

Because what moves you is only part of the equation.

You also need to know what sustains you, what drains you, and what throws you off course.

You need to recognize when pressure turns to paralysis... when self-talk becomes sabotage... and when effort stops feeling like your own.

Emotional intelligence isn't a bonus skill.

For ADHD minds, it's a *survival tool*—and a blueprint for thriving.

In the next section, we'll learn how to monitor emotions like signals, how to decode internal feedback without getting stuck in shame, and how to build resilience that's flexible, not forced.

The journey from chaos to clarity doesn't end with strategy.

It deepens into self-understanding.

Let's move forward—and inward.

✦ Part IV: Thinking Clearly, Feeling Fully—Emotional Intelligence as the Bridge Between Motivation and Action

If you've ever said, "I know what I need to do—I just can't seem to make myself do it," then you've already met the invisible wall between knowing and doing. That strange motivational Bermuda Triangle where ADHD minds often sail in... and vanish.

In Part Three, we explored the factors that drive motivation in ADHD, including signals, salience, emotional amplification, the need for spontaneity, meaning, and movement. We mapped the terrain of inner roles—the Visionary, Producer, and Editor—that shape how ADHD minds dream, decide, and do.

However, even the most well-structured internal team can falter when emotions flood the system. Motivation can short-circuit—execution stalls. And self-talk turns from a coach into a critic. That's where emotional intelligence steps in—as the bridge between knowing and doing, between having a plan and being able to follow it.

🧠 Clarity Before Action
Before you can act on motivation, you need to feel it clearly.

And before that, you need to know *who's doing the feeling*—and whether the emotion matches the moment.

That's why this part of the book begins by listening inward.

You'll start by exploring your **Nested Selves**—the many internal voices and emotional layers that have been shaped by time, expectation, and often trauma. These parts aren't broken. They're echoes of experience—and learning to understand them is the first step toward emotional clarity.

Once you can name the inner voices, the next challenge is sorting their signals. That's where **critical thinking** comes in—not as cold logic, but as a tool for untangling thought distortions and emotional confusion.

And from there, you'll begin building the skill that turns emotion into motion: **emotional intelligence**.

When thoughts race or distort—as they often do in ADHD—emotions get scrambled. Panic masquerades as urgency. Shame dresses up as laziness. Guilt, grief, fear, and desire get tangled up in a pile of mental laundry you'd rather just ignore.

Critical thinking untangles that mess. It doesn't suppress emotion—it reveals it. And that's where emotional intelligence begins.

🎲 Span of Apprehension—Why We Drop Everything All at Once

In Chapter 2, we introduced the concept of Span of Apprehension (SOA)—the mental "tray" we use to juggle thoughts, feelings, and priorities in real-time.

Anything you invest attention, emotion, or effort into takes up space on that tray. And when the tray gets full—when you exceed your SOA—what happens?

You don't set things down carefully.

You drop them.

All of them.

This is why ADHD moments of collapse feel so sudden:

You're managing a deadline, a social conflict, a sense of failure, and maybe your blood sugar—and then one more thing lands, and boom! ... The tray flips.

One second, you're holding it together—the next, you're shut down.

Here's what it might look like:

o **Emotionally**: You're already feeling frustrated, and then a minor mistake triggers rage or despair.
o **Energetically**: You've been pushing through all day, then you misplace your keys and suddenly feel like you can't handle life at all.
o **Cognitively**: You're juggling multiple thoughts and lose track of what you're doing mid-sentence, then forget what you were even trying to remember.

These aren't failures of character. They're failures of capacity—the kind that emotional intelligence can help you predict, understand, and recover from.

And sometimes, the overwhelm doesn't come from what's in the tray.

It comes from what's been piling up behind you—the invisible emotional weight you've been dragging without even realizing it.

○ What Emotional Intelligence Means

Emotional intelligence isn't about being calm all the time or never losing your temper.

It's not about bottling up your feelings or becoming a walking TED Talk.

It's about being able to read your internal signals without shame—to understand what your emotions are telling you, and to respond in ways that give you more choices, not fewer.

It's also deeply ADHD-friendly—especially when taught with compassion and real tools. Emotional intelligence is a skill, not a personality trait. And for those of us with ADHD, it often holds the key to getting unstuck.

🎯 The Opportunity of Motivation

In the **MMO model**—Method, Motive, Opportunity—we often spend so much time trying to figure out the "how" (method) or waiting to feel the "why" (motive), that we forget the third piece: **opportunity.**

And here's the twist: emotional intelligence is what *creates* opportunity.

It tunes our attention toward signal rather than noise, helping us recognize what matters, and what can be safely set down.

It removes emotional blockers.

It transforms anxiety into information.

It turns demotivation into signal.

It gives your intention a place to land—and a reason to move.

🔍 What This Section Will Explore

In the chapters ahead, you'll learn:

- How nested emotional selves shape your inner world, and how to relate to them with compassion
- How **critical thinking** supports emotional regulation and protects your **span of apprehension**
- A practical, ADHD-informed model for **emotional intelligence**
- How **internal language and self-talk** shape emotion, identity, and motivation

- o   How to break free from **shame and rejection-based beliefs**
- o   How to monitor and balance your **energy, stress, and internal capacity**
- o   Plus, personal reflections and sidebars on **shame, identity**, and how ADHD minds **think, feel, and function** in high-stakes moments

Each chapter is designed to help you lighten the tray, widen your bandwidth, and choose your next move with more clarity—and less collapse.

📱 A New Kind of Emotional Power
Motivation doesn't start with willpower.

It starts with clarity—of thought, of emotion, of identity.

And that clarity begins with the courage to observe your internal world without flinching.

You don't have to carry it all.

You just need to know what's actually yours—and how to hold it differently.

Let's begin.

Chapter 13

Gender, Culture, and the ADHD Lens

"Until the lion learns to write, every story will glorify the hunter."
—African proverb

📓 How to Use This Chapter

This chapter explores how gender, culture, and identity shape the way ADHD is expressed, diagnosed, and supported—or missed altogether. It reveals how our understanding of ADHD is filtered through social expectations, diagnostic bias, and invisible labor. Using real-world examples and signal-based tools, it invites readers to see beyond stereotypes and uncover the hidden stories behind behavior.

This chapter follows the same three-part format used throughout the book, offering tailored insights for different audiences:

🔍 What You'll Get From This Chapter:

How gender and cultural identity shape ADHD expression

- Why some students are diagnosed early, and others are missed entirely
- The emotional cost of masking, misdiagnosis, and misunderstanding

- o How race, class, and gender intersect with diagnostic bias
- o What it means to build systems that actually *see* neuro-divergent minds

🧠 For People with ADHD—Students, Workers, and Curious Minds

I've sat with students and clients across every gender expression you can imagine—some diagnosed early with ADHD, others not until adulthood. Over the years, I've watched the same condition wear very different masks depending on who's wearing it. A boy bouncing in his chair might get sent to a psychologist by third grade. A girl staring out the window? She's dreamy. Emotional. Maybe anxious. Probably just sensitive. Rarely disruptive enough to raise flags. And so, she slips through the cracks—until she's drowning in college, doubting herself despite her potential.

This is the intersection of gender and ADHD.

We tend to think of ADHD as a hyperactive boy's disorder. That's what early research focused on. That's how the diagnostic criteria were shaped. But that story is incomplete. ADHD isn't one thing; it's a shapeshifter, molded by context, culture, and expectation. And gender, in all its social and biological complexity, adds another layer to the story.

The Cost of Being Missed

Girls and women often learn to mask their symptoms. They internalize. They try harder. They develop elaborate compensations—perfectionism, people-pleasing, and emotional labor. These adaptations "work" until they don't. And when they finally collapse under the weight of their own strategies, they're labeled anxious, depressed, or failing. But the root system is often ADHD that no one saw, or chose not to see.

Meanwhile, many boys are identified early, but that doesn't

mean they're thriving. The diagnosis can come with stigma, lowered expectations, and social friction. Boys are often told to "man up" when they experience emotional dysregulation or are punished more harshly for impulsivity. When those expectations collide with an executive function disorder, shame often takes root.

Why Women Are Catching Up—and Surpassing

Ironically, the same societal pressures that delay diagnosis in girls may also cultivate resilience and adaptability. Women with ADHD, by the time they are identified, have often developed deep wells of grit. They've navigated years of subtle failure and internal tension, and when they do find support— therapy, coaching, community—they tend to use them. Studies now show women outperforming men in college enrollment, persistence, and even some life measures of well-being. But that comes at a cost: exhaustion, burnout, emotional overload.

Intersectionality Isn't a Buzzword—It's the Blueprint

And then, there's the bigger picture. Gender doesn't exist in a vacuum. ADHD interacts not just with sex or gender identity, but with race, class, culture, and neurodiversity itself. A non-binary student of color navigating ADHD in a rigid academic system faces different barriers than a white cisgender boy in a suburban school. Intersectionality helps us understand why one person is seen as gifted, another as troubled, and another as invisible.

Culture Shapes What We See—And What We Miss

The lens of ADHD doesn't just distort along gender lines. Race, class, and cultural expectations twist the view even more. Research shows that Black and Latino children are significantly less likely to be diagnosed with ADHD, despite equal or higher levels of impairment. One reason? The behaviors of children of color are often interpreted through a lens of defiance or disruption, not neurodivergence. A white child might be seen as inattentive; a Black child with the same behavior may be labeled disrespectful.

Even when ADHD is present, many children of color are misdiagnosed with conduct disorders, or are routed into discipline instead of support systems. Language barriers, teacher bias, and lack of access to culturally competent clinicians all contribute to this diagnostic gap. Without diagnosis, students miss out on accommodations, support plans, coaching, and medication. And over time, they may start to believe what the system reflects back: that they're lazy, disobedient, or not trying hard enough.

We Need a New Lens

To support people with ADHD, we must move past the old categories. The diagnosis needs to be fluid enough to see the boy who shuts down instead of acting out. The girl who seems fine until she isn't. The gender-diverse teen whose brilliance is camouflaged by exhaustion from trying to be understood. The child of color whose creativity is mistaken for defiance. The college student who spent years adapting but never learned to rest.

Let's build systems that see nuance. Let's develop diagnostic tools that listen to context. Let's stop asking "What's wrong with this person?" and start asking "What's the story this person is living—and how can we help them thrive in it?"

Because ADHD doesn't discriminate, but the systems around it still do.

✐ For Parents, Educators, Clinicians, Coaches, and Curious Minds

If you're working with students, clients, or children with ADHD, consider the lens you're using to see them. Are you noticing behavior through a culturally sensitive framework? Are you aware of how gender norms might shape the way someone expresses (or hides) their ADHD? And most importantly, are you asking yourself what kinds of invisible labor—emotional, social, or cultural—they may already be doing just to survive in a system that doesn't fit?

🪄 Culture as Signal Filter

Internal signals don't operate in a vacuum—they're filtered through what we've learned is acceptable, safe, or dangerous to express. A child socialized to suppress frustration may not appear dysregulated but could be carrying an invisible emotional weight.

⚱ Internalized Signaling Suppression

Many individuals learn to override their internal signals—like "I'm overwhelmed" or "This isn't working"—because they've been conditioned to believe those signals will be ignored or punished.

🧩 Representation Shapes Recognition

When ADHD is only depicted through narrow stereotypes—like the hyperactive white boy—people outside that mold may never recognize their own neurodivergence. Representation helps people understand their experiences not as personal failings, but as neurological realities.

🚧 Bias in the Diagnostic Path

Boys are more likely to be flagged for impulsivity. Girls are more likely to be mislabeled with anxiety. Students of color may be punished instead of referred. Each of these pathways reflects how systems see behavior—and whose struggles get noticed.

🏆 Culture-Specific Strengths and Stigmas

Some cultures prize emotional control, achievement, or family duty. These values may lead to increased masking, or a reluctance to seek help. But they can also cultivate unique resilience and community support structures. Effective intervention must honor both challenge and strength.

🔎 Reclaiming the Narrative

To support people with ADHD, we must move past one-size-fits-all categories. The diagnosis must be flexible enough to see the quiet child who's shutting down instead of acting out. The teen who seems "fine" on the surface but is burning out inside. The student whose creativity is misread as rule-breaking.

Research indicates that diagnostic bias is a real phenomenon. But so is repair. When we name these gaps, we can start to close them. When we widen the frame, we create room for stories that were previously unwelcome.

This chapter isn't about blame. It's about better vision. Seeing clearly so people with ADHD don't have to suffer invisibly. So they can be met with understanding, not assumptions.

📚 References for Further Reading

o Coker, T. R., Elliott, M. N., Toomey, S. L., Schwebel, D. C., Cuccaro, P., & Schuster, M. A. (2016). Racial and ethnic disparities in ADHD diagnosis and treatment. Pediatrics, 138(3). This study highlights how Black and Latino children are underdiagnosed and undertreated for ADHD compared to white children, even when symptoms are similar.

o Hinshaw, S. P., & Scheffler, R. M. (2014). The ADHD Explosion: Myths, Medication, Money, and Today's Push for Performance. Oxford University Press. Explores how socioeconomic, educational, and cultural factors influence ADHD diagnosis and treatment trends across the U.S.

o Morgan, P. L., Staff, J., Hillemeier, M. M., Farkas, G., & Maczuga, S. (2013). Racial and ethnic disparities in ADHD diagnosis from kindergarten to eighth grade. Pediatrics, 132(1), 85–93. This longitudinal study confirms significant disparities in ADHD diagnosis based on race and ethnicity, independent of actual symptom severity.

o Nadeau, K. G., Littman, E. B., & Quinn, P. O. (2020). Understanding Girls with ADHD: How They Feel and Why They Do What They Do. Advantage Books. Essential reading on how gender norms shape the emotional and behavioral presentation of ADHD in girls and women.

o **Thomas, J. (2025).** Beyond the Edge of Chaos: ADHD, Identity, and the New Science of Thriving. Sleepy Creek Press. This book presents a signal-based framework for understanding ADHD motivation, emotional regulation, and identity development. It also introduces the Visionary–Producer–Editor model and tools for navigating complex systems and inner conflict.

➡ Segue to Chapter 14: Nested Selves

What begins on the outside doesn't stay there. When society misreads your attention, mislabels your emotions, or overlooks your neurodivergence entirely, it alters how you perceive yourself. You internalize the story you're given—until it becomes your own inner voice.

In the next chapter, we'll meet those voices. The Critic. The Protector. The part of you still hiding. The part still hoping to be seen. To truly support emotional intelligence in individuals with ADHD, we must start by listening to the selves within.

Chapter 14

Nested Selves—Internal Voices, Roles, and Self-Compassion

"We are not just one person over time—we are a chorus of selves, layered across our experiences. And sometimes, they argue."
—Jon Thomas

▧ How to Use This Chapter

This chapter introduces a compassionate framework for understanding the inner roles and emotional voices that shape how ADHD minds experience conflict, identity, and healing.

- ○ 🧠 **For People with ADHD—Students, Workers, and Curious Minds**
  - Discover why your inner dialogue can feel so loud—or so divided.
  - Meet your Inner Critic, Protective Self, and Vulnerable Self—and learn how they formed.
  - Use the Nested Selves Map to spot emotional patterns, develop healthier internal conversations, and practice signal-based self-compassion.

- ○ ✎ **For Parents, Clinicians, Educators, and Coaches**
  - ▪ Explore how developmental layers of self—from early vulnerability to adult masking—interact in ADHD identity formation.
  - ▪ Learn how to support clients and students in building self-awareness without shame.
  - ▪ Use the Nested Selves Map and the "Signal Words" tool to help reframe stuck thinking and internalized stigma.
- ○ ♀ **Key Tools and Takeaways**
  - ✓ The Nested Selves Model (Critic, Vulnerable, Adaptive/Protective, and Core Self)
  - ✓ Signal Words – internal language that stabilizes or scrambles the signal
  - ✓ Exercises for restoring compassionate inner dialogue
  - ✓ Practices for witnessing internal voices without identifying with them

---

💡 This chapter helps readers become observers of their inner experience—not to silence the voices within, but to understand them, honor their origins, and write a new script.

Introduction

Young adulthood is often described as a time of "finding yourself." But for many students with ADHD, the problem isn't a lack of self—it's because there are too many selves competing for airtime. One minute, they feel like a confident, driven adult; the next, they've slipped into the mindset of a frustrated middle schooler or a scared little kid. The experience is disorienting. It's not a crisis of identity—it's a traffic jam of identities, each with its own voice, needs, and baggage.

🧠 For People with ADHD—Students, Workers, and Curious Minds

Nested Selves: A Fractal View of Identity

Think of identity as a set of Russian dolls—selves within selves, layered over time. These "nested selves" develop through stages, roles, and major experiences. We carry:

- The child self who feared being different.
- The teen self who masked or rebelled.
- The college self, struggling with independence.
- The ideal self who lives in some imagined future.
- The social self, shaped by how we're perceived.

They don't vanish. They get activated. They show up in different situations. For neurotypical students, there's often enough inner coherence to keep them loosely aligned. But for students with ADHD, the volume knobs are broken. One self shouts while the others sulk in silence or pop up uninvited.

ADHD and the Problem of Integration

Students with ADHD are especially vulnerable to fragmented self-experience. Here's how:

1. Time blindness Disrupts the Self-Timeline

ADHD is often called a disorder of time perception (Barkley, 2008). It's not that students don't care about the future—it's that they can't feel it. The "future self" seems like a stranger, someone else's responsibility. The past self is equally distant or distorted. So they're left anchored in the "now self," reacting instead of planning.

"I know I should care about my final grade," one student told me. "But future-me always feels like a theoretical person."

2. Emotional Flooding Revives the Younger Self

Under stress, people with ADHD often regress. They may lash out, shut down, or procrastinate—not out of immaturity, but because a younger, overwhelmed self has taken the wheel. That younger self may have been humiliated in third grade, misunderstood in eighth, or labeled "lazy" by a well-meaning adult. When emotional regulation breaks down, that old wound becomes the present reality.

3. Variability of Performance Fractures Self-Image

ADHD students often swing between extremes:

- Crushing an exam one week, forgetting to show up the next.
- Getting praise for insight in class, then being penalized for missing a deadline.

These contradictions confuse others—but more painfully, they confuse the student. They begin to form parallel selves:

- o One that's gifted.
- o One that's a failure.
- o One that's pretending.
- o One that's just tired.

And they don't know which one to believe.

4. Masking and Mirroring Lead to Performed Selves

Many students with ADHD become social chameleons. They read the room, play the role, and mirror expectations. One moment they're the jokester, next they're the golden child, and later, the burnout. These masks are adaptive—but over time, the student may lose track of who they really are beneath the roles.

"Everyone says I'm smart and funny," a student once told me. "But I don't know if that's me or just who I've learned to be to survive."

Developmental Time Travel: How Old Selves Shape Today's Struggles

The Nested Selves aren't imaginary. They're real echoes of who we once were—formed at different developmental stages and triggered by present-day stress.

A missed assignment might awaken the 8-year-old who was labeled "lazy." A social rejection might re-activate the 13-year-old who never fit in. The college self who almost dropped out might come roaring back at the slightest hint of failure.

The goal isn't to silence them. It's to parent them. To listen with compassion, not compliance.

As Dr. Joel Nigg reminds us, identity in ADHD is shaped not just by biology, but by layered emotional learning. And those layers can be remapped.

" ... ADHD is not a single-issue brain disorder, but a multi-layered interplay of biology, environment, and self-regulation—shaped over time. Our sense of self in ADHD is similarly layered. From the externally visible 'performing self' to the inward 'questioning self' to the hidden 'hurting self,' these identities don't replace one another—they nest and interact across contexts, constantly shaping how we show up in the world."

Restoring the Inner Dialogue

The goal isn't to "fix" this nesting—it's to listen to it.
Integration means:

- o Letting the hurt younger self speak without letting them drive.
- o Helping the future self become more than a fantasy.
- o Recognizing the performed self as protective, but incomplete.
- o Choosing which self gets the mic, and when.

This is the emotional intelligence work we often overlook—not calming down, but listening inward, clearly, and without shame.

When we begin to recognize these internal voices, something important shifts: they stop seeing themselves as broken and start seeing themselves as plural—layered, responsive, and dynamic.

But awareness alone isn't enough. Because sometimes the loudest voices we hear aren't out in the world—they're the ones echoing in our own minds.

🏆 Changing the Channel: Signal Words and the Language of Internal Power

These voices speak a language we've often absorbed unconsciously, word by word, over time.

And in the minds of those with ADHD, **language doesn't just reflect emotion—it amplifies it.**

The words we whisper inward—especially under pressure—can either stabilize our signals or distort them. They can spark resistance, or they can invite agency. They can open a path forward, or quietly plant a seed of sabotage.

That's why one of the most overlooked—but powerful—tools for self-integration is something straightforward: **learning to change the words we use with ourselves.**

Before we go deeper, consider this:

> *"Thinking is the talking of the soul with itself."*
> **—Plato**

And when we talk to ourselves in this way, we listen.
Especially when we're afraid.

Especially when we're unsure.
Especially when iwe need a reason to keep going.
Because in moments like that, our words stop being merely narration and start acting like instructions:

- o   To our nervous system.
- o   To our motivation.
- o   To our belief system.
- o   To the future self we're still becoming.

Words are magic spells.
Especially the ones we say to ourselves.

🎭 Hidden Scripts: How Our Words Shape Reality

Let's look at some everyday phrases:

- o   "I can't mess this up…"
- o   "I should have already done this…"
- o   "If I pass this test…"
- o   "I haven't failed yet…"

They might sound like motivation. But each one carries a quiet suggestion—a **hidden belief**. These aren't neutral statements. They're **post-hypnotic suggestions**.

🔍 What's a post-hypnotic suggestion?

It's a phrase that embeds a mental command, often bypass-ing resistance. Moreover, when we say it to ourselves, our brain tends to listen, without filtering—and obey.
   Let's break a few of these down:

- "I haven't failed yet" may sound encouraging. But it presupposes you will eventually fail—just not *now*.
- "If I pass..." carries a built-in doubt. That uncertainty doesn't go away—it lingers in the background, quietly reinforcing fear.
- "I should have..." tells your brain you're already behind, activating shame, pressure, and internal scolding—not momentum.

Because we're the ones saying these things (to ourselves), we rarely question them. We treat them as truth and then act accordingly.

And that is the trick: **language becomes belief when it slips in unchallenged**.

🎏 The Words That Trigger Resistance

There's another class of words that don't trigger compliance—they trigger rebellion.

Words like:

- "Should"
- "Have to"
- "Ought to"
- "Better"
- "Gotta"

These signal **pressure**. Even when they come from our own voice, they carry the weight of external expectation. They feel like a command, not a choice. And that's precisely what triggers what we described in Chapter 6 as the **"uneasy-in-the-harness"** response—a tension that comes from being given an agenda that doesn't feel like your own.

ADHD minds often bristle at that.

We don't respond well to pressure disguised as self-motivation.

It backfires.

We push back, stall out, or rebel.

🔁 Rewriting Internal Scripts: From Pressure to Permission

Words can either block our signals or restore them.

Here's how common self-talk phrases can be rewritten to unlock agency, possibility, and forward movement:

🚫 Old Phrase (Blocks Signal)	☑ New Phrase (Restores Signal)
"I should have done this already."	"I'm doing this now—and that matters."
"I have to finish, or I fail."	"I'll take a step and see what's next."

⃠ Old Phrase (Blocks Signal)	☑ New Phrase (Restores Signal)
"If I pass…"	"When I pass…" or "Here's how I'll pass…"
"I never follow through."	"Sometimes I stall, but I know how to restart."
"I'm so behind."	"This is the point I'm starting from."
"I don't even know where to start."	"I'll find a small place to begin."

Signal Words don't deny reality—they reframe it in a way that restores **agency**.

They widen our **working space**—the mental pause between emotion and action—where motivation can grow.

🧠 Why It Matters for ADHD Minds

ADHD brains are wired to respond to **salient language**, especially when it's emotionally charged or self-referential. That's why phrases like *always, never, can't, should, have to* land with such force. They act like emotional tripwires—igniting guilt, fear, shame, or perfectionism that blocks action instead of supporting it.

In the SASMA Pathway (Chapter 5), these phrases often act as **amplifiers**—distorting the original signal and turning it into resistance or overdrive.

But when we replace them with **Signal Words**—phrases that cue **possibility, permission,** or **progression**—something shifts. We don't just change our behavior.

We change how we feel about what's next.

And in ADHD minds, that emotional reframe is often the key to unlocking action.

🔧 Practice Prompts

Try experimenting with this over a few days. Here's how to get started:

1. **Notice your self-talk.** Catch moments when you say "should," "can't," or "if I..."
2. **Ask:** Is this voice helping me—or hijacking my signal?
3. **Reframe with Signal Words.** Try: "I choose to..." or "I'm ready to..." or "Here's what I can do."
4. **Record it.** Make a short voice memo to your future self using signal-based language—like Matt did in his video before a run: sweaty, tired, proud he showed up.
5. **Play it back.** Especially when you're stuck, over-whelmed, or doubting yourself.

🎯 The Bottom Line

Signal Words aren't just semantics.
They're **behavioral primers**.
They tell your brain:

- What to expect.
- How to feel.
- What role to play.

When we speak in fear, guilt, or doubt, our actions follow suit.
But when we speak with clarity, alignment, and owner-ship—we move differently.
And we believe differently.
And belief—especially the kind we say out loud to ourselves—is the most powerful post-hypnotic suggestion there is.
So listen closely.

Signal your future.

Change your words—and you just might change your world.

🗺️ Tool: The Nested Selves Map

To support this journey, we've created a tool called the **Nested Selves Map**—a reflective worksheet that helps students name, describe, and navigate among their various selves.

It asks:

- Who are the "selves" you carry from past, present, and future?
- What role do they each play?
- What situations activate each one?
- What does each self want or fear?
- How might you invite them into alignment?

Consider this an inner **coalition-building exercise**.

The goal isn't consensus—it's **coordination**.

🗡️ Example: Completing Your Nested Selves Map

Sometimes it helps to see how this looks in practice. Below is a sample map with some common inner voices that often show up for people with ADHD. Notice how each self has a role, triggers, fears, and ways it can be invited into alignment. Your own answers will look different—that's the point. Everyone carries a unique combination of selves, shaped by experience, identity, and history. Use this example as a guide, not a template.

🗺️ Nested Selves Map—Example Worksheet

Here's a sample Nested Selves Map to illustrate how you might complete the worksheet.

You may discover different nested selves so your answers

will look different, but notice how each self has a role, triggers, fears, and ways it can be invited into alignment.

Self Name	Role / Purpose	Situations That Activate This Self	Wants / Fears	How to Invite Into Alignment
Inner Critic	Tries to prevent failure by being harsh	After mistakes, before deadlines	Wants success; fears rejection	Remind it of past growth and reframe mistakes as learning
Protective Self	Shields Vulnerable Self from pain	Conflict, criticism, high stakes	Wants safety; fears exposure	Acknowledge its role, offer reassurance, allow safe risks
Vulnerable Self	Holds early wounds and raw feelings	Failure, shame triggers, feeling left out	Wants belonging; fears abandonment	Listen with compassion, give it space to be heard
Future Aspiring Self	Pushes toward growth and goals	Opportunities, inspiration, future planning	Wants purpose; fears stagnation	Clarify values, set small steps, celebrate progress
Integrated Self	Coordinates and balances all selves	Reflection, journaling, therapy, coaching	Wants harmony; fears chaos	Use maps, tools, and self-talk to invite dialogue

Notice: The goal is not to eliminate or silence any self, but to understand each one's role and help them coordinate.

✳ Nested Selves vs. Integrated Selves: Where the Visionary–Producer–Editor Fit In

If the Nested Selves are emotional time capsules—echoes of who you were at different points in your life—then the **Visionary, Producer, and Editor** are **functional roles** you can consciously inhabit today.

They aren't replacements for your inner child, performer, or protector.

They're the **guides** who can listen to those voices but still make intentional decisions.

- o The **Visionary** holds your dreams and longings—even the ones your younger self was told to hide.
- o The **Producer** acts on those dreams, without shaming the part of you that's scared to start.
- o The **Editor** reflects, protects, and plans—but with kindness, not cruelty.

When these integrated adult selves take the mic, your Nested Selves don't disappear—they just don't have to run the show.

The **Visionary–Producer–Editor model** offers a next step:

Conscious, intentional adult functioning that includes—but isn't run by—the Nested Selves.

From Listening Inward to Thinking Clearly

As you begin to understand your inner voices—and recognize the parts of you that react, protect, perform, and dream—a new kind of awareness starts to take shape.

You're not just feeling differently.

You're starting to **see** differently.

But what do you do when those inner voices contradict each other?

When part of you wants to move forward, and another part pulls you back?

That's where **clear thinking** comes in.

The next chapter introduces the third major pillar of thriving with ADHD: **Critical Thinking and Cognitive Clarity**. We'll explore the traps ADHD minds tend to fall into—like black-and-white thinking, catastrophizing, or internalizing every bit of feedback—and how to
climb out of them with compassion, curiosity,
and logic.

Because once you can hear yourself think without shame...

You can begin to think yourself free.

For Parents, Educators, Clinicians, Coaches, and Curious Readers

- o Many students with ADHD experience self-fragmentation due to developmental trauma, emotional flooding, or inconsistent feedback. Helping them build self-awareness tools grounded in compassion can dramatically shift motivation and resilience.
- o Encourage students to name and externalize their internal voices through narrative, drawing, or journaling.
- o Teach that integration is not erasure—it's learning when to listen, when to soothe, and when to lead.
- o The Visionary–Producer–Editor model complements the Nested Selves by giving students practical roles to grow into, without dismissing the younger parts that still show up.
- o Pair emotional awareness work with regulation tools and motivational scaffolding.

✧

Additional Guidance for Supporters

Students with ADHD often experience "time travel" when stressed—suddenly reacting as though they were much younger. When you notice a student's response feels out of sync with their age, it may be a past self taking the mic. Approaching these moments with curiosity ("Which part of you feels hurt right now?") can shift the dynamic from confrontation to compassion.

The Nested Selves Map can also be used directly in therapy, coaching, or classroom settings. Invite students to externalize their selves through drawing, storytelling, or role-play. By naming the Inner Critic or Protective Self, shame decreases and perspective grows: "This isn't all of me—it's one voice inside me."

For families and teachers, it helps to recognize that tone and context often activate specific selves. A scolding voice may summon the 8-year-old who once felt humiliated; rigid rules may activate the Rebellious Self. Instead of escalating, experiment with language that invites agency: "What would your future self want here?" or "How could your protective self help, without shutting everything down?"

Finally, the Nested Selves model pairs well with the Visionary-Producer-Editor framework. While the Nested Selves help students honor their history, the VPE roles give them tools to act in the present. Together, they provide both compassion and structure—an inner compass for moving forward without abandoning the younger selves who still need care.

📖 References for Further Reading

o **Barkley, R. A. (2008).** *Executive functions: What they are, how they work, and why they evolved.* Guilford Press.
This foundational work explains the role of executive function and time perception in ADHD. It supports the chapter's exploration of time blindness and the difficulty that ADHD students have in connecting with future or past versions of themselves.

o **Hallowell, E. M., & Ratey, J. J. (1994).** *Driven to distraction: Recognizing and coping with attention deficit disorder from childhood through adulthood.* Touchstone.
A classic ADHD text that introduced the concept of emotional flooding and regression in moments of stress. This is cited in the section on the younger self being reactivated under emotional overload.

o **Nigg, J. T. (2017).** *Getting ahead of ADHD: What next-generation science says about treatments that work.* Guilford Press.
This work presents a multi-layered understanding of ADHD as a developmental and regulatory condition shaped by environment, biology, and emotion. It underpins the Nested Selves concept introduced in this chapter and connects to the broader theme of recursive identity in individuals with ADHD.

🔄 Next Chapter: From Nested Selves to Clearer Thinking

When you begin to recognize your internal voices—not just the loudest, but the hidden ones—something fundamental shifts. You stop reacting blindly. You start listening inward.

But now comes the next challenge:

What do you do when those voices disagree?

One part of you wants to move forward.

Another part is convinced you'll fail.

A third part just wants a snack and a nap.

This isn't weakness. It's the natural result of a complex, layered inner life—one shaped by ADHD's emotional intensity, time distortion, and recursive feedback loops.

To navigate this chorus of selves, you don't just need self-awareness.

You need a strategy for thinking clearly when your mind feels noisy, scattered, or stuck.

That's where we're going next:

Critical Thinking for ADHD Minds.

Not in the academic sense—but in the real-world, every-day sense of catching faulty logic, decoding mental traps, and interrupting self-sabotage.

You've met your voices.

Now it's time to help them talk to each other—with clarity, curiosity, and compassion.

Chapter 15

Critical Thinking—The Third Pillar of Thriving with ADHD

"Thinking is difficult, that's why most people judge."
—Carl Jung

▨ How to Use This Chapter

Chapter 15: Critical Thinking—The Third Pillar of Thriving with ADHD follows the layered structure used throughout the book. Whether you're an ADHD learner, a supporter, or simply curious, each section offers tailored insight for different readers—and tools that translate insight into action.

- ○ 🧠 **For People with ADHD—Students, Workers, and Curious Minds**
  Learn how ADHD minds process thoughts, emotions, and logic differently—and how to catch distorted thinking before it spirals. Explore tools like *Cards Against Faulty Thinking*, fast vs. slow thinking strategies, and reframing prompts designed to support clarity without shame.

- ○ 🔬 **For Parents, Clinicians, Educators, and Coaches**
  Dive into the neuroscience and emotional patterns that affect logic and decision-making in ADHD. Use the ADHD-specific fallacies chart, metacognitive prompts, and structured tools to support students in building flexible, compassionate thinking skills.

o 💡 **Key Concepts and Tools You'll Find Here**
- ✓ Fast vs. Slow Thinking (System 1 vs. System 2)
- ✓ ADHD Logical Fallacies & Thinking Traps Table
- ✓ "Cards Against Faulty Thinking"—a practical reframing tool
- ✓ Reframing Language and the Role of Signal Words
- ✓ Working Space: Creating Internal Conditions for Thought
- ✓ Integration with the Editor Role in the Visionary-Producer-Editor Model

---

> 💡 This chapter isn't about thinking harder—it's about thinking more clearly, by slowing down just enough to see your thoughts as signals, not absolute truths.

🧠 For People with ADHD—Students, Workers, and Curious Minds

We talk a lot about focus when it comes to ADHD—sustaining it, shifting it, losing it like a sock in the laundry. But what we don't talk about enough is how ADHD affects how we evaluate our own thoughts.

Clear thinking isn't just about intelligence. It's about meta-cognition—the ability to reflect on your thoughts before reacting. For many with ADHD, that reflective pause either shows up late or not at all. Thoughts become truths. Feelings become facts. Panic becomes the plan.

Thoughts like "I'm failing," or "They're mad at me," or "It's already too late" might feel automatic—but that doesn't mean they're accurate.

This chapter is about taking back your mental filter. And it begins by understanding how your brain processes information—from fast to slow and everything in between.

⚖️ System 1 vs. System 2 Thinking (Kahneman, 2011)

To understand where this mental filter breaks down—and how to rebuild it—we need to explore how your brain processes information.

Psychologist Daniel Kahneman famously explained that the brain runs two thinking systems:

- ○ System 1: Fast, automatic, emotional, reactive
- ○ System 2: Slow, deliberate, logical, effortful

For individuals with ADHD, System 1 tends to dominate. That's not inherently bad—intuition and speed can be superpowers. But when you need perspective, restraint, or strategy, System 1 is like a toddler holding the car keys.

That's where critical thinking comes in. Not as judgment or overthinking, but as a balance beam. A way to pause, step back, and ask, "What else might be true?"

💼 Working Space—The Bridge Between Impulse and Insight

Have you ever thought of the perfect thing to say—ten minutes too late? Or remembered the test answer right after handing it in?

That's not failure. That's "Working Space."

People with ADHD often need time after the pressure is

gone for ideas, clarity, and emotional understanding to surface. It's not a flaw—it's a process. Working Space is the interval between stimulus and insight, a kind of mental workshop where System 2 can finally come online.

This is where System 2 has a chance to speak—not louder, but clearer.

We often think ADHD is about speed. But sometimes the greatest gift we can give our brains is an intentional pause.

Working Space allows:

- Curiosity to replace panic
- Reflection to catch up with emotion
- Ideas to emerge without urgency shouting over them

It's the space where "What just happened?" becomes "What does this mean?"—and eventually, "What can I do next?"

So, if you need time to think things through, take it. That's not a delay—*it's your brain doing the real work.*

🏛 ADHD and the Architecture of Thought

Let's be honest: ADHD throws noise into the brain's editing department. Thoughts rush in, powered by urgency or emotion, and there's little filtration before action.

Executive functions, such as inhibition, working memory, and flexible thinking, often struggle to keep up. It's like trying to proofread a document while someone is shouting, your phone is buzzing, and your chair is on fire. For ADHD minds, reflection isn't absent—it's just harder to hear through the noise.

And in that storm, false beliefs take root. Thoughts like "I'm doomed," "Everyone hates me," or "This always happens" become headlines instead of hypotheses.

These thinking traps aren't personal flaws—they're fast-thinking shortcuts our brains take under stress. And with a little distance, they can be spotted, softened, and reworked.

And in our hyper-digital world—where social media algorithms amplify drama over nuance—these shortcuts get reinforced constantly.

🕵️ Thinking Traps: Classic Fallacies and ADHD Examples with Antidotes

Fallacy / Distortion	What It Is	ADHD Example	Antidote / Reframe
All-or-Nothing Thinking	Seeing things in extremes, no middle ground	"If I don't ace this, I'm a total failure."	"I can do well without being perfect."

Confirmation Bias	Only noticing info that supports your fear	"I always bomb these tests—this proves I'm hopeless."	"What else do I know that might counter that?"
Overgeneral-ization	Making broad conclusions from one event	"One rejection means I'll never succeed."	"This was one moment. It doesn't predict all the others."
Catastroph-izing	Expecting worst-case scenario as inevitable	"If I mess this up, I'll get fired and end up homeless."	"Even if this goes badly, I can recover."
False Cause	Assuming cause where there's only correlation	"I wore green socks and failed—green socks are cursed."	"Coincidence doesn't mean cause."
Ad Hominem	Attacking the person instead of the idea	"He's annoying, so his feedback is wrong."	"Even frustrating people can say useful things."
Appeal to Authority	Relying blindly on experts or influencers	"The productivity guru said it'll work, so I must be broken."	"Their tool might help—but I still get to choose."
Emotional Reasoning	Thinking that feelings are facts	"I feel overwhelmed, so I must be failing."	"Feelings are real, but not always reliable data."

		"Emotions are messengers, not maps."	
Personaliza-tion	Blaming yourself for events outside your control	"They're quiet today, I must have done something wrong."	"Maybe it's not about me."

🖊 Sidebar: Signal Words and the Editor—Rewriting Internal Logic

When we discuss distorted thinking, we typically envision obvious fallacies—such as catastrophizing, black-and-white thinking, and emotional reasoning. But sometimes, the distortion is more subtle. It hides inside everyday phrases we whisper to ourselves:

"I always mess this up." "I should have already done this." "If I fail this, I'm done."

These aren't just emotional reactions. They're post-hypnotic suggestions—internal scripts we speak in moments of stress that bypass logic and go straight into belief.

This is where your inner Editor—the reflective, curious, compassionate part of you—can step in and ask: "Is that true? Or just how it feels right now?"

Signal Words, introduced in Chapter 13 (Nested Selves), are one of the simplest tools to help catch and reframe these phrases. When you shift your inner language from pressure to permission, panic to clarity, you're not just thinking better—you're editing your mental script in real time.

> ✍ Rewriting "I never get this right" into "Sometimes I struggle, but I know how to restart" isn't just reframing. It's metacognition in action.

Metacognition—The Mirror Behind the Thought

📖 The Story That Changed Everything

When I first began teaching executive function to college students, I asked them to track not just what they were doing, but what they were thinking in the moments they got stuck. One student's journal entry changed my career:

"I sat down to write. Then I heard the voice in my head say: 'This is going to suck. You're probably going to blow it again.' So I decided to clean the kitchen."

That sentence—"I heard the voice in my head say..."—was metacognition. It wasn't the thought itself. It was awareness of the thought. And that awareness created a tiny bit of distance. In that space, the student could choose differently. Awareness, not just willpower, became the turning point.

🧭 What Is Metacognition? Metacognition is the capacity to notice your own thinking. It's the mental mirror that lets you see what's happening inside your mind—not just the content, but the process.

It's what happens when you realize:

- "Oh wow, I'm really spiraling right now."
- "This isn't even my belief. I'm just repeating what my dad used to say."

o   "My brain is avoiding this task because it feels overwhelming."

The key isn't to stop the thought. It's to see the thought. Once it's seen, it can be named, challenged, redirected, or gently replaced.

ADHD and Invisible Thinking

People with ADHD often live in a world of invisible influences. Automatic shame scripts. Looming catastrophes. Emotional flashbacks disguised as logic. Distraction loops that feel like laziness. These aren't failures of logic—they're failures of awareness.

Without metacognition, we don't even notice the lens we're looking through.

With metacognition, we can say:

"This is a lens. It's not the truth."

Thinking Loops and Feedback Spirals

Your brain loves patterns. Once a certain thought pattern becomes familiar, it's easier to fall into again. That's not a moral failing—it's just how neural networks work.

Here's the cycle:

You think a thought ("I always mess this up.")

That thought shapes emotion (shame, anxiety)

Emotion creates behavior (avoidance, freeze)

Behavior leads to results (unfinished work)

Results reinforce the original thought

This is a feedback spiral. The way out is not brute force—it's interruption. A metacognitive pause.

🗓 Metacognitive Pause: A Tool
When you feel stuck, ask:

- What am I thinking about this right now?
- Is that thought helping me or hurting me?
- Where did I learn to think this way?
- What might a different thought feel like?

Even just writing the thought down—externalizing it—can change its power. As one student told me:

"When I saw it on paper, I realized it sounded like my high school band director, not me."

🎛 College, Career, and Real-World Consequences

- In School: A student with ADHD misreads a critique on an essay as proof they're stupid and shuts down.
- In Career: An employee misses a deadline and assumes they should quit the job entirely.
- In Relationships: A friend forgets to text back, and the ADHD brain jumps to "They hate me."

In every case, fast thinking overrides reflection. System 2 never gets a chance to step in.

🔧 Thinking Clearly Isn't Just a Skill—It's a practice. You can't change your default wiring overnight. But you can install circuit breakers. This is where your Working Space becomes a lab for clarity—where messy thoughts meet gentle scrutiny.

One powerful way? Externalize your thinking. Speak it. Write it. Share it.

Try this Cognitive Trap Check-In:

- What's actually happening?
- What story am I telling myself about it?
- What logical fallacy might I be using?
- What evidence supports or contradicts that story?

These questions slow the spiral. They make room for better questions. And better outcomes.

That's why we created Cards Against Faulty Thinking—a game that helps people with ADHD name, defuse, and reframe thinking errors with humor and self-kindness. (Find sample prompts and downloads in the appendix or at the companion website.)

As Dr. Russell Barkley reminds us: "ADHD is not a disorder of knowing what to do, it's a disorder of doing what you know." That gap is never more dangerous than when we're reacting without reflection.

🖹 Tool: Reframing Prompts for People With ADHD

- "Is this feeling a fact, or a flag?"
- "What would I tell a friend in this situation?"
- "What might be missing from my mental picture?"
- "If this goes wrong, what's a softer landing plan?"

These don't just clarify thought. They unlock agency.

✧

Clarity as a Superpower

Critical thinking isn't about being cold, rigid, or robotic. It's about creating space between emotion and action.

It's about asking, "What else might be true?" before you write the ending.

In ADHD life, clarity is not just a skill. It's a lifeline. A source of resilience. A path to self-trust.

You don't have to think faster. You just need to think truer—and give that quieter part of your brain room to speak.

✧

Fractal Intelligence: A Pattern-Seeking Brain Needs a Reflective Filter

People with ADHD tend to excel at spotting connections others miss—echoes, metaphors, recurring dynamics. This "fractal intelligence" is a powerful gift, particularly in creativity, systems thinking, and problem-solving.

But in moments of stress or urgency, that same pattern sensitivity can turn against us. We don't just see what's happening—we *jump* to conclusions, often fueled by past pain or untested assumptions. One friend doesn't text back, and suddenly it's "No one ever wants me around."

Critical thinking isn't the opposite of fractal intelligence—it's the **anchor** that keeps it from spiraling. It's the filter that asks, "Is this a true pattern—or just a strong feeling looking for evidence?"

When you pair ADHD's pattern-seeing gifts with the tools of metacognition, you get something rare: insight *with* accuracy. Creativity *with* discernment. A mind that can connect the dots—without being trapped by them.

Sidebar: Thinking With, Not Instead Of Why ChatGPT Doesn't Make You Dumber

By Jon L. Thomas, EdD, LPC

A recent MIT study warned that using ChatGPT might lead to "cognitive atrophy"—a weakening of critical thinking, reflection, and metacognitive skills. Suddenly, headlines exploded:

"ChatGPT is making people dumber." "AI is hurting our brains." "Using ChatGPT kills cognition."

But that's not the whole story—especially for people with ADHD.

As a therapist, educator, and ADHD specialist—and someone with ADHD myself—I'd like to offer a different perspective. One that comes from decades of watching students struggle with executive function, writing paralysis, and burnout—and also from watching some of them thrive, once they had the right tools, mindset, and guidance.

The Nonspecific Amplifier—What That Means for ADHD

In emerging therapies using ketamine, psilocybin, or MDMA, we hear these compounds referred to as nonspecific amplifiers. They don't direct you. They amplify what's already happening in your brain, your nervous system, and your environment. When paired with thoughtful support, they can facilitate breakthroughs. When used in isolation, they can amplify confusion or escape.

It means this: the tool doesn't fix you. It amplifies what's already present—your mindset, your blind spots, your strengths, your habits.

ChatGPT is the same. It doesn't make you smarter. It doesn't make you dumber. It reflects and amplifies the quality of the thinking you bring to it.

Come to it with laziness? It will reinforce laziness.

Come to it with curiosity? It will open doors.

Come to it with a poorly formed question? It will spin confusion into confident-sounding mush.

Come to it with an insight you're still shaping? It will help you test, iterate, and refine.

And if you're a person with ADHD struggling to move ideas into action, it can be the bridge that lets you move again.

Not by thinking instead of you.

By thinking with you.

Product vs. Process—and Why It Matters for ADHD Brains

Here's what the MIT study missed: it measured the product, but not the process.

Yes, ChatGPT helped participants generate usable outputs faster—and yes, when they were later tested on logic tasks, they performed worse than those who had written from scratch. But that doesn't prove the tool caused the deficit. It only shows they didn't engage deeply with the thinking process.

This happens everywhere. A student copies a paper from a friend. A professional reuses a stale PowerPoint. A teacher downloads a worksheet they've never read.

Shortcuts are everywhere. But AI isn't the problem. Skipping the process is. Shortcutting is the problem.

For many students with ADHD, ChatGPT doesn't remove the thinking process—it supports it. When used well, it helps externalize working memory, test ideas safely, scaffold transitions, or break writer's block. These students aren't skipping steps. They're finally accessing the ones they couldn't reach before.

This doesn't make students dumber. It makes students braver by creating a feedback loop that rewards action, reflection, and iteration.

Research on ADHD and executive function confirms that external scaffolding can significantly improve task initiation, working memory, and planning (Barkley, 2012).

Real-Life Amplifiers—and How ADHD Users Respond
We're all already surrounded by nonspecific amplifiers—and their impact depends on how we use them.

Caffeine – Enhances alertness for task engagement | Intensifies anxiety or overfocus

Group work – Boosts energy, creativity, accountability | Triggers overwhelm or avoidance

Time pressure – Sparks urgency, narrows attention | Causes shutdown or panic

Music - Calms or energizes based on preference | Distracts or overstimulates if mismatched

Open-book tests - Supports memory limits, encourages application | Enables surface-level cramming

ChatGPT fits right in. It amplifies mindset, context, skill, and intention.

So when we treat it like a shortcut—"Just have the bot do it!"—we get shallow thinking.

When we treat it like a thinking partner—"Let's wrestle with this together"—we get growth.

You Are the Author. AI Is the Amplifier.

In my work with ADHD students, we teach a core principle:

You are the author. AI is the amplifier.

That means you're still responsible for:

- o Asking the deeper question
- o Revising the messy draft
- o Owning your voice
- o Deciding what to keep and what to discard

ChatGPT can suggest. Challenge. Mirror. Provoke. But it can't own the outcome. That's yours.

So let's stop asking whether ChatGPT is "good" or "bad." That's like asking whether a guitar is dangerous. Or whether glasses are unfair.

The better question is:

Are we teaching learners to use this amplifier with creativity, integrity, and critical thought?

How ADHD Learners Can Use ChatGPT to Grow—Not Just Get By

Used well, ChatGPT doesn't bypass growth—it accelerates it.

Not just by improving the final product, but by strengthening the thinking process that leads to it.

When ADHD students engage with AI intentionally, reflectively, and iteratively, it can help them:

- o **Strengthen executive function**—by organizing thoughts, sequencing ideas, externalizing working memory, and structuring tasks in manageable steps
- o **Amplify metacognition**—by turning invisible processes (like self-questioning or mental rehearsal) into visible drafts they can inspect, revise, and learn from
- o **Improve critical thinking**—not by handing over the answer, but by offering a space to test arguments, challenge assumptions, and refine logic in real time

These aren't shortcuts to polished results.

They're scaffolds for building better mental habits.

When we focus on process over product, we stop asking "Did the bot do it?"

And we start asking, "Did the learner grow through it?"

What the Research Says About ADHD and Cognitive Tools

- o ADHD learners often struggle not with knowing what to do, but with initiating and sequencing action—especially in open-ended tasks. (Barkley, 2012)

- o Metacognition and self-monitoring are executive functions that can be supported through visual or conversational tools—including AI writing aids. (Dawson & Guare, 2010)
- o ChatGPT may serve as an "externalized working memory," allowing learners with ADHD to offload mental steps while staying engaged with meaning and structure. (Author interpretation)

And Here's the Good News
If you bring curiosity, honesty, and purpose to the keyboard, this tool will help you grow.

If you don't, it will echo back the shortcuts you already take.

But the power stays with you.

For Parents, Educators, Clinicians, Coaches, and Curious Readers

People with ADHD often respond fast and regret later. They may:

- o Mislabel their thoughts as facts
- o Overreact to ambiguous cues
- o Internalize failure instead of questioning assumptions

To support clearer thinking:

- o **Normalize reflective pauses**—model curiosity about

"What else could be true?" before reacting.

- o **Teach common fallacies playfully**—use tools like *Cards Against Faulty Thinking* or real-life "spot the distortion" games to build awareness without shame.
- o **Model metacognition**—say out loud, *"Here's how I questioned my first reaction."* Hearing adults do this makes reflection visible and learnable.
- o **Create safe revision space**—emphasize that drafts, do-overs, and corrections are part of learning, not evidence of failure.

Most importantly, remind them: thinking is not identity. Thoughts can be improved, updated, or even laughed at later. That perspective builds **cognitive resilience**—the confidence that minds can stretch, adapt, and recover rather than collapse under pressure.

📑 References for Further Reading

- o **Barkley, R. A. (2008).** *Executive Functions: What They Are, How They Work, and Why They Evolved.* New York: Guilford Press.
A foundational work by leading ADHD researcher Dr. Russell Barkley that explains how executive functions operate and why individuals with ADHD struggle with reflective decision-making. This book underpins many of the behavioral and neurological insights referenced in this chapter.

- o **Brown, T. E. (2013).** *A New Understanding of ADHD in Children and Adults: Executive Function Impairments.* New York: Routledge.

Dr. Brown explores how ADHD affects complex decision-making, emotional regulation, and metacognition—key ingredients in critical thinking. His executive function
model adds nuance to Kahneman's System 1/System 2 lens.

o **Dvorsky, M. R., & Langberg, J. M. (2016).** Predicting academic outcomes in college students with ADHD: The role of executive functions and motivation. *Journal of Clinical Child & Adolescent Psychology, 45*(4), 442–456.
This study links ADHD-related executive function deficits—especially in planning and inhibition—to academic performance, reinforcing the need for structured critical thinking strategies in ADHD populations.

o **Goldstein, S., & Naglieri, J. A. (Eds.). (2014).** *Handbook of Executive Functioning.* New York: Springer.
A comprehensive overview of executive function research, including chapters on how impulsivity and working memory limitations interfere with critical evaluation and strategic thinking in ADHD.

o **Kahneman, D. (2011).** *Thinking, Fast and Slow.* New York: Farrar, Straus and Giroux.
Nobel laureate Daniel Kahneman's seminal text explaining the dual-system model of thinking—fast, intuitive System 1 vs. slow, logical System 2. This framework provides the backbone for understanding impulsive vs. reflective cognition, particularly in ADHD.

o **Zelazo, P. D., & Lyons, K. E. (2012).** The potential benefits of mindfulness training in early childhood: A developmental social cognitive neuroscience perspective. *Child Development Perspectives, 6*(2), 154–160.

While not ADHD-specific, this article explores how reflective awareness (i.e., metacognition) can be enhanced through mindfulness—a strategy shown to improve critical thinking and emotional regulation in ADHD.

⟳ Next Chapter: From Thinking Clearly to Feeling Wisely

Critical thinking helps you spot distortions.

It helps you question assumptions.

It gives you the power to pause—and choose a better path.

But logic alone doesn't move us.

Because ADHD minds aren't just driven by thought—they're *fueled* by emotion.

That's why clear thinking and emotional intelligence aren't opposites. They're partners.

You can't manage what you don't understand.

And you can't think your way through a feeling you haven't yet named.

In the next chapter, we'll explore how to work with emotions the same way we've learned to work with thoughts:

- o   With awareness, not avoidance.
- o   With permission, not panic.
- o   With tools—not shame.

Because under every stuck thought is often a stuck feeling.

And when ADHD minds learn how to feel what they feel—without getting overwhelmed or hijacked—clarity becomes not just a skill, but a state.

Let's go deeper.

🪨 Chapter 16

Emotional Intelligence—Understanding What You Feel and Why

"Emotions are not problems to be solved.
They are signals to be understood."
—Anonymous workshop participant

"What really matters for success,
character, happiness, and lifelong
achievements is a definite set of
emotional skills—your EQ—not just purely cognitive
abilities that are measured by conventional IQ tests."
—Daniel Goleman

🪨 How to Use This Chapter

Chapter 16: Emotional Intelligence—Understanding What You Feel and Why follows the three-layered format used throughout this book. It helps readers make sense of emotional experiences, decode the role of feelings in ADHD motivation and meltdown, and build emotional regulation as a skill.

- 🧠 **For People with ADHD—Students, Workers, and Curious Minds**
  - Learn how emotions affect your focus, memory, motivation, and self-talk

- Discover how to monitor, name, and interpret emotions without getting flooded
- Use tools like the Three E's Model, the Caldron of Emotion, and Signal Words to regulate emotions in real time

○ ✏ **For Parents, Clinicians, Educators, and Coaches**

- Understand the emotional amplification patterns common in ADHD minds
- Support students in building skills across the four domains of emotional intelligence: monitoring, naming, interpreting, and managing
- Use tools like the Signal Compass, the Caldron Exercise, and Emotion Check-Ins to build emotional literacy

○ ♀ **Key Concepts and Tools You'll Find Here**

- ✓ Monitoring Emotions Without Judgment
- ✓ Naming What You Feel—and Why That Matters
- ✓ Interpreting Emotional Data vs. Reacting Automatically
- ✓ Managing Emotions With Signals, Not Suppression
- ✓ The Three E's Model (Experience-Evaluation-Emotion-Expression)
- ✓ The Caldron of Unexpressed Emotion
- ✓ Signal Words and Self-Talk in Emotional Regulation
- ✓ Working Space: Building Room for Reflection

💡 Emotional intelligence isn't about suppressing emotion—it's about learning to *work with it* as part of your signal system. This chapter helps you understand what you feel, why you feel it, and what to do next.

🜨 Introduction

Before we can manage the outer systems of life—stress, energy, and balance—we need to understand our inner system. That means learning how to work with emotion, not against it. For people with ADHD, emotional intensity isn't a flaw—it's a feature. But without tools to read and respond to emotional signals, we get overwhelmed, shut down, or pushed around by feelings we don't fully understand. Emotional waves come crashing in, and instead of surfing them, we wipe out—or pretend they're not happening until we can't ignore them anymore.

Emotional intelligence is the skillset that helps us stay afloat. It lets us track what we're feeling, understand where it's coming from, and decide what to do next. It's not just about being "in touch" with emotions—it's about using this knowledge to steer your life.

In this chapter, we'll explore the four core emotional skills that ADHD minds often miss out on growing up:

- o Monitoring what you feel
- o Naming the feeling clearly

- o Understanding what it means
- o Managing your response to the feeling with intention

These aren't luxuries. They're survival skills. They affect everything—from your motivation to your relationships to your ability to recover from stress. They're also learnable.

Psychologist Daniel Goleman helped popularize the idea that emotional intelligence (EQ) predicts success more reliably than IQ. But ADHD minds need a different roadmap—one that accounts for emotional sensitivity, difficulty shifting mental states, and a brain that sometimes screams when it's trying to speak. That's what we'll build here: a signal-based, ADHD-friendly framework for emotional intelligence—starting with how your body speaks.

🧠 For People with ADHD—Students, Workers, and Curious Minds

Emotional intelligence is not the opposite of intelligence; it is not the triumph of heart over head—it is the unique intersection of both."
—David Caruso

🧠 Section 1: *Your Body Speaks in Three Languages—Are You Listening?*

Have you ever made a decision that looked great on paper—but felt completely wrong?

Maybe your head said *yes*.

Your heart hesitated.

And your gut clenched.

This isn't just a metaphor. It's neuroscience.

Your body has **three major intelligence centers**—the **brain**, the **heart**, and the **gut**—and each one speaks a different language. According to emerging research in neurocardiology, gut-brain science, and systems neuroscience, these three systems work together (and sometimes compete) to shape your emotions, choices, and behavior.

- Your **gut** is the first responder. It's fast, visceral, and mostly unconscious. It checks for threat and safety before you even realize something's off.
- Your **heart** brings your values online. It asks, *Do I care? Does this matter?*
- Your **head** brings strategy and logic. It asks, *What's the plan? What makes sense?*

When these three systems are in sync, you feel grounded, clear, and decisive.

When they're in conflict, you stall, spiral, or snap.

And for people with ADHD, that **internal misalignment can feel amplified**. One part of you is already moving, another part is hesitating, and a third part is panicking. You might shift between clarity and confusion in seconds—or feel like three different people trying to drive one car.

💡 Note on Metaphor and Science

When we talk about the "head, heart, and gut" as intelligence centers, we're not saying your stomach holds little professors or your heart keeps a filing cabinet of values. The metaphor works because these regions *do* contain dense networks of neurons that influence how you feel and decide.

- **Gut:** The enteric nervous system—sometimes called the "second brain"—has ~500 million neurons. It processes threat and safety cues lightning fast and signals the brain through the vagus nerve (Gershon, 1998). That's why a bad hunch can literally feel like a gut punch.
- **Heart:** The heart has its own ~40,000 neurons and sends more signals *to* the brain than it receives. Neurocardiology research suggests it shapes emotional salience—in other words, it helps you know what matters to you (McCraty et al., 2009).
- **Head:** The prefrontal cortex and related circuits are still the master planners—weighing options, delaying impulses, and structuring action.

So yes—it's a metaphor, but one rooted in biology. These centers form a kind of *neural chorus*: the gut keeps you safe, the heart tunes you to meaning, and the head builds the plan.

Emotional intelligence begins with listening to this internal conversation.

It's not about always choosing heart over head or gut over logic—it's about recognizing that all three are speaking. And learning how to translate what they're trying to tell you.

If you've already started identifying your core values or

learning to spot distorted thinking, this next piece connects the dots. Because when your thoughts, values, and emotional signals start working together—instead of fighting for control—your whole internal system begins to make more sense.

This is your first step toward emotional fluency—and the foundation for everything else that follows.

Why This Is Hard for ADHD Brains (and Why It Matters Even More)

"You have to name it to tame it."
—Dr. Dan Siegel

Challenge 1: Monitoring Lag
Emotional intelligence doesn't come naturally to most of us with ADHD—not because we're broken, but because we're running a different kind of operating system.

We often feel things **more intensely** but **notice them later**.

We get flooded with feelings we can't immediately name.

And by the time we realize what we're feeling, it may already be leaking out sideways—in our voice, our body language, or our decisions.

This isn't about immaturity. It's about **monitoring lag**—a delay between emotional activation and self-awareness. Add to that a weak internal vocabulary, fast-switching states, and shame about "overreacting," and it's no wonder so many people with ADHD grow up feeling emotionally confused, unsafe, or out of control.

✦

Challenge 2: Too Many Words. Too Many Feelings.

One reason emotional intelligence is hard for ADHD minds. **Language overload.**

There are hundreds of feeling words in the English language. Even a standard "feelings wheel" has dozens of options radiating outward. For someone with ADHD—already dealing with signal noise, language retrieval difficulty, and emotional ambiguity—this becomes a recipe for shutdown.

And that's just *one* feeling.

ADHD minds often experience **multiple emotions at once**—We might feel excited and terrified, hopeful and ashamed, angry and lonely—*simultaneously*.

ADHD brains are already managing signal overload—sounds, sights, thoughts, memories, and shifting emotions. When we try to name a feeling, we're often faced with dozens of options:

Are you disappointed?

Frustrated?
Embarrassed?
Discouraged?
Ashamed?
Mad?
Hurt?

That kind of decision tree is overwhelming—and under pressure, we shut down or guess wrong.

☑ Solution: The Five Core Feelings
We simplify it. Five core emotions, easy to remember, backed by decades of psychological research:

- **Glad**
- **Sad**
- **Mad**
- **Afraid**
- **Ashamed**

Everything else is a variation or blend.

Instead of asking "Which of 37 words best fits what I'm feeling right now?"

You ask: *Which of these five are happening right now—and how strong are they?*

Naming—Language as Emotional Precision

"If you can't name what you feel, you can't work with it."

That's not just a poetic truth—it's neurological. Emotional signals that stay vague or unspoken tend to either flood the system or fade into the background, creating internal noise that interferes with decision-making, motivation, and connection.

Naming what you're feeling is like switching on a light in a dark room. You may not like what you see—but now you can choose how to respond.

Why Naming Helps

- **Validation** – "This feeling is real, and it matters."
- **Communication** – "Here's what I'm feeling—and what I need."
- **Self-awareness over time** – "I've been hitting Mad-8 every Thursday before my team meeting. What's that about?"

As the saying goes: *You can't manage what you don't measure.*

And for ADHD minds, *you can't reframe what you can't name.*

Naming is the first move in reclaiming your emotional agency.

⚠ Challenge 3: More Than One Emotion at a Time

ADHD minds often feel **multiple emotions at once**. You might be:

- Glad to see your friend
- Mad they showed up late

- o Ashamed for snapping at them
- o Afraid they're pulling away
- o And Sad about how hard connection feels lately

And this could all be happening *in the same five minutes.*

☑ Solution: The 1–10 Emotional Intensity Scale

Instead of trying to "pick one," you **rate each** feeling from 1 (barely there) to 10 (all-consuming).

This helps you:

- o Make sense of emotional layering
- o Notice which emotion is dominant right now
- o Track patterns over time
- o Communicate your internal state without collapsing into it

Example Check-In:

"I'm Mad–3, Sad–6, Afraid–5, Ashamed–2, and a little Glad–4 that I'm finally noticing."

Glad	Sad	Mad	Afraid	Ashamed
10.	10.	10.	10.	10.
9.	9.	9.	9.	9.
8.	8.	8.	8.	8.
7.	7.	7.	7.	7.
6.	6.	6.	6.	6.
5.	5.	5.	5.	5.
4.	4.	4.	4.	4.
3.	3.	3.	3.	3.
2.	2.	2.	2.	2.
1.	1.	1.	1.	1.

It's not clinical. It's human.

And for folks with ADHD, **externalizing the inner world** like this can be transformational.

🌍 Emotional Development Isn't Evenly Distributed

There's also a cultural side to this.

Historically, emotional fluency has been encouraged differently based on gender and role. In many societies, boys have been rewarded for stoicism and punished for vulnerability, while girls have been expected to
read emotional cues and soothe others from an early age.

Some evolutionary theorists suggest this division may have ancient roots:

- o Men, acting as hunters or soldiers, may have benefited from quick action and emotional suppression.
- o Women, managing caregiving and community, may have developed deeper emotional nuance to keep relationships and systems intact.

Whether or not those roles were universal, the emotional expectations *certainly were*—and their echoes still shape how children are raised today.

⚠️ But Here's the Thing: No One Gets a Pass Anymore

In today's world, **emotional intelligence is not optional**.

It's the skill behind leadership, partnership, parenting, teamwork, recovery, and growth.

It's what helps you navigate conflict, build trust, and know when you're about to crash.

It's what lets you live from your values—not just your reactions.

And for ADHD minds—which already experience life more intensely—emotional intelligence is **not a luxury skill**. It's survival infrastructure.

You don't need to become a therapist. But you do need to learn how your internal systems work. Otherwise, you'll keep making decisions that seem right on paper but *feel wrong in your gut*—and you won't know why.

Monitoring—The Inner Map

> *"Emotions are data. They're not directions."*
> —Brené Brown

You don't have to crash and burn to know you're running hot.

But if you've disconnected your internal sensors—or never learned where to find them—it's easy to miss the warning signs until you're already in a spiral. For ADHD minds, this doesn't happen because we're careless or weak-willed. It happens because we often operate at the **Edge of Criticality**—that intense place where passion, focus, and overload coexist.

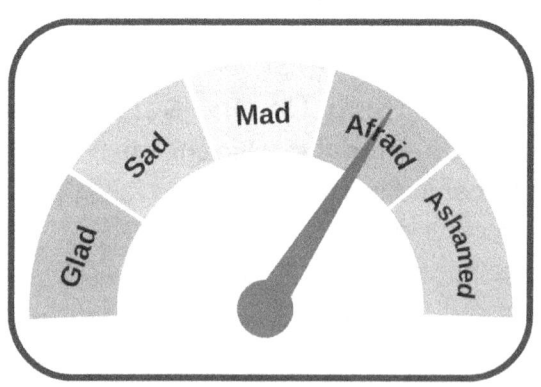

Monitoring your emotions isn't about suppressing them. It's about **checking your internal dashboard** before your engine overheats. It's the skill that lets you notice when you're moving from centered to shaky—and gives you a chance to adjust before the blowout.

🚐 The Lost Dashboard

As kids, our parents (if emotionally attuned) often acted as our external dashboards. They noticed when we were tired, overstimulated, hungry, or headed toward a meltdown.

But as adults, we're expected to self-monitor.

And many of us with ADHD were never taught *how.*

The result? Even high-functioning adults end up emotionally undernourished, overstimulated, and out of balance—not because we're reckless, but because we're untrained.

✦ Tool: The Feeling Signal Map

Start simple. Before you act, speak, or plan, pause and ask:

- What am I feeling right now? *(Glad, Sad, Mad, Afraid, Ashamed)*
- How strong is it? *(1–10)*
- What triggered it?
- What story am I telling?
- What action or expression will help me move forward?

This five-point map turns emotional noise into directional clarity. It's a way to chart your inner landscape—and steer before you stall.

🐾 Tool: BREATHE—The Signal Scan
A quick reset for emotional overload

Sometimes, you don't even know what you're feeling—just that something is "off."

That's where this tool comes in. **BREATHE** is a five-point system scan designed for people with ADHD: fast, intuitive, and built for moments when your system feels scrambled.

Adapted from clinical tools developed by Jon Thomas, LPC, through the ADHD College Success Guidance Program, INC.

BREATHE: The Signal Scan
B – Breath
Am I holding my breath or tightening up without realizing it?
→ Pause. Inhale slowly. Exhale fully. Repeat twice.

R – Recovery
Am I still carrying stress or emotion from something that just happened?
→ Acknowledge lingering tension or emotional hangover.

E – Effort
Am I using energy to suppress or avoid something I don't want to feel?
→ Identify the hidden work. Avoidance drains the system.

A – Ache
Is there something small that hurt—a micro-wound I ignored?
→ Name it. Even brief hurts add weight if unprocessed. *ADHD minds are often startled by interruptions—sudden noises or shifts can land like a slap when we're deep in focus or thought. Those jolts count too.*

T – Too Much

Is everything too loud, too fast, or too much right now?

→ Overwhelm isn't weakness. It's a signal to pause or simplify.

H – Held Back

Is there something I want to express or do—but feel blocked?

→ Notice what's stuck. Expression is a pressure release.

E – Exit Path

What does this emotion need now? Expression? Action? Stillness?

→ Emotion is energy. Give it a path to move forward.

You don't need to analyze every detail. Just **breathe**—and notice.

This scan won't solve everything, but it will reconnect you with your emotional system—and help you choose your next step with more clarity.

Interpreting—Making Meaning from Feelings

"Between stimulus and response there is a space.
In that space is our power to choose our response.
In our response lies our growth and our freedom."
—Viktor E. Frankl

Emotions don't just "happen." They're created.

Not out of thin air—but from the stories we tell ourselves about what's happening around us.

Two people can go through the same experience and feel completely different things. Why? Because what we feel is shaped by how we *evaluate* what's going on.

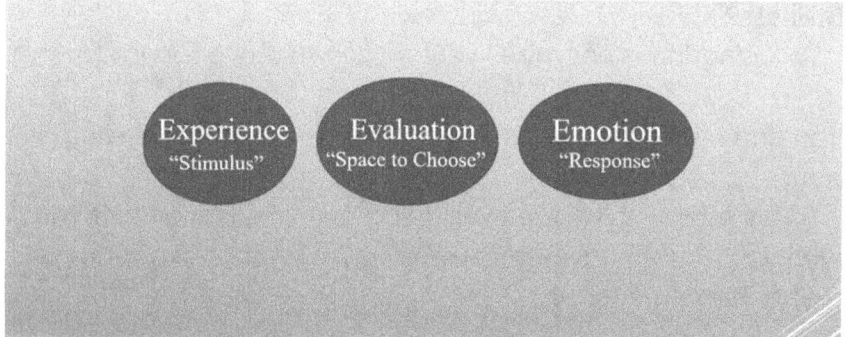 The Three E's Model: Event → Evaluation → Emotion

Here's the emotional sequence most people never get taught:

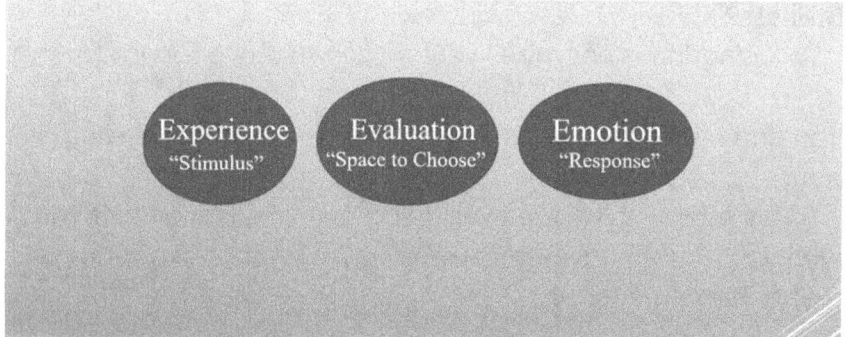

1. **Event** – Something happens.
2. **Evaluation** – You interpret what that event means.
3. **Emotion** – You feel something based on that interpretation.

It's not the *event* that causes the emotion—it's the *story* you attach to it.

🪧 Example: Same Event, Different Evaluations
Your friend doesn't text back for two days.

- You think, *"They're mad at me. I messed up."* ➤ You feel anxious and ashamed.

- o You think, *"They're probably busy."* ➤ You feel patient and mildly concerned.
- o You think, *"They always ghost. I'm done."* ➤ You feel angry and detached.

Same event. Different evaluations. Completely different emotional experience.

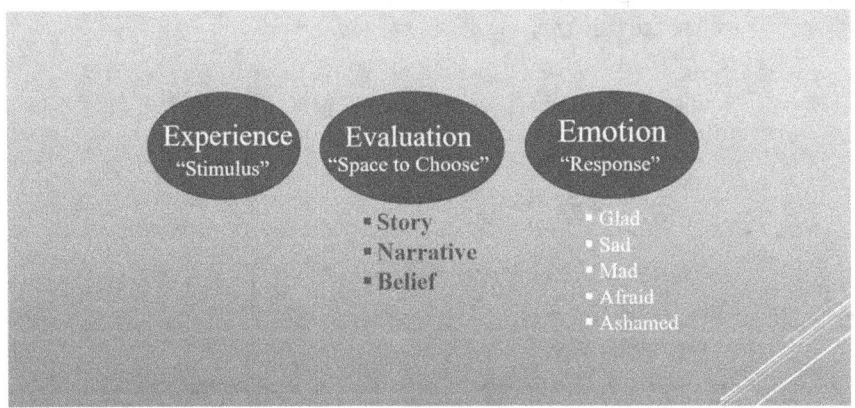

🔄 Reframing Is Not Lying

Reframing doesn't mean denying your feelings.
It means **opening up your interpretation** to a wider perspective.

You might still feel sad, or mad, or afraid. But now, you have room to ask:

- o *Is there another possible explanation?*
- o *Am I making assumptions based on old patterns or past wounds?*
- o *What else could be true here?*

These questions don't erase emotions. They help you **understand where they came from**—and what they're trying to tell you.

✧

The Caldron of Unexpressed Emotion

When emotions go unnamed or unprocessed, they don't disappear. They **accumulate**.

They sink to the bottom of your awareness and thicken over time—like a stew left simmering too long.

- Unspoken sadness becomes numbness or depression
- Repressed anger turns into chronic shame
- Uncelebrated joy curdles into cynicism
- Denied fear becomes background anxiety
- Suppressed hope becomes quiet resignation

This is the **Caldron of Unexpressed Emotion**—a heavy, bubbling mix of what's never been said, felt, or allowed.

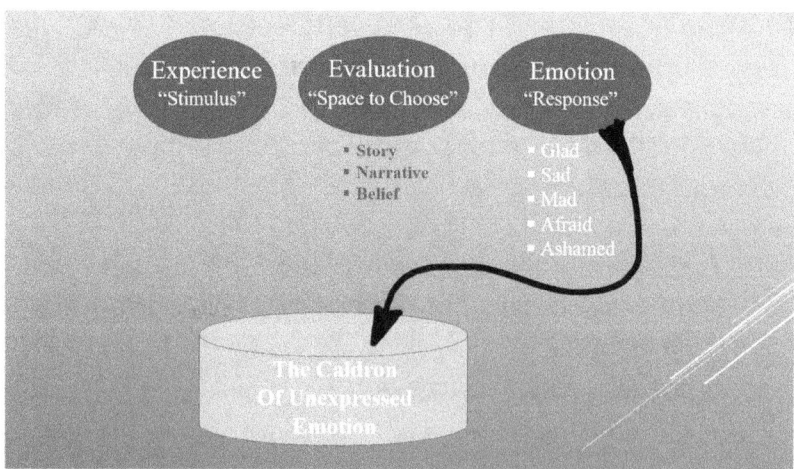

You don't need to "dump it all out." But you do need to **stir it**, name it, and let some of that heat release.

Understanding what you're feeling—and why—is how you stop adding to the caldron without realizing it.

Some of What's in the Caldron Isn't Just Emotion—It's Belief

Over time, unexpressed emotions don't just sit—they solidify. They become stories. Beliefs. Personal "truths" that shape how we see ourselves—and what we think we're capable of.

For ADHD minds, these beliefs often form early and hard:

- o "I'm not college material."
- o "I'm lazy and undisciplined."
- o "No one takes me seriously."
- o "I'll never be consistent."
- o "I have to hide how I really am—or I'll be rejected."

These beliefs may not be true—but they *feel* true, because they've been reinforced by years of emotional struggle and mis-fired efforts. So when you stir the cauldron, don't be surprised if what comes up isn't just a feeling... ...it's a voice. A belief. A sentence that's been running in the background for a long time.

Changing that isn't about forcing positivity. It's about seeing clearly what's there—and beginning to shift the story.

That's what we'll explore next: **How beliefs are formed, why they stick—and how to rewrite them from the inside out.**

Caldron Self-Check—What Are You Still Carrying, and Why?

Unexpressed emotions don't just accumulate randomly. Sometimes, we *hold onto them on purpose*—even if we don't realize it.

Ask yourself:

o What emotion have I been carrying that hasn't been expressed or released?
o When did I start holding it?
o What belief or story is it reinforcing?
o Is it protecting me from something I'm not ready to face?
o Is it trying to *prove* something—about me, or about someone else?
o What might this emotion want me to do?
o What would it feel like to gently *start* doing that?

You don't need to dump the whole cauldron. But you can stir gently. And decide what's ready to be released—and what still needs space, context, or support.

Managing—From Feeling to Action

> *"Feelings are much like waves. We can't stop them from coming, but we can choose which ones to surf."*
> —Jonatan Mårtensson

Once you've identified what you're feeling—and understood why—you've reached a critical crossroads.

What happens next **matters**. Because emotion is not inert.

It's not a thought or a wish. It's **electrical energy.** And energy needs a circuit.

If there's no path, that energy doesn't just fade away. It gets trapped.

And what gets trapped turns into tension, anxiety, avoidance, or collapse.

⚡ Emotion Needs a Next Step

Every emotion is a message *and* a movement. It asks:

What now?

You have three core choices:

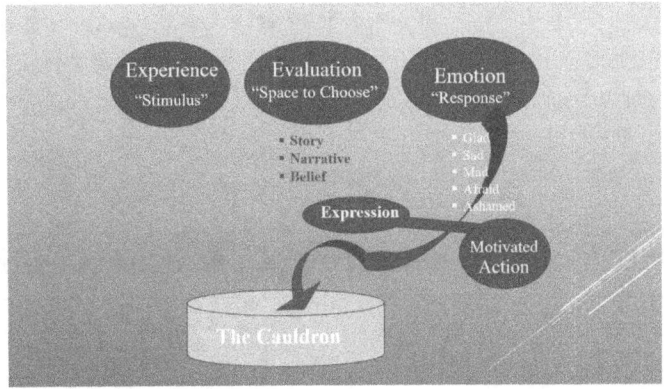

1. **Express it**
   - Say it, write it, move it, create with it
   - Let the emotion exit the system through safe release
2. **Channel it**
   - Use the energy as fuel for action, boundary-setting, or change
   - Convert emotion into momentum
3. **Contain it**
   - Hold it temporarily when expression isn't possible
   - Requires emotional capacity (and a plan to return to it later)

✏️ When Containment Becomes Overload

Sometimes you can't cry in the moment. Can't rant, pause, or move.

So you hold it—you contain it. That's okay. Containment is a valid skill.

But containment only works when there's room in the system.

If the **Caldron of Unexpressed Emotion** is already full—with years of unspoken grief, unheard anger, or denied fear—containment becomes overload. There's no space left. That's when emotions leak out sideways... or explode.

✴️ Emotional Translation Questions

These reflection prompts help turn awareness into aligned action:

- What is this emotion asking for?
- Do I need to express it, channel it, or contain it (for now)?
- If I don't act, where will this energy go?
- What response would be most aligned with who I want to be?

This is where emotional intelligence becomes more than awareness.

It becomes **direction. Choice. Power.**

Emotion is energy.

The question is: *Where will you send it?*

✎ **Sidebar: *Emotion as Signal, Not Symptom***

You're not broken because you feel something.

You're receiving a signal.

Each core emotion carries information. When you learn to decode it, you stop reacting blindly—and start responding intentionally.

Here's what each of the five core emotions often points to:

Emotion	Possible Signal
Glad	Alignment, connection, resonance, success, meaning
Sad	Loss, change, unmet need, grief, longing
Mad	Boundary violation, injustice, frustration, unmet expectations
Afraid	Anticipated threat, danger, risk, uncertainty, lack of control
Ashamed	Internal value conflict, perceived failure, disconnect from self-worth

---

Ask yourself:

- *What is this emotion trying to show me?*
- *What boundary, value, or need is being highlighted here?*
- *What would happen if I stopped judging this emotion—and started listening to it?*

The goal isn't to suppress emotion.

It's to **understand what it's pointing to**—and respond with clarity.

Social Intelligence—The Mirror of Connection

Emotional intelligence doesn't end with self-awareness.

It extends outward—into how we connect, communicate, and repair.

This is where **social intelligence** comes in: the ability to understand other people's emotions, respond with empathy, and regulate interactions in real time.

For ADHD minds, this can be especially challenging. Not because we don't care—but because the signals are fast, layered, and easy to miss.

ADHD and Theory of Mind

Many people with ADHD struggle with **Theory of Mind**—the ability to imagine what someone else is thinking or feeling in the moment. Combine that with impulsivity, emotional flooding, or rejection sensitivity, and it's easy to misread others—or overreact to a signal that wasn't even about us.

We may:

- Interrupt out of excitement and be perceived as rude
- Miss subtle shifts in tone and think everything's fine—until it's not
- Over-apologize, under-express, or withdraw when the stakes feel high
- Spiral into shame when feedback comes, even gently

These aren't character flaws. They're signal-processing challenges.

🧠 Why It's Called a Theory— And Why That Matters

We call it *Theory* of Mind because the mind itself is invisible. You can see someone's face, hear their voice, notice their behavior—but you can't see their thoughts. We *theorize* that other people have minds like ours: filled with values, memories, fears, and hopes that shape how they see the world.

This mental modeling is what lets us get out of our own head and ask:

- o *What event might they be reacting to?*
- o *How are they evaluating it?*
- o *What emotion could that be stirring up for them?*

When we bring the Event → Evaluation → Emotion model into relationships, it becomes a bridge—not just a solo skill. It helps us approach others with curiosity instead of judgment. And when we *name the theory out loud*—"Hey, I wonder if maybe when I said that it came off like X, and it felt like Y?"—we give the other person space to clarify, connect, or correct.

That's not just emotional intelligence. That's social fluency in action. And it starts with the radical move of imagining another mind—and being willing to check your theory.

🎯 Intention vs. Impact—One of the Hardest Social Lessons

A key part of emotional and social intelligence is recognizing that **what you meant** and **how it landed** aren't always the same thing.

You might say something jokingly—but it stings. You might offer advice—but it feels like judgment. You might mean to help—and instead, trigger hurt.

That gap between *intention* and *impact* is where misunderstandings often live. And in relationships, **it's the impact that matters first**—because that's what the other person is actually experiencing.

For ADHD minds, this distinction can be hard to spot at first. We may feel unfairly blamed for things we didn't "mean," or hurt when our good intentions go unrecognized. But being able to pause and say:

"That's not what I meant—but I can see how it landed, and I'm sorry for that impact."

is one of the most powerful forms of repair.

It's also an advanced form of Theory of Mind. Because it shows you're able and willing to consider the emotional model *inside someone else's head*—not just your own.

⚒ Tools for Social–Emotional Fluency

The good news: social intelligence is **trainable**—especially when you've already started monitoring and naming your own emotions.

Here's how to strengthen the bridge between inner signals and outward connection:

- ○ **Normalize repair**
  - ➤ Misfires happen. Say: "That didn't come out right. Let me try again."

- o **Externalize emotional cues**
  - ➤ Try: "I'm a little overwhelmed right now, but I care about this."
- o **Co-regulate with safe others**
  - ➤ Find people who can calm you—not just challenge you. Practice emotional pacing together.
- o **Expect misinterpretation—and stay in the learning loop**
  - ➤ Social fluency isn't about getting it right every time. It's about adjusting in real time and not giving up when it gets messy.

Emotional Mapping—Pulling It All Together

You've learned a lot in this chapter:

That emotions are signals.

That ADHD minds process them differently.

That naming, interpreting, and responding to them takes real skill—not just sensitivity.

Now it's time to put that into a practice you can actually use.

Tool: The Emotional Signal Map

This tool combines everything we've covered into a fast, re-peatable check-in—one you can use when you're stuck, over-whelmed, or just trying to understand what's going on inside.

Use it during journaling, therapy, or coaching. Or just run through it mentally when something feels "off."

✸ The Five-Step Map

1. **Feeling**
   - ➤ What core emotions are present? *(Glad, Sad, Mad, Afraid, Ashamed)*
2. **Intensity**
   - ➤ Rate each from 1 (low) to 10 (high)
3. **Trigger**
   - ➤ What just happened that may have sparked this?
4. **Story**
   - ➤ What are you telling yourself about what happened?
5. **Needed Expression or Action**
   - ➤ What would help move this emotion forward—expression, channeling, or containment?

Example Check-In:

"I'm Sad–6 and Mad–4. The trigger was a colleague interrupting me.

The story I'm telling myself is that I'm not respected.

I think I need to calmly name it and ask for space to finish next time."

This isn't just emotional hygiene. It's navigation.

It's how you steer by internal signals instead of external pressure or emotional chaos.

The more you practice, the more fluent you'll become.

And emotional fluency builds something ADHD minds deeply need: **agency, alignment, and stability.**

⚗ For Parents, Educators, Clinicians, Coaches, and Curious Readers

Emotional dysregulation is one of the most misunderstood symptoms of ADHD.

It doesn't stem from immaturity or volatility.

It stems from underdeveloped *internal monitoring systems*—often compounded by poor emotional modeling, unmet needs, and chronic shame.

☄ What Helps

To build emotional intelligence in ADHD learners and clients, focus on:

- ○ **Validation**
  - ➤ Affirm the emotional experience before addressing the behavior.
  - ➤ "That was hard" lands better than "You need to calm down."
- ○ **Language Scaffolding**
  - ➤ Provide feeling word banks, emotion wheels, or the 5-feeling/1–10 scale.
  - ➤ Use modeling: "I think I'm Mad-3 and Sad-5 right now."
- ○ **Frameworks**
  - ➤ Teach repeatable tools like the **Emotional Compass** and **BREATHE** scan.
  - ➤ Practice aloud. Embed in transitions, coaching, or classroom routines.
- ○ **Meaning-Making**
  - ➤ Help the individual identify when an emotional response may be linked to:
    - ○ an *old belief,*
    - ○ an *unprocessed memory,* or
    - ○ a *misinterpreted signal*
- ○ **Agency through Options**
  - ➤ Don't just ask, "How do you feel?" Ask: "What do you want to do with this feeling?"

- ➤ Provide choices: express, channel, contain—and return later.
- o **Meet Them at Their Model of the World**
  - ➤ Some learners and clients arrive with very little emotional awareness. Others may feel deeply but lack the structure to interpret or manage what they feel.
  - ➤ Either way, it helps to meet them where they are—without judgment—and introduce tools like the Five Core Feelings, the 1–10 intensity scale, or the Event → Evaluation → Emotion model as **primer-level emotional literacy**.
  - ➤ Even clients with strong emotional intelligence often benefit from revisiting these fundamentals. Simplifying emotion into signal, story, and action provides clarity—and often, a surprising sense of relief.

✧

EFCBT—Executive Function–Cognitive Behavioral Therapy

Traditional CBT assumes linear thinking, strong working memory, and emotional regulation—all of which can be impaired in ADHD.

That's where **EFCBT** comes in: a **signal-based adaptation** of CBT for ADHD minds.

This model integrates:

1. **Signal Awareness**
   - ➤ Identify emotional, sensory, and environmental triggers
   - ➤ Separate signal from noise
2. **Cognitive Reframing with Support**
   - ➤ Break distortions into manageable pieces
   - ➤ Scaffold rethinking with visuals or scripts

3. **Emotion–Action Bridging**
   - ➤ Ask: "What is this emotion asking for?"
   - ➤ Use chaining to build from feeling → insight → action
4. **Time Anchoring and Future-Self Work**
   - ➤ Use messages to and from the Future Self to break time blindness
5. **Signal Stacking**
   - ➤ Pair important behaviors with emotional drivers: belonging, purpose, novelty

EFCBT aligns beautifully with the tools in this book—and is being developed into a full visual practitioner guide for use with students and adults.

Note on EFCBT—How This Model Emerged

Over the years of developing and using the **Event → Evaluation → Emotion** model with ADHD students and adults, we noticed how naturally it echoed elements of **Cognitive Behavioral Therapy (CBT)**—particularly the idea that our thoughts shape our emotional responses and actions.

But ADHD minds often need more than traditional CBT offers. They need **help noticing the signal** in the first place. They need tools that scaffold working memory, reduce overwhelm, and bridge emotional insight to action in real time.

That's where our adapted approach—**Executive Function– Cognitive Behavioral Therapy (EFCBT)**—was born.

EFCBT builds on core CBT principles but adds a signal-based ADHD lens, including:

- o Emotion–Action Bridging
- o Signal Awareness
- o Time Anchoring
- o Chaining
- o Signal Stacking

This isn't a replacement for CBT. It's an evolution—designed to meet ADHD minds where they are and give them tools to move forward with more clarity, agency, and emotional resilience.

As emotional intelligence increases, so does **agency**.

And with agency comes **resilience**, confidence, and connection—all things ADHD minds deserve, and can build. Top of Form

📖 References for Further Reading

o **Barkley, R. A.** (2008). *Executive functions: What they are, how they work, and why they evolved.* New York: Guilford Press.
A foundational work on executive functioning, self-regulation, and behavioral inhibition in ADHD. Helps explain why emotional monitoring often breaks down in neurodivergent individuals.

o **Gershon, M. D.** (1998). *The second brain: A groundbreaking new understanding of nervous disorders of the stomach and intestine.* HarperCollins.
Introduced the concept of the enteric nervous system and the gut as a decision-making and emotional processing center—a key basis for the "gut speaks first" metaphor.

o **Goleman, D.** (1995). *Emotional intelligence: Why it can matter more than IQ.* New York: Bantam Books.
The book that launched emotional intelligence into mainstream psychology, offering a compelling framework for why EQ is essential for long-term success—both personally and professionally.

o **Greenberg, L. S., & Paivio, S. C.** (1997). *Working with emotions in psychotherapy.* Guilford Press.
Focuses on the role of emotion in personal transformation, offering models for helping clients access, understand, and shift emotional responses—especially useful in ADHD-informed therapy.

o **McCraty, R., Atkinson, M., Tomasino, D., & Bradley, R. T.** (2009). The coherent heart: Heart–brain interactions, psychophysiological coherence, and the emergence of system-wide order. *Integral Review, 5*(2), 10–115.
Reviews research on heart–brain coherence and its role in emotion regulation, decision-making, and resilience.

o **Royaards, W., & Drevitch, G.** (2025, July 21). *Your brain speaks three languages: What neuroscience reveals about your decisions.* Psychology Today.
Popularized the head–heart–gut model with updated neuroscience, providing accessible metaphors that align with polyvagal and systems theory.

o **Satir, V.** (1988). *The new peoplemaking.* Science and Behavior Books.
A classic in family systems and emotional development; offers insight into how early emotional roles and scripts shape adult regulation patterns.

o **Thomas, J.** (2025). *EFCBT: Executive Function–Cognitive Behavioral Therapy for ADHD minds* [Unpublished clinical framework].
Developed as a signal-based adaptation of CBT that integrates emotion–action bridging, signal awareness, and time anchoring. Created to support emotional regulation and behavioral momentum in ADHD learners and adults.

🔄 Chapter Handoff: Beliefs—The Stories That Shape Us

By now, you've learned how emotional intelligence gives you a way to feel what's happening, understand why, and choose your next step with clarity.

But there's one more layer beneath emotion—and it's powerful.

That layer is **belief**.

What we believe about ourselves, about others, and about how the world works doesn't just affect how we think—it shapes what we *feel*. It influences what signals we even notice, how we interpret them, and whether we feel hope, shame, motivation, or despair.

And here's the tricky part: **many of our most deeply held beliefs aren't based on truth.**

They're based on experience, emotion, and survival.

Especially for ADHD minds, beliefs often form in the heat of failure, frustration, or rejection—then harden into identity:

- "I'm not smart enough."
- "I'll never follow through."
- "I have to hide who I really am."

Sometimes we hold on to these beliefs because they feel functional—even if they're painful. As philosopher Hans Vaihinger wrote, *"We believe not what is true, but what is useful."*

So in the next chapter, we'll begin uncovering those internal stories:

- Where they come from
- How they reinforce themselves
- And how to shift them—gently, with insight, not force

When you understand what you feel—and why—you reclaim your agency. That makes it possible to challenge the beliefs you've been carrying, often silently, all along.

Chapter 17

The Stories We Tell Ourselves—Beliefs, Identity, and Emotional Logic

"The most powerful beliefs are the ones we don't even know we're carrying."

"Until you make the unconscious conscious, it will direct your life, and you will call it fate."—Carl Jung

🗞 How to Use This Chapter

This chapter explores how the beliefs we carry—often shaped early, unconsciously, and emotionally—become internal scripts that influence our behavior, motivation, relationships, and sense of self. It follows the same three-part format used throughout the book, offering tailored insights for ADHD learners, supporters, and professionals.

✧

- o   **For People with ADHD—Students, Workers, and Curious Minds**
  - ▪   Learn how ADHD can lead to the formation of

limiting beliefs rooted in misunderstanding, shame, or past failure

- Discover how belief systems form—and how to rewrite them using signal-based tools
- Identify internalized labels and stories that no longer serve you, and begin replacing them with flexible, compassionate narratives

- 🖋 **For Parents, Clinicians, Educators, and Coaches**
  - Understand how emotional reasoning, RSD, and time-blind memory influence belief development in ADHD minds
  - Use tools like the "Belief Inventory," the "Is It True?" reframe, and narrative coaching to support identity reconstruction
  - Recognize common ADHD-related belief distortions (e.g., "I'm lazy," "I always mess up," "I don't belong") and how to gently challenge them

- 🔎 **Key Concepts and Tools You'll Find Here**
  - ✓ Emotional Logic—why feelings can "feel like facts"
  - ✓ The Role of Rejection Sensitivity in Belief Formation
  - ✓ Story Mapping: Identifying the old scripts that shape your self-view
  - ✓ Belief Checkpoints—reflective prompts that disrupt automatic internal narratives
  - ✓ Chaining Back to Origins—tracing current beliefs to formative signal moments
  - ✓ Signal Words and Identity Language
  - ✓ Tools for Self-Reclamation and Reframing

💡 *You are not the story you inherited—or the one your failures wrote. This chapter gives you the tools to become your own narrator.*

Introduction

There are things we feel that don't have language yet.

Things we carry that we've never spoken aloud.

Things we believe—not because they're true, but because they helped us survive.

In the last chapter, we explored how emotions speak—through signals, intensity, story, and response. But now we shift focus to something deeper. Not just what we feel, but **what we've come to believe**.

Beliefs aren't just thoughts. They're emotional frameworks.

They shape what we see, how we interpret it, and what we expect from the world—and from ourselves.

And here's what's wild:

Most of our beliefs didn't start as beliefs at all.

They started as **stories**—the meaning we gave to something that hurt.

Then they got repeated. Reinforced. Echoed by shame, silence, or failure.

Eventually, the story became a **narrative**—a familiar script.

And the narrative hardened into a **belief**—something that feels like fact.

This chapter is about those inner frameworks.

The ones that filter what gets through.

The ones that tell us what's possible, what's off-limits, and who we are.

Some of those beliefs are empowering.

But many were written too early, under too much pressure, and without the tools to question them.

Now it's time to go back.

Not to blame.

Not to erase.

But to **reclaim** the story.

Because once you see the belief clearly, you're no longer trapped inside it.

It's now another fish in the pond.

And you get to ask the question that changes everything: "What else might be true?"

🧠 For People with ADHD—Students, Workers, and Curious Minds

🎮 I. From Event to Emotion— Where Beliefs Begin

By now you know the pattern:

Event → Evaluation → Emotion.

Something happens. We evaluate it. That evaluation triggers a feeling.

But here's the part that often goes unseen:

Evaluation = story. It's the narrative we tell ourselves about what the event means.

And that story? It changes the emotion.

If someone bumps into me, and I tell myself, *"She did that on purpose"*—I'm angry.

If I think, *"She didn't see me,"* I feel surprised, maybe a bit flustered.

The event didn't change. The story did.

Now imagine that same story gets told again and again, reinforced by strong emotion. Over time, it hardens into something more than just a story.

It becomes a **narrative**—a running explanation we carry with us.

Keep going a little further, and the narrative turns into something deeper: A **belief.**

And here's where it gets tricky:

Beliefs don't just *respond* to experience. They begin to *filter* it.

What you believe changes what you even notice.

We don't get all the data the world offers. We get the bits that match our filter. So when a belief takes hold, it doesn't just shape how we *interpret* reality—it shapes what we *see.*

Beliefs are perception engines. Once they kick in, they steer the ship.

✧

II. The Belief Map—Three Concentric Circles

Beliefs don't just float around randomly. They organize themselves into layers—like rings around a core.

And where a belief *lives* affects how easily it can be changed.

We call this the **Belief Map**—and it's adapted from the work of psychologist and NLP researcher Robert Dilts, who developed what he called the *Neurological Levels of Change.*

Dilts' original model describes how experience and belief are layered across six levels: environment, behavior, capability, belief, identity, and purpose.

We've adapted that structure here to reflect how ADHD

minds experience belief—emotionally, experientially, and developmentally—in three core layers:

✧

Layers of Core Beliefs

Level	Focus	Example Beliefs
🌍 World	How the world works	"People can't be trusted." "Success requires perfection."
📱 Capability	What I can do in the world	"I'll never finish what I start." "I'm not creative."
🧬 Self	Who I am at the core	"I'm broken." "I'm lazy." "I'm not enough."

✧

The outer ring—🌍 **World**—is often the easiest to shift. We update these beliefs all the time: about politics, relationships, careers.

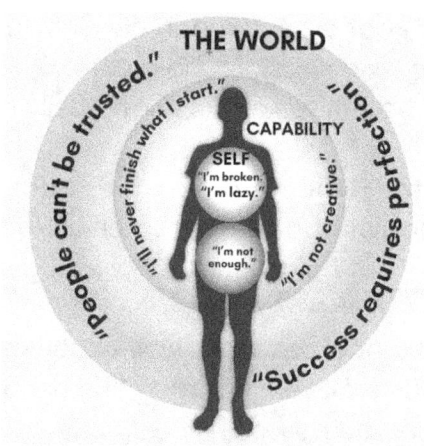

The middle ring—📱 **Capability**—takes more effort. It often changes through experience, feedback, and practice.

But the inner ring—🪃 **Self**—is the hardest. These are identity-level beliefs, often absorbed early and held unconsciously. They *feel* like truth. Even when they're not.

And here's where Dilts' insight matters most:

🌀 Change at a deeper level affects everything above it. Shift a belief at the **Self** layer, and suddenly what you think you're capable of—and how you see the world—changes too.

This model doesn't just describe *what* you believe.

It shows you *where* that belief lives.

And that gives you a map—for reflection, healing, and intentional change.

✦

🏺 III. The Caldron Revisited— Emotion Becomes Belief

Remember the Caldron of Unexpressed Emotion? Now we stir it again.

Some beliefs don't come from logic. They come from emotional residue.

Grief. Shame. Rejection. Embarrassment. Loneliness.

When those feelings are stored, not spoken, they don't just fade.

They form layers. They congeal. And eventually, they start whispering truths:

- ○ "No one listens to me."
- ○ "I'm too much."
- ○ "I'll never get it right."

They *feel* true. Because they've been lived. Even if they weren't challenged.

Sometimes beliefs keep the cauldron full. Other times, the cauldron *births* the beliefs.

📺 IV. Vaihinger's "As-If" ... Functional but False

Philosopher Hans Vaihinger offered a radical insight:

We don't just believe what's true. We act on what's useful.

We live *as if* certain things are true—because it helps us function. Even if they aren't true.

ADHD minds are survival-based learners. We adapt fast:

- o   "Don't ask for help—you'll look dumb."
- o   "Push through everything—rest is failure."
- o   "Stay small—it's safer."

These beliefs helped you get through *then*.

But are they helping you move forward *now*?

Sometimes we hold onto painful beliefs, limiting, or even self-defeating—not because we *want* to, but because they once served a purpose. They made sense in a specific time, place, or emotional context. They protected us, motivated us, or helped us avoid shame.

It can be frustrating—even painful—to notice this in ourselves or others.

Why would anyone cling to a belief that causes suffering?

Because it once helped us survive.

But beliefs, like habits, tend to stay in motion until something interrupts them.

And when we *see* that a belief no longer serves us—really see it—something remarkable can happen:

It can dissolve.

It can let go of *us.*

And in its place, a more functional belief can emerge—one that moves us forward, not just gets us through.

The Stories We Tell Ourselves—Rewriting Beliefs With Emotional Intelligence

"The most powerful stories aren't the ones we read—they're the ones we repeat quietly to ourselves when no one else is listening."

People with ADHD don't just struggle with attention—they struggle with what they pay attention to about themselves.

Over time, the brain develops an internal narrator: a storyteller that tries to explain our successes, failures, and emotional experiences. But when you live with chronic overwhelm, inconsistent performance, and rejection sensitivity, that narrator often goes off script—and not in a good way.

The Hidden Machinery of Shame

Two psychological forces work in tandem to entrench limiting beliefs in the ADHD brain:

1. Rejection Sensitivity Dysphoria (RSD)—a hair-trigger emotional response to perceived failure or criticism. RSD doesn't just make us feel bad—it makes us feel worthless, instantly.
2. The Zeigarnik Effect—a cognitive bias where the brain fixates on incomplete thoughts, tasks, or narratives until they're resolved.

Put these together, and the ADHD brain becomes wired to ask painful questions—and then answer them in the most emotionally damaging ways:

- Why didn't I turn it in on time? → "Because I'm lazy."
- Why can't I just do what everyone else does? → "Because I'm broken."
- Why does everyone seem mad at me? → "Because I'm a failure."

These are the brain's attempts to complete the emotional story. But when shame is your narrator, the story always ends in tragedy.

Beliefs Are Loops—Not Truths

A belief is just a sentence we've decided to keep repeating.

And for ADHD learners, especially those undiagnosed until later in life, many of those sentences were formed without context:

- "You're not trying hard enough."
- "You're so smart, but you don't apply yourself."
- "You always forget important things."

Over time, these become self-reinforcing loops: The belief becomes the lens. The lens shapes what you see. What you see confirms the belief. Round and round it goes.

Interrupting the Loop—Emotional Intelligence in Action

Emotional intelligence isn't just about understanding others—it's about catching yourself in the act of narration and deciding to edit the script.

I call this the emotional loop trap—and it's one of the most common patterns I help clients rewrite.

This chapter invites readers to practice three core skills:

1. Recognition—Noticing when a negative belief has been triggered.
2. Reflection—Identifying the underlying question or emotional loop.
3. Reframing—Rewriting the belief with context, compassion, and cognitive flexibility.

Reflective Tool: Closing the Loop With Truth

Use this 5-step journaling prompt to challenge limiting beliefs shaped by RSD and the Zeigarnik effect:

1. Identify the Trigger
   What just happened? What thought or feeling showed up?
2. Name the Question
   What question am I asking myself right now? (e.g., "Why do I always mess this up?")
3. Catch the Default Completion
   What's the answer my mind automatically fills in? (Be honest.)
4. Interrupt the Narrative

What's another explanation—one that's true, kind, and more complete?

5. Create a Replacement Thought
   Write a belief that helps you move forward instead of locking you in place.

Example:

- Default: "I can't get started because I'm lazy."
- Reframe: "I need a better starting signal. Once I'm in, I usually get things done."

Why This Matters

Until we rewrite the stories we tell ourselves, no strategy will fully stick. Beliefs shape behavior. Behavior reinforces belief.

That's why this chapter isn't just an emotional sidebar—it's the operating system underneath motivation, resilience, and executive function.

If you've been living in a loop of unfinished questions and shame-based conclusions, it's not because you're broken. It's because your mind is trying to close an open loop with the wrong pen.

You get to write the ending now.

👕 V. The T-Shirt Workshop—A Story in Fabric and Fire

Here's one of the most powerful things we do in our workshops: We give students a plain white T-shirt. And ask them to draw their limiting belief. It may be as simple as a one-word sentence or an elaborate and detailed drawing. But the message is clear. And usually painful and devasting:

- o "I ruin everything."
- o "I'm disgusting."
- o "I'm invisible."

Then we ask: *Where did that come from?*
Do you still believe it?
Is it yours—or was it handed to you?

Finally, we give them a choice:
Keep the shirt.
Or destroy it.

Some burn it in a fire.
Some tear it up.
Some keep it folded as a reminder.

And then: they design a **new shirt.** One that carries an updated belief.

"I'm not a failure. I'm learning." "I'm not broken. I'm building." "I'm not invisible. I'm here."

👀 VI. Why ADHD Minds Absorb Beliefs So Fast

Here's the formula:

Repetition + Emotion = Belief.

ADHD minds often experience:

- More perceived failures
- More intense emotion
- Less working memory or regulation to buffer the impact

That's the perfect storm.

A missed homework becomes a character flaw. A moment of overwhelm becomes "I'm weak." And without tools to update that story? It sticks.

🏚 VII. Rewriting the Narrative— What You Can Do

Beliefs aren't fixed. They're learned. And anything learned can be unlearned and updated.

Tools that help:

- o   Belief Journaling (What do I believe? Why?)
- o   Self-inquiry: Where did this belief come from?
- o   CBT tools: Catch it, Challenge it, Change it
- o   Rituals: Write and burn. Rewrite and wear.
- o   "As-If" Explorer: Is this belief true, or just familiar?

You don't have to attack your beliefs. You can meet them. Talk to them. See if they still fit.

Then decide: *What do I want to believe now?*
What story do I want to live?

That's where change begins.

And here's something else to remember:
When an old belief dissolves, it leaves space behind.
And nature abhors a vacuum.

Something *will* begin to grow in that space—a new belief, a new story.

The question is: **What kind of belief do you want to take root?**

Some new beliefs are fragile—like a small fire in a cold, rainy forest. You'll need to protect them, feed them slowly, keep the wind off until they catch.

Others are like sturdy campfires—burning steadily, needing only the occasional log.

And sometimes, a new belief feels like it was always wait-ing—self-sustaining, quietly powerful, feeding itself on the truth of your present.

No matter what kind of belief it is, one thing matters most:
Know what stage it's in.
Protect it accordingly.
Tend it like something that matters.
Because it does.

🪓 When Beliefs Become Bottlenecks

Beliefs don't just shape how we *feel*. They shape what we *do*.
A limiting belief is like a bottleneck in your internal sys-tem—no matter how much motivation or strategy you pour in, it won't flow through.

- A student who believes they're "just bad at school" will stop before they start.
- A worker who thinks "I always mess it up" may procras-tinate or self-sabotage.
- A young adult who feels "I'm not enough" might avoid opportunity to avoid being exposed.

That's why belief work isn't a luxury.
It's infrastructure.
And for ADHD minds, it's often the place where growth begins—or stops.

🔧 **Sidebar: Keeping the Fire Lit—Simple Actions to Support New Beliefs**

If your new belief feels fragile, here are a few ways to keep the fire burning:

- o Write it somewhere you'll see it daily—a post-it, a phone wallpaper, or a journal cover.
- o Speak it out loud, especially when old beliefs try to return.
- o Surround yourself with people or media that reinforce it.
- o Keep a "belief evidence log": short notes about when this new belief *felt* real.
- o Pair it with a small action—even a 2-minute win that reflects this new truth.

You don't have to force the fire.
Just feed it.

🔧 For Parents, Educators, Clinicians, Coaches, and Curious Minds

ADHD learners often develop limiting beliefs not because they lack ability, but because they have repeatedly bumped into a world that doesn't accommodate the way their brains work. Over time, these emotional collisions form internal scars—stories about who they are and what they're worth. When those stories go unexamined, they harden into beliefs. And beliefs shape everything: what we notice, what we expect, what we dare to try.

This chapter offers a structured, compassionate framework

for understanding how ADHD learners construct, reinforce, and (with support) revise those beliefs.

🔍 Why This Matters

- o Beliefs are more than just thoughts—they're emotional survival strategies.
  ADHD learners often form "defensive beliefs" to protect themselves from repeated failure, shame, or exclusion. These may not be factually true, but they're functionally protective in the short term.
- o Without intervention, limiting beliefs become self-fulfilling. Students who believe they are "bad at math" may unconsciously avoid effort, reinforcing failure. A teen who believes "people like me don't go to college" may never even explore options.
- o Belief work is identity work.
  At their core, beliefs shape how a learner sees themselves in relation to the world. That's why belief change must be relational, respectful, and timed appropriately.

🛠 What Helps

Meet the learner at their model of the world.
A person with low emotional awareness may first need a *primer-level introduction* to the Event → Evaluation → Emotion model, or a basic five-feeling scale. Even for emotionally attuned learners, returning to these basics helps ground insight and reveal distortions in long-held narratives.

Normalize belief formation as a survival response.
Beliefs like "I'm stupid" or "I always mess up" often originate from painful moments of overwhelm, not logical reasoning. Recognizing this removes shame—and opens the door to change.

Use embodied tools and rituals.
In our workshops, students design t-shirts showing the belief they've been "wearing" emotionally for years. These visual, creative, and kinesthetic activities make belief work real—and culminate in meaningful re-authoring rituals like shirt-burning ceremonies or replacement with a new, updated design.

Help students identify levels of belief.
Using the "concentric circle" model (World → Capability → Self), help students name not just *what* they believe, but *where* that belief lives. The deeper it sits, the more it may need emotional support—not just logical rebuttal.

Make belief change actionable.
Offer signal-based tools like chaining, reframing prompts, and the BREATHE scan to help students notice when a belief is active—and try something different, right in that moment.

📖 References for Further Reading

o **Beck, A. T. (1976).** *Cognitive therapy and the emotional disorders.* International Universities Press.
The foundational text for Cognitive Behavioral Therapy (CBT), emphasizing how beliefs and cognitive distortions shape emotional and behavioral responses.

o **Burns, D. D. (1980).** *Feeling Good: The New Mood Therapy.* William Morrow and Company.
A popular and accessible book on CBT, including a catalog of distorted thinking patterns that form the basis of many limiting beliefs.

○ **Dilts, R., Hallbom, T., & Smith, S. (1990).** *Beliefs: Pathways to Health and Well-being.* Meta Publications.
This foundational text presents the Neurological Levels of Change model and explores how beliefs function across behavior, capability, and identity. The adapted belief map in this chapter is based on this framework, reinterpreted through the lens of ADHD motivation and emotional learning.

○ **Dweck, C. S. (2006).** *Mindset: The New Psychology of Success.* Random House.
Introduces the growth vs. fixed mindset theory, offering insight into how beliefs about ability shape motivation, learning, and resilience.

○ **Goleman, D. (1995).** *Emotional Intelligence: Why It Can Matter More Than IQ.* Bantam Books.
A foundational work connecting emotional intelligence to success, decision-making, and belief formation.

○ **Nadeau, K. G. (2005).** *ADHD in the Schools: Assessment and Intervention Strategies.* The Guilford Press.
Addresses the emotional and cognitive development of students with ADHD, including belief systems around capability and academic identity.

○ **Ross, L. (1977).** The intuitive psychologist and his shortcomings: Distortions in the attribution process. In L. Berkowitz (Ed.), *Advances in Experimental Social Psychology* (Vol. 10, pp. 173–220). Academic Press.
A key paper in attribution theory, supporting the idea that people draw faulty conclusions about causes and identity based on limited observations—often reinforcing negative self-beliefs.

o **Sleeper-Triplett, J. (2010).** *Empowering Youth with ADHD: Your Guide to Coaching Adolescents and Young Adults for Coaches, Parents, and Professionals.* Specialty Press.
Offers a strengths-based approach to belief and identity development in ADHD youth, including tools to support positive belief change.

o **Vahinger, H. (1924).** *The Philosophy of 'As If': A System of the Theoretical, Practical and Religious Fictions of Mankind.* (C. K. Ogden, Trans.). Harcourt, Brace & Company.
Explores how people hold beliefs not because they are true, but because they are functional—a concept that supports compassionate inquiry into limiting beliefs that may once have served a protective role.

🔁 Chapter Handoff: From Beliefs to Balance

We've done the inside work:

You've learned to recognize your emotional signals, challenge your thoughts, and rewrite the beliefs that hold you back.

But insight alone isn't enough.

Life keeps moving. Expectations keep showing up. And ADHD doesn't always come with built-in brakes.

That's why we're closing this part of the journey with a chapter on **alignment**—the daily practice of protecting your energy, monitoring your stress, and making space for the version of yourself you're becoming.

Because the real test of belief isn't what you write in your journal.

It's how you **live**—how you respond to overload, how you reset when things go sideways, and how you build a life that reflects what you now know to be true.

Chapter 18

Living in Alignment—Stress, Energy, and Life That Works

"Funny how falling feels just like flying... for a while."
—Jeff Bridges, The Ballad of Bad Blake

🛠️ How to Use This Chapter

Chapter 18 follows the book's three-layer format. It integrates practical insights about stress, emotional processing, and life balance—with a special focus on signal awareness and burnout prevention for ADHD minds. It includes tools like the Cauldron, the Stress Wagon, and the Signal Check worksheet to help you build an internal dashboard that works.

- ○ 🧠 **For People with ADHD—Students, Workers, and Curious Minds**
  This chapter helps you recognize early stress signals, understand emotional overload, and build new ways to monitor energy before you hit burnout. It's not about feeling perfect—it's about staying aligned.
- ○ 🏫 **For Parents, Educators, and Professionals**
  You'll gain insight into how ADHD individuals often miss internal signals until it's too late—and why emotional intelligence, energy awareness, and restorative practices matter more than ever in education, work, and home life.

- ○ ⊛ **Core Concepts and Tools**
  - ▪ The Cauldron—where unprocessed emotions go
  - ▪ The Three E's—Experience, Evaluation, Emotion
  - ▪ Emotional Intensity Scale—Five Core Feelings + levels
  - ▪ The Stress Wagon—what you're hauling and how to lighten it
  - ▪ The Signal Self-Check—a tool for alignment and daily reflection
  - ▪ Monitoring restoration needs and energy drain patterns
  - ▪ Putting it all together—a dashboard for sustainable thriving

⊛ For People with ADHD—Students, Workers, and Curious Minds

⊛ Hitting the Wall with ADHD—Surge Capacity and the Long Crisis

The Slow Burn of a Long Crisis

Not everyone burned out at once. Some fizzled early. Others crashed spectacularly. But by the time the pandemic passed its first year, nearly everyone had run out of road. And for people with ADHD, we didn't just encounter the wall—we sprinted straight into it.

Burnout, exhaustion, executive function fog—these weren't new to us. But something about the pandemic revealed the deeper patterns beneath them. It wasn't just about being overwhelmed. It was about staying "on" too long, too intensely, without knowing how to shut off or restore.

We call that **surge capacity depletion**.

It's a mouthful, but it's one of the most important concepts we can understand if we want to build a life that doesn't run on crisis mode. Especially for ADHD minds, which thrive on urgency—until they don't.

The Canary Crashes First

At the start of the pandemic, I felt strangely alive. Focused. Activated. While many around me were dazed and disoriented, I charged forward.

"I was born for times like these," I told my colleagues.

It wasn't a boast—it was an instinct.

As a therapist with ADHD, I know what it feels like to thrive in chaos. Novelty. Urgency. Purpose. I filled my schedule. I volunteered. I took on projects. I wrote, I trained, I supported frontline workers. It was exhausting—but it was meaningful. And it kept the fear and helplessness at bay.

Until it didn't.

A few months in, the charge wore off. My energy tanked. My mood sank. I couldn't think clearly or recover my footing. I wasn't just tired—I was **depleted**.

And I didn't understand why... until I found the work of psychologist **Ann Masten**.

What Is Surge Capacity—and Why Did It Fail Us?

Surge capacity, Masten explains, is *"a collection of adaptive systems—mental and physical—that humans draw on for short-term survival in acutely stressful situations, such as natural disasters."*

It's the inner reserve that helps us rise to the occasion. It kicks in during hurricanes, earthquakes, mass trauma—helping us make decisions, take action, support others, and survive.

But here's the catch: it's designed for **short-term** use.

Most natural disasters follow a rough arc: beginning, middle, end. The crisis happens. The body responds. Then comes recovery.

But the pandemic didn't end. For over a year, we sat at the beginning—waiting for the middle. Waiting for certainty. Waiting for normal.

And while we waited, we kept surging.

Our inner reserves were never meant to stretch that far. And for ADHD minds—always on the edge of overwhelm—that prolonged crisis mode became especially dangerous. Because it wasn't just our energy that ran dry. It was our sense of agency, motivation, and self-trust.

The Edge of Criticality—and the Cost of Living There

As we explored back in Chapter 2, people with ADHD often thrive on that unstable edge—the place where systems become most adaptive, most responsive, and most alive. It's the threshold between chaos and order where our minds light up and leap into action.

But that same edge is also unstable. Living there can be exhilarating, but it comes at a cost. During the pandemic, with no clear recovery window, many of us stayed at the edge too long.

And eventually, **the edge gave out**.

ADHD, Urgency, and the Trouble with Restoration

People with ADHD often shine in short bursts. We rise to challenges. We respond to novelty. We're drawn to the fire—not the slow burn.

But surge capacity doesn't just rely on activation. It relies on **recovery**. And that's where ADHD minds often struggle the most.

- o   We don't always notice when we're depleted—until we collapse.
- o   We don't always stop when we're full—because we're afraid the motivation won't come back.
- o   And when our usual sources of restoration disappear, we're left wondering what to do with ourselves.

This looked different depending on temperament. **Introverts** often found themselves with too much of a good thing—isolation, quiet, solitude. But even they eventually lost the intentionality of alone-time and began to drift.

For **extroverts**, especially those who rely on social energy to reset, the experience was even more jarring.
No coffee shop buzz. No in-person brainstorming.
No unplanned adventures. No kinetic exchange with others.

The pandemic stripped away many of our natural ADHD coping tools.

So we kept trying to sprint through a marathon.

Until the fuel ran out.

As one person put it: We were all in the same storm, but we had different boats.

What Recovery Really Looked Like

When I finally admitted that I was burned out, I stepped back. Not out of wisdom—out of necessity.

But in the quiet, I began to notice something important:

I hadn't just used up my time or energy. I had **burned through my identity fuel**.

I was so used to being in motion that I had forgotten how to be without the doing.

So I started small.

- o   I set limits on work.
- o   I referred clients when I needed to.
- o   I made space for breathwork, yoga, and stillness—even when it felt boring.
- o   I reached out to friends more intentionally.
- o   I reconnected with simple pleasures: music, cooking, nature, quiet.

And gradually... something returned.
Not the surge. Not the adrenaline.
But something steadier. Quieter.
A strength I hadn't known before.

Lessons From the Edge

People with ADHD often live close to the edge. We wait for the last minute. We run on urgency. We mistake intensity for effectiveness—until something breaks.

But we can learn from these moments.

We can read our signals **before they become sirens**.

- o   Notice energy dips before collapse.
- o   Inventory your surge levels the same way you track time or tasks.
- o   Create restoration plans that work even when life gets boring.
- o   Remember: motivation may spike in a crisis—but that doesn't mean you're thriving.

This isn't a sprint.
It never was.
And now we know.

✱ The Lost Dashboard—Learning to Read Your Inner Map

You don't have to crash to know when you're running hot. But if you've **disconnected your internal sensors**—or never learned where they are—it's easy to miss the warning signs until you're in free fall.

That's especially true for ADHD minds.

We often live at the **edge of criticality**—that exhilarating threshold where urgency, novelty, and challenge collide. It's the zone where ADHD brains are most alive... and most at risk.

In that state, we lose track of fuel levels. Of rest needs. Of subtle emotional shifts. We push forward because we're finally activated—even if we're burning out in the process.

To avoid this cycle, we need something most of us never learned:

A way to read our **Inner Map**.

👦 From Parental Regulation to Self-Monitoring

As children, we had external regulators—parents, teachers, coaches. Ideally, they helped us monitor energy, food, sleep, stimulation, and stress. They told us when to rest, eat, reset. They were our dashboard.

But now?

You're the adult.

No one is coming to shut your laptop at 2 a.m.

No one is going to hide your phone, refill your water, or remind you to breathe.

And for many of us with ADHD, **there was never a clear handoff** from outer regulation to inner awareness. Even high-performing students and professionals can find themselves **under-resourced, overstimulated, and emotionally brittle—without realizing it.**

That's not a character flaw.
It's a missing skill.

⚒️ Rebuilding the Dashboard

The rest of this chapter is about building that dashboard—
learning to check your signals before they become sirens.
We'll use tools like:

- o The **Caldron** metaphor—understanding where emotions go when unprocessed
- o The **Three E's** model—decoding the relationship between experience, evaluation, and emotion
- o The **Five Core Feelings + Intensity Scale**—to name and track your emotional state
- o The **Signal Self-Check Worksheet**—a simple but powerful habit to recalibrate daily or weekly

And we'll finish with a practical reminder:
Emotional health isn't about feeling good all
the time.

It's about noticing what's true—and responding wisely.
Let's start with where emotions go when we don't.

💥 Emotional Fuel and Friction—The Role of Feelings in Stress and Energy

In Chapter 16, we explored emotional intelligence as a foundational skill—how emotions function as signals and how understanding those signals can shift our experience of ADHD.
Now, we return to those tools with a different goal in mind:
Stress recovery, energy balance, and internal alignment.
Emotions aren't just internal weather. They are forms of

energy—and if left unprocessed, they can drain us. But when understood and expressed, they can become renewable fuel.

This section explores how emotional awareness becomes the first lever in **sustainable living**—especially for ADHD minds living near the edge of criticality.

💧 The Cauldron—Where Emotions Go When They're Ignored

Imagine you have a cauldron inside you—not a witch's pot, but a container. A vessel where all unspoken, unprocessed emotions go.

Every time you say "I'm fine" when you're not...

Every time you swallow your anger to keep the peace...

Every time sadness rises and you distract yourself instead...

It goes in the cauldron.

At first, it's manageable. A low simmer. But over time, that emotional residue builds up. And for ADHD minds, which often feel things intensely and struggle to process them fully in real time, the cauldron can fill fast.

It doesn't just hold sadness or anger. It holds *any* emotion that didn't get named, expressed, or completed. Joy that wasn't shared. Fear that was minimized. Shame that was never soothed.

And the problem isn't just emotional—it's energetic.

Emotions are a form of energy. If they're not expressed or metabolized, they don't vanish. They stagnate. They thicken. And they distort our reactions in the present.

Sometimes when you explode at a tiny frustration, it's not because the moment was big—it's because your cauldron was already full.

Sometimes what looks like anxiety or depression is really just the steam trying to escape.

And sometimes, the thing that finally tips us into burnout isn't the last straw itself—it's the heat that's been rising beneath it for weeks, or months, or years.

✧

The Three E's—A Model for Emotional Awareness

If you want to understand your emotions, don't start with how you *feel*.

Start with what you *experienced*, and what you *told yourself about it*.

That's the core of the **Three E's** model we introduced in Chapter 16 and revisit now:

1. **Experience**—Something happens.
2. **Evaluation**—You interpret what happened.
3. **Emotion**—You feel something *based on that interpretation*.

Let's say someone doesn't respond to your text.

That's the *experience*.

If your evaluation is, *"They must be mad at me,"* your emotion might be fear, guilt, or shame.

But if your evaluation is, *"They probably got distracted,"* you might feel neutral—or even compassionate.

Same experience. Different evaluation. Different emotional outcome.

This is emotional intelligence at its core:

The ability to slow down between experience and emotion—and notice the story in the middle.

For people with ADHD, that middle part—the evaluation—often gets skipped.

We jump from input to feeling in a flash, especially under stress.

That's why pausing to ask, *"What am I telling myself right now?"* can be so powerful.

In the next sections, we'll explore ways to name your emotions more precisely—and express them in ways that lighten your cauldron, not add to it.

🎧 Naming the Fish—Language as Emotional Precision

If emotions are signals, then naming them is how we tune the frequency.

But for many people with ADHD, especially those who grew up masking or moving fast, emotional vocabulary can be limited. You might feel "bad," "off," or "not okay"—without knowing exactly *what* that means.

That's why we use a simple system borrowed from men's work, trauma therapy, and emotional development models:

The Five Core Emotions:

- o   **Glad**
- o   **Sad**
- o   **Mad**
- o   **Afraid**
- o   **Ashamed**

Everything else is a variation or a blend.

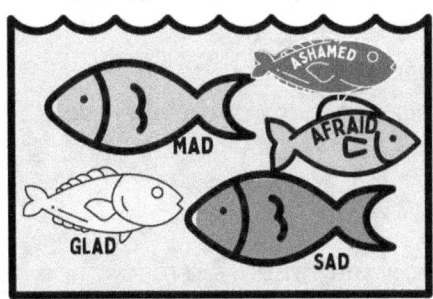

When we teach this in coaching and group settings, we often say:
"You don't have to name the fish by its Latin genus. Just catch it, hold it up, and say, 'Looks like a fish to me.'"
That's enough to start.

🔬 Bonus Tool: Scaling Emotions

For even more clarity, we add a number from 1–10:

- o   "Mad–2" might mean irritated.
- o   "Mad–9" could mean enraged.
- o   "Afraid–3" might be unease.
- o   "Afraid–8" is panic.

This does two things:

1. It gives language to the experience.
2. It creates a data point for patterns. (Are you always at a "Sad–7" after certain social situations? Are your "Glad" moments increasing with better sleep?)

Naming the fish doesn't just help you understand how you feel—it keeps the cauldron from overflowing.
Because every unnamed fish you toss in there?
It keeps swimming.

🔬 Emotions as Signals, Not Problems

In our model, **emotions aren't distractions**.

They aren't malfunctions.

They aren't problems to fix.

They're *signals*—data from the inner world.

Here's how the five core emotions signal something specific:

- o **Glad** signals **alignment**—a resonance between intention and outcome.
- o **Sad** signals **loss**—something meaningful is gone or at risk.
- o **Mad** signals **violation**—a boundary, value, or expectation has been crossed.
- o **Afraid** signals **danger**—real or perceived, physical or emotional.
- o **Ashamed** signals **misalignment with values**—personal or social.

Most people try to *stop* negative emotions. But what if instead, we *read* them?

"Mad–8" isn't just anger.

It might be a signal that your values are under threat.

That your time is being wasted.

That your boundaries are being trampled.

"Afraid–5" might not mean you're weak—it might mean you're about to stretch into something big.

What we resist tends to amplify. But what we *listen to* often de-escalates.

Especially for ADHD minds—who are often labeled "too sensitive" or "too reactive"—this reframing is a relief. It validates the signal instead of invalidating the person.

So the next time a strong feeling hits, try this:

Instead of asking:

"How do I stop feeling this?"
Ask:
"What is this feeling pointing to?"
Emotions are messengers.
You don't have to shoot them.
Just receive the message.

🔄 From Evaluation to Expression— Keeping the Circuit Moving

Emotions aren't meant to sit.

They're meant to **move**.

Just like a completed electrical circuit allows energy to flow, an emotional circuit completes through **expression** or **action**. If that doesn't happen, the signal gets stuck—and the charge builds up.

This is the unspoken rule of the Cauldron:

What isn't expressed gets stored.

And the Cauldron doesn't discriminate. It holds everything:

- That sigh you didn't let out
- The tears you swallowed
- The anger you "managed" by pushing it down
- Even the joy you minimized to avoid seeming "too much"

Eventually, it shows up somewhere else:

- Muscle tension
- Emotional fatigue
- Brain fog
- Overreactions
- Numbness

So how do you complete the emotional circuit?

🛠 Some ways ADHD minds can express emotional energy:

- ○ Journal it (especially with prompts or open structure)
- ○ Voice note it (speak your thoughts out loud, no filter)
- ○ Move it (walk, shake, lift, run—anything that lets energy out)
- ○ Share it (talk to someone you trust)
- ○ Make something (music, art, food, playlists, memes— anything expressive)
- ○ Laugh or cry intentionally (yep, both are regulation tools)

Remember: Expression isn't the same as reaction.

You don't need to punch a wall or confront someone to express anger.

You don't have to collapse in public to honor your sadness.

You just need to give the signal a place to go.

And when you do?

The signal calms down.

The circuit closes.

The system resets.

🔔 Sidebar: When Cues Become Signals

People with ADHD often rely on alarms, reminders, or other external prompts to stay on track. But not all cues are created equal. A cue is just a prompt—but a **signal** is something that gets through.

Here are two real-world examples that show how cues can be transformed into signals:

- **Waking Up from Deep Sleep:** Some people with ADHD sleep so deeply that they set multiple alarms—and still sleep through them. A sound alone isn't always enough. Adding a **kinesthetic layer** like a vibrating mattress pad creates a multisensory experience, helping the brain register the signal and transition into wakefulness.

- **Leaving for Zumba Class:** One client valued both her exercise routine and her time spent talking with a close friend. She set a phone alarm to remind her when to leave—but the sound often faded into the background. So she changed the alarm to **play Zumba music** instead. That cue carried emotional and contextual meaning, triggering recognition, movement, and action. It helped her transition out of conversation and into the next part of her day.

These examples show how **layering a cue**—with music, vibration, emotional tone, or meaning—can turn it into a **signal**. When a reminder becomes recognizable, relevant, and action-triggering, it cuts through distraction and hyperfocus. And that's the heart of good signal design.

🜨 Social Intelligence—The Emotional Mirror

You've learned to name your feelings.

You've learned to express them.

But emotional intelligence doesn't end with *you*.

Social intelligence is the next layer—the ability to recognize, respond to, and **co-regulate** with others.
For ADHD minds, this can be tricky. We're often either:

- o Hyper attuned to others' moods (hello, rejection sensitivity), or
- o Oblivious to social nuance until it's too late.

Either way, it can make relationships feel confusing, overwhelming, or just exhausting.
But here's the good news:
Social intelligence is a learnable skill.

🧠 Two Foundations of Social Intelligence:

1. **Theory of Mind**—Realizing that others have different inner maps than you.
2. **Empathy**—Imagining what their map might feel like.

When you build these skills, you start to notice:

- o "She's quiet—maybe she's anxious, not angry."
- o "He snapped—but it might not be about me."
- o "They didn't respond—maybe they're overloaded."

This unlocks emotional generosity.
It also helps you stop taking everything personally—a common loop for ADHD and trauma-sensitive brains.

❀ A Word on Co-Regulation

Humans don't regulate emotions in isolation. We do it *together.*

Think of a baby crying. They don't need a lecture—they need a calm presence. That's co-regulation.

Now fast-forward. You're an adult, melting down at work or zoning out in class. What do you need?

Sometimes:

- A grounding friend
- A voice that says, "You're okay"
- A moment of eye contact, laughter, or shared breath

Social intelligence is the ability to offer—and receive—that connection.

And here's a twist people with ADHD often miss:

The more emotionally intelligent you become, the more likely you are to feel safe in community, and the less likely you are to burn out trying to regulate everything on your own.

📺 Sidebar: Love Island and the Illusion of Intimacy

When connection becomes performance, we lose the very thing we were chasing.

In a world where attention is currency and vulnerability feels dangerous, shows like *Love Island* offer something strangely comforting: a version of connection that's curated, controlled, and consumable.

It looks like intimacy—flirtation, confession, affection, dramatic declarations. But it's not vulnerability. It's a performance of closeness designed for viewers, not participants. Nothing is truly at risk.

So why is it so compelling, especially to younger audiences? Because it scratches an itch many don't know they have: the hunger to matter, to be seen, to connect—without the fear of rejection, awkwardness, or emotional exposure.

In ADHD minds, where emotional sensitivity is often turned up to eleven, this kind of stylized connection can be especially appealing. It promises stimulation, novelty, and the *signal* of mattering without the uncomfortable friction of real-world relationships. But like any emotionally hollow substitute, it leaves us emptier in the long run.

Reality shows like *Love Island* reflect a deeper cultural signal: that being validated is more important than being known. That *looking* connected is safer than *actually connecting*.

But the truth is:

Connection without vulnerability is a simulation.
Validation without authenticity is noise.
And performance, no matter how polished, is not presence.

If we want relationships that nourish us—not just entertain us—we need to risk showing up for real. Not with perfect lighting. Not with a practiced script. But with the messy, unfinished truth of who we are. That's where real connection begins.

🚌 The Stress Wagon—What Are You Carrying?

Imagine you're pulling a wagon behind you.

It's not flashy. It's not loud. But it's always there.

STRESS WAGON

As you move through your day, things get tossed in—some deliberately, others without you noticing. A difficult conversation. A deadline. A sleepless night. A missed medication dose. That unresolved email thread. A flicker of shame that simmers from something small and unspoken.

At first, the load seems manageable. But over time, it builds.

Eventually, you feel off—foggy, irritable, restless, or suddenly immobilized.

You wonder, *"Why am I like this?"*

But it's not a mystery.
You just haven't checked the wagon.

🧠 ADHD Minds and Load Blindness

People with ADHD often don't notice their internal load building until it tips. We move fast. We're focused on the next thing. And we're notoriously bad at recognizing when we're overwhelmed until we're already deep in shutdown, meltdown, or flameout.

What makes it trickier is that stress doesn't show up in just one way.

Our wagons get filled with all kinds of weight:

- ○ **Cognitive Load**—decisions, problem-solving, task-switching

- o **Logistical Load**—scheduling, managing stuff, preparing for transitions
- o **Emotional Load**—feelings we've absorbed or ignored (hello, Caldron)
- o **Social Load**—masking, code-switching, RSD triggers, or strained dynamics
- o **Sensory Load**—noise, light, crowds, physical discomfort
- o **Invisible Weight**—shame, self-doubt, the mental chatter of unfinished tasks

Each item might seem small on its own. But together, they become crushing.

💎 Crystal, Steel, and Plastic—Not All Items Weigh the Same

In our coaching work, we teach clients to sort their stressors by type:

- o **Plastic**: Light and flexible. Can be tossed or rescheduled without major impact.
- o **Steel**: Heavy but manageable. Needs planning or support to carry well.
- o **Crystal**: Fragile and high stakes. Must be handled with care—think relationships, health, major deadlines.

When you don't inventory what's in your wagon, you treat it all the same—or worse, ignore the Crystal until it shatters.

The Hidden Load—What's Beneath the Pile?

Sometimes the heaviest object in your wagon is buried under a pile of more visible ones.

A forgotten grief. A lingering resentment. An unspoken fear. Often, these emotional weights were tossed in long ago and quietly reshaped how you move through the world.

This is why emotional intelligence isn't a separate skill from stress management. It's central to it. Emotional overload is often the hidden weight that tips the wagon—not because it's the biggest, but because it's the one we refuse to name.

✧

🔁 The Wagon Check-In—A Tool for Daily Use

The goal isn't to empty your wagon completely. That's impossible.

The goal is to check it regularly. To ask:

- o What am I carrying today?
- o What's light? What's heavy?
- o What's most important ... least important?
- o What can I offload, delegate, postpone, or ritualize?
- o What needs naming, expressing, or resolving?

This chapter's companion worksheet walks you through this process. Like a dashboard for your stress and energy systems, it helps you build the habit of checking in before the breakdown.

Because when you monitor your wagon, you prevent the crash.

And that's what alignment is really about.

✳ Monitoring Energy and Life Balance—The Missing Metrics

You've checked your wagon. You've named your feelings. You've tracked the stress that's been riding along unnoticed.

But there's one more system to tune into—and it's one we almost never get taught:

Your energy patterns.

⚡ ADHD and the Myth of Consistent Output

Traditional productivity models assume steady-state performance: get up, work for 8 hours, sleep, repeat. But ADHD doesn't work that way. We don't run on a flat line—we run in cycles. Bursts. Surges. Collapses.

We may:

- Hyperfocus for 10 hours and crash the next day
- Stay awake till 3 a.m. then sleepwalk through the morning
- Feel flatlined all day until one hour before a deadline, when we suddenly come alive

It's not laziness. It's not inconsistency. It's **neurological variability**—a natural fluctuation in executive function and activation energy. But when we don't recognize it, we end up blaming ourselves for not "keeping up" with a model that was never made for us.

◎ Life Balance Isn't Symmetry—It's Signal Awareness

Forget perfect equilibrium. **Balance**, for ADHD minds, isn't about making every area of life equal. It's about learning when a signal is out of range—when something's drawing too much energy, or getting too little attention.

We call these **signal imbalances**. Common ones include:

- o All work, no rest
- o Constant stimulation, no recovery
- o Helping everyone else, but not yourself
- o Managing logistics while ignoring emotions
- o Living in the future (plans) or past (mistakes), but never present

And just like with the wagon, the weight often accumulates without conscious notice.

Until something breaks.

That's why balance is best monitored not by external standards, but by **internal reflection**—asking questions like:

- o Am I restoring energy as much as I'm expending it?
- o Are my daily rhythms aligned with how I actually work best?
- o What's getting sacrificed in the name of urgency?
- o Am I ignoring small signals that something is off?

🔖 Curiosity as a Map: What Restores You?

Most people can list what depletes them. But far fewer know how to **deliberately restore** themselves.

If you're not sure where to start, get curious:

- o What activities make you feel more **alive** after doing them—not just distracted or numbed out?
- o What kinds of environments energize you (or drain you)?

o   Who are the people that **restore** you—and who tends to **cost** more than they give?
o   What have you done in the past that helped you feel grounded, creative, or whole?
o   What haven't you tried yet—but suspect might help?

Some of the most restorative practices don't look "productive" on the surface:

o   Wandering in nature
o   Making something with your hands
o   Letting yourself daydream without guilt
o   Playing, singing, swimming, dancing
o   Being alone, or being seen—depending on your wiring

You don't need a research paper to prove it's good for you. If it helps you come back to yourself—it counts.

✧

Restore, Don't Just Recharge

People often say "recharge" like we're batteries. But ADHD minds don't just need to be plugged in—we need to **restore missing elements.**

For some, that means:

o   **Movement** (not just exercise, but kinetic stimulation)
o   **Social connection** (especially for extroverts)
o   **Creative flow** (projects that light you up)
o   **Spaciousness** (for introverts and deep thinkers)
o   **Low-stimulation environments** (to soothe sensory overload)

This isn't a "treat." It's **maintenance.**

When we build in restoration intentionally, the crashes become less frequent—and the peaks less costly.

Energy Bars and Life Meters—How Full Are You?

In our workshops, we often borrow from video game language:

Think of your life like a character with a visible **energy bar**—how full is it today?

You might ask:

- o What's draining my bar the fastest right now?
- o What kind of "health pack" do I need to restore it?
- o Are there background programs (like shame, indecision, emotional residue) that are quietly eating up energy?

Try visualizing your **life meter** once in the morning, midday, and evening. It's a simple but powerful way to build **interoception**—the skill of reading your internal signals before they become crisis alarms.

✸ Sidebar: Introvert vs. Extrovert Restoration

During the pandemic, introverts got too much of a good thing. Extroverts got too little. The result? Both burned out in different ways.

Extroverts often restore through interaction, novelty, and social energy. The isolation of lockdowns cut off their oxygen.

Introverts restore through solitude, reflection, and lower stimulation. The constant anxiety of the outside world disrupted their inner quiet.

ADHD doesn't map cleanly onto introvert vs. extrovert—many of us are a mix—but understanding your own **restorative channels** is key.

As one person put it:

"We were all in the same storm—but we had different boats."

🐝 Putting It All Together—Living in Alignment

Throughout this chapter, we've taken a deep dive into stress, energy, and emotional regulation—not as isolated problems, but as interconnected systems within your life. We've seen how surge capacity depletes under chronic pressure, how emotions accumulate when ignored, how beliefs shape your inner experience, and how unexamined loads quietly fill the wagon you're pulling.

Now it's time to pull the threads together. Because none of these are just mental health concerns—they're *life design* concerns.

When ADHD minds are at their best, they're creative, resourceful, driven by purpose, and capable of stunning insight. But those capacities can't flourish in survival mode. And they won't activate on command if you're disconnected from the internal signals that power them.

Living in Alignment Means...

- Understanding what fuels you—emotionally, cognitively, and physically.
- Recognizing what drains you—including subtle stressors and false beliefs.

- ○ **Building systems that protect your energy**—not just spend it.
- ○ **Checking your signals regularly**—not just waiting for the crash.
- ○ **Choosing actions that align with your core values**—so you don't have to rely on crisis to find meaning.

Tools for Alignment
By now, you've collected a full dashboard of tools:

- ○ **The Three E's Model** for recognizing how emotions form
- ○ **The Caldron** metaphor for understanding emotional buildup
- ○ **The Stress Wagon** for tracking mental and logistical load
- ○ **The Signal Check-In Sheet** for staying calibrated
- ○ **The Energy Bar Metaphor** to monitor depletion and restoration
- ○ **Belief Mapping** to uncover and revise the stories beneath your feelings
- ○ **Curiosity Practices** to explore what actually restores you

Together, these aren't just emotional tools—they're navigational ones. They help you turn inward with clarity instead of fear. They help you reclaim authorship of your life instead of reacting to it.

Alignment Is a Practice, Not a Personality Trait
You don't have to become someone else to live in alignment. You don't need to "fix" your brain. But you do need to learn how to hear it—and how to respond with intention.

Alignment isn't perfection. It's presence. It's noticing when you're veering off course and making small, compassionate adjustments. Again and again.

And when you do that, even the most chaotic life begins to feel coherent.

✧

For Parents, Educators, Clinicians, Coaches, and Curious Readers

ADHD is often framed in terms of distraction, impulsivity, and task failure—but one of its most overlooked impacts is in the realm of **stress accumulation** and **energy mismanagement**. People with ADHD often operate in a "sprint" mode—moving from crisis to crisis, unaware that they're living close to depletion until they crash.

This chapter offers insight into the **internal regulation gaps** that make self-monitoring more difficult—and the tools that can help bridge those gaps. Emotional signals are often misread or missed entirely. Energy depletion goes unnoticed until burnout. And restorative practices, when absent, leave even high-performing individuals brittle and dysregulated.

This matters in classrooms, clinics, families, and workplaces.

- In school, a child who seems unmotivated may actually be **emotionally overloaded** or chronically overstimulated. What looks like defiance may be depletion.
- At home, parents may miss early stress signs until their child is in meltdown—or may model burnout cycles themselves.
- In therapy and coaching, we can support clients in building **signal awareness**, **recovery habits**, and **emotional fluency**—long before a major collapse.

The metaphors in this chapter—*the Cauldron, the Stress*

Wagon, and the *Dashboard*—are teaching tools. They help make invisible processes visible. They can be used in IEP meetings, counseling sessions, or family conversations. ADHD brains don't just need motivation strategies. They need **energy literacy**—and adults who know how to model it.

We all live in a world that runs too hot. But for neurodivergent learners and workers, restoring the ability to read internal cues is vital for long-term success.

📖 References for Further Reading

o **Arnsten, A. F. T. (2009).** *The emerging neurobiology of attention deficit hyperactivity disorder: The key role of the prefrontal association cortex. Journal of Pediatrics*, 154(5), I–S43. Arnsten outlines how stress directly impairs executive function and prefrontal cortex regulation—providing a neurological link between chronic stress and ADHD symptom expression.

o **Brown, B. (2012).** *Daring Greatly.* Gotham.
Brown's work on shame, vulnerability, and wholehearted living helps explain why ADHD individuals may internalize emotional exhaustion as failure—and why recovery must include self-compassion and reframing.

o **Levine, P. A. (1997).** *Waking the Tiger: Healing Trauma.* North Atlantic Books.
Levine emphasizes how trauma and chronic stress can be held in the body. His "completion of the stress cycle" idea connects to the Cauldron metaphor and emotional discharge models used here.

o **Masten, A. S. (2014).** *Ordinary Magic: Resilience in Development.* Guilford Press.

Masten's work on "surge capacity"—the emergency system humans draw on during acute stress—provided the foundation for the chapter's discussion on burnout and prolonged crisis mode. Essential reading on resilience science.

o **Nigg, J. T. (2017).** *Getting Ahead of ADHD: What Next-Generation Science Says About Treatments That Work—and How You Can Make Them Work for Your Child.* Guilford Press. Nigg's model of ADHD development offers a framework for understanding self-regulation, emotional scaffolding, and executive dysfunction. His insights help contextualize the need for internal monitoring tools.

o **Porges, S. W. (2011).** *The Polyvagal Theory: Neurophysiological Foundations of Emotions, Attachment, Communication, and Self-Regulation.* W. W. Norton. Porges' theory helps explain why ADHD individuals often live in sympathetic overdrive—constantly scanning for urgency and struggling with down-regulation. The vagus nerve and social engagement system are deeply relevant to the stress-recovery cycle.

o **Siegel, D. J. (2010).** *Mindsight: The New Science of Personal Transformation.* Bantam. Siegel's work supports the idea that increased internal awareness—mindsight—can lead to emotional healing and regulation. A key conceptual foundation for developing the Inner Compass and emotional dashboard tools.

o **Taylor-Klaus, E. (2020).** *The Essential Guide to Raising Complex Kids with ADHD, Anxiety, and More.* Fair Winds Press. Taylor-Klaus provides practical approaches for parents navigating complex emotional and energy patterns. Her emphasis on self-care, emotional literacy, and compassionate coaching aligns well with this chapter's tools.

⬅ Closing Reflection to Part IV

The Factory I Never Left—A Dream Reflection on Shame, Struggle, and Identity

As we turn toward the practical challenges of work, calling, and real-world navigation, I want to share a recurring dream that has followed me for years. It's rooted in the past—but it reveals something vital about how beliefs, stress, and self-worth shape the paths we choose.

I worked in a mobile home factory in my late teens and early twenties, trying to pay my way through college. The place was grim. Pre-OSHA. Dangerous. Filthy. Bleak. It was the kind of environment Dickens might've imagined if he were writing about Waco, Texas instead of Victorian London. The people I worked with were mostly ex-offenders, undocumented immigrants, or men stuck in hard lives with no exits. Some didn't speak much English. Some couldn't read. Everyone was tired, bruised, and watching the clock.

I was tired too—physically, emotionally, existentially. There were days I felt like I might never escape. Like maybe this factory wasn't just a stop along the way, but a destiny I couldn't reroute. I didn't know yet whether I had the horsepower to build a different life. So I kept working. And studying. And wondering.

Running in the background, like a cruel radio I couldn't turn off, was something my high school math teacher once told me: *"You're just not college material."* That sentence stuck. It shaped how I interpreted every failure, every setback. That belief—that maybe I wasn't cut out for something more— made the noise of the factory even louder and the path forward even darker.

What's haunted me isn't just the memory of that place— it's the fact that it's followed me for decades in my dreams. Always the same mobile home factory. Sometimes gritty and brutal, like it really was. Other times, surreal—modernized, efficient, even high-tech. Once it looked like a level 5 clean room where they make microchips. And in more recent versions of the dream, I'm not a grunt—I'm a supervisor. Or I sneak back in, undercover, pretending to be one of the guys again. Like I'm testing something. Or honoring something. Or checking to see if it could still swallow me.

I think these dreams are a signal—a message from a deeper layer of me, a place where shame and grit and worthiness still wrestle. Because the truth is, I was afraid I might never leave that place. And I was equally afraid I might not deserve to.

But the factory has changed. And so have I.

The part of me that survived that early chapter still lives in me. He's the reason I don't give up on people who are struggling. He's the reason I can look a kid in the eye who's failing out of school and say, "You're not broken. You just haven't found your way out yet."

I no longer live in that factory. But I know my way around

it. And if I return in dreams, it's not to be trapped. It's to re-member who I was when I had no map—and to thank him for getting me here.

Sometimes healing isn't about burning the past. It's about walking back in with the lights on, knowing the exit, and real-izing you're not stuck anymore.

This story isn't just about a factory—it's about a belief. One that started as a comment, became a story, and eventually shaped my internal narrative. That's how beliefs form: we ex-perience something, we tell ourselves what it means, and that meaning becomes a habit of mind.

According to the emotional intelligence model used throughout this book, emotions are not random—they're reac-tions to the stories we tell ourselves about events. And when those stories go unexamined, they harden into beliefs. Beliefs shape our moods, our confidence, our behavior—and they of-ten do so invisibly, until we find ourselves reacting to life from a place we don't even recognize.

That old belief became an operating system—not just for how I worked, but for how I felt about myself. It took years to rewire. Years to realize that I could still care deeply about the people who were stuck—without believing I had to stay stuck with them. That I could honor my roots without living under-ground. That the identity I forged in that place was shaped by fear and effort, a desperate hope that I wouldn't always feel this loss.

You may never fully forget the adversity you came from. The beliefs forged there may echo longer than you expect. But when those echoes arrive, you'll be more equipped to meet them. Not with fear, but with clarity. Not with shame, but with signal.

This reflection isn't just about where I've been—it's about what I bring with me. The grit, the shame, the hope. They're all part of the compass I use now to guide students, workers, dreamers, and ADHD minds finding their way in a world that often misreads them.

In the next section, we move from the inner world to the outer one—where these skills meet opportunity, and where the right work can become more than survival. It can become signal.

Introduction to Part V: Real-World Skills, Career Navigation, and Life Beyond the System

✺ *A World in Flux—Why ADHD Minds Are Built for the Future*

*"What do I do with my life when
the rules keep changing?"*
—a high school senior with ADHD

That question wasn't asked out of curiosity—it was asked out of quiet panic.

The student who said it wasn't confused. She was awake. She'd watched her older brother drop out of college. She'd read headlines about scientists leaving the U.S., teachers leaving classrooms, and entire industries becoming automated. She didn't want to waste years following a path that might disappear—or worse, betray her. She wasn't lazy. She wasn't cynical. She just didn't see a future she recognized.

And honestly, who could blame her?

We're living in a time of massive transition—socially, politically, economically, even ecologically. And it's not some distant future crisis. It's happening *now*.

Across the country, young people are graduating into a system that no longer works the way it used to. The social contract is fraying. Long-trusted paths to stability—public service, higher education, science, healthcare—are being destabilized. Policies rooted in austerity, deregulation, and cultural division are reshaping everything from immigration to education to mental health support. Many of the scaffolds that neurodivergent students once relied on are being dismantled or priced out of reach.

We're watching a slow-motion collapse of old systems, even as new ones haven't fully formed.

For ADHD students—for anyone navigating the edge between potential and overwhelm—this creates a uniquely difficult challenge. But it also presents a critical opportunity.

🌱 Living at the Edge—and Learning to Build

If you've made it this far in the book, you already know: ADHD is not a deficit in willpower or intelligence. It's a difference in how we process signals, build motivation, and engage with the world.

You've learned how ADHD minds thrive in pattern-rich environments, follow signals rather than schedules, and struggle when forced into systems that don't reflect their operating style. You've also seen how powerful those minds can become when they're properly supported.

But here's the truth: support isn't coming from the system. Not consistently. Not equitably.

If anything, many of the systems we were told to rely on—educational institutions, healthcare structures, public infrastructure—are now places of strain and contradiction. And that strain often falls hardest on people who need the most clarity to succeed.

That's why this section—and this moment—matters so much.

✧

You Already Have the Tools. Now Use Them to Build Your World.

Everything you've learned so far—every signal you've mapped, every amplifier you've noticed, every internal voice you've strengthened—is a piece of *internal infrastructure*. And now, in this final section, it's time to take those tools out into the world.

You'll revisit:

- **Signal Mapping**: to know what really moves you, even when the world is loud and full of noise
- **Chaining**: to turn insight into action, one link at a time
- **The Visionary–Producer–Editor model**: to manage your own creativity, productivity, and reflection
- **Sprint Thinking**: to work in bursts, recalibrate when needed, and avoid burnout
- **Emotional Intelligence and Critical Thinking**: to

process what you feel, filter what you hear, and protect your focus

These are not luxuries. They are your armor and compass.

Because the world doesn't just need compliant workers anymore.

It needs *adaptive minds*—ones that can detect pattern in chaos, improvise in motion, and build new systems when old ones break down.

In other words: it needs you.

🔭 Moving Forward—and Making it Yours

This isn't the world your parents prepared for. And it may not be the world you were promised.

But ADHD minds have never truly belonged to someone else's blueprint. We've always lived closer to the edge—where risk meets possibility, where disruption meets invention.

The road ahead won't be smooth. But it will be *real*. And with the right tools, with the signal-based awareness you now carry, you can build a future that reflects who you are—not just what the world demands.

So ask yourself again:

What do I do with my life when the rules keep changing?

And now answer it:

I learn the patterns. I follow the signal. I build something new.

Let's begin.

Chapter 19

The Polymath Mind— ADHD, Curiosity, and Fractal Intelligence

Thriving at the Intersection of Curiosity, Complexity, and Connection
"A jack of all trades is a master of none—but oftentimes better than master of one."
—Popular proverb, origin disputed; earliest known written use, 1612

🪨 How to Use This Chapter

This chapter is designed with three perspectives in mind. You don't have to read it all at once—and you're free to skip to what's most relevant for you.

- 🧠 **For People with ADHD—Students, workers, and curious minds:** This section explores what it means to be a polymath with ADHD—someone who learns in spirals, not straight lines. You'll find stories, tools, and reframes to help you organize your many interests without giving up any part of who you are.
- 🔬 **For Parents, Educators, Clinicians, and Coaches:** If you support someone with a wide-ranging ADHD mind, this section offers insight and support strategies—including how to scaffold structure, affirm

identity, and help polymath learners thrive in systems that weren't built for them.

- o ♀ **Key Concepts and Takeaways:** Throughout the chapter, you'll find visual metaphors (like the spiral staircase and constellation thinking), practical tools (like Signal Mapping and Sprint Thinking), and examples to help apply fractal intelligence in learning, work, and life.

♀ You can read this chapter straight through—or use it like a compass, returning to the parts that speak to your experience, your learner, or your next creative leap.

Introduction: A Different Kind of Knowing

In a world that demands specialization, ADHD minds often show up as "too much"—too curious, too distracted, too scattered, too unfocused. But what if that wasn't a failure to conform?

What if it was a different kind of intelligence—not linear, but layered... not singular, but interconnected?

In this chapter, we explore the Polymath Mind: the ADHD tendency toward wide-ranging, deep-diving, interdisciplinary thinking. It's the mind that learns in webs, not wires. That follows signal rather than schedule. That doesn't just chase knowledge—it connects it.

We call this style of learning *fractal intelligence*—a recursive, integrative way of making meaning that deepens in spirals, not straight lines. And in an increasingly fragmented world, this may be the thinking we need most.

🧠 For People with ADHD—Students, Workers, and Curious Minds

🜂 Perspective Is the Pattern

Earlier in this book, we explored how ADHD minds often prioritize perspective over procedure. That idea comes full circle here.

- 🐘 **The Six Blind Men and the Elephant**: Each touched one part and mistook it for the whole. The polymath mind tries to touch all the parts—not for certainty, but for synthesis.
- 🕰 **The Hands of the Clock**: ADHD learners may not always track exact time, but they intuit how systems move and shift—especially when they're free to build their own rhythm.
- 🔭 **Beginner's Mind**: Polymaths return to topics again and again—not because they forgot, but because they've grown. Each return adds nuance, depth, and new insight.

This is not aimless drifting. It's recursive, layered learning—the mind's version of zooming in, reframing, and returning with sharper tools each time.

🌿 What Is a Polymath?

A polymath is someone whose curiosity doesn't stay in one lane. They ask questions that don't fit on a single syllabus. They learn in constellations, not silos. And they're often misunderstood by systems that expect a straight path.

Polymathy isn't about knowing everything—it's about seeing how everything relates. It's about synthesis, flexibility, and signal sensitivity.

Historically, polymaths shaped eras of innovation. Leonardo da Vinci wasn't just an artist. He was a scientist, inventor, anatomist, engineer. And like many ADHD minds today, he left projects unfinished—not because he didn't care, but because he cared about too much.

For many with ADHD, polymathy shows up as:

- Passion that changes direction (but never dies)
- Deep dives into topics with no clear endpoint
- A love of integration, analogy, metaphor, and systems thinking

In other words: it shows up as the very thing our culture says it values, but often punishes in practice.

◎ Fractal Intelligence—Thinking in Spirals, Not Ladders

Fractal intelligence is the pattern-mind's natural architecture.
It means:

- o Revisiting themes over time with increasing insight
- o Applying knowledge across fields
- o Building recursive understanding—like tree rings, not straight lines

Think **spiral staircase**, not elevator. Same height, but with more perspective at every turn.

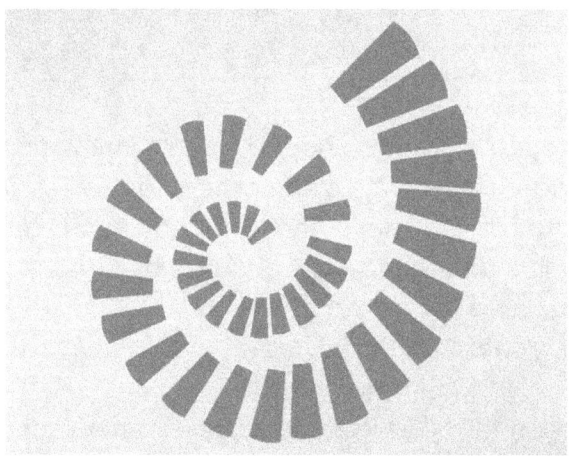

ADHD polymaths often show learning that deepens in spirals. They might not recall a formula on command—but they'll see how it applies across unrelated fields. They may not always finish every book—but they remember the pattern it helped reveal.

Fractal thinkers don't just revisit—they revise, reframe, and re-integrate. This isn't failure. It's function.

But this way of learning looks very different from traditional expectations. Here's how polymath minds compare with more linear thinkers:

Two Ways of Thinking—Linear vs. Polymath

Linear Thinkers	Polymath Thinkers (Fractal)
Prefer depth in one domain	Thrive on depth *across* domains
Follow step-by-step sequences	Work in recursive cycles, spirals, and bursts
Value focus and completion	Value connection, synthesis, and meaning
Often specialize early	Often explore widely before integrating
Clear path and milestones	Fluid path shaped by curiosity and signal
Strength: Mastery through repetition	Strength: Insight through pattern recognition
May struggle with too many inputs	May struggle with narrowing down
Succeed in structured systems	Succeed when allowed to design their own systems

 One is not better—just different. We need both in a changing world.

✧

📋 Tools That Help the Polymath Mind Thrive

1. **Signal Mapping**
   Identifies which passions are active right now—and which ones are dormant but still meaningful. Creates clarity without shutting anything down.

2. **The Crystal–Steel–Plastic Model**
   Helps sort tasks and priorities based on their emotional and practical weight. Prevents overinvesting in plastic tasks while crystal priorities go neglected.
3. **Sprint Thinking**
   Uses short bursts of focused effort (1–2 weeks) toward a defined outcome. Polymaths flourish when work is modular, time-bound, and followed by a pivot.
4. **Visionary–Producer–Editor Roles**
   An internal model for managing multiple ideas:
   - The **Visionary** captures inspiration
   - The **Producer** turns it into action steps
   - The **Editor** refines, assesses, and adapts
   This supports switching gears without losing momentum.

⚠ When the Polymath Mind Struggles— And How to Support It

Even when gifted, driven, and full of potential, ADHD polymaths often find themselves at odds with systems built for linear specialization. The result? Internal confusion, external underperformance, and a long trail of "almosts."

1. **Trouble Committing to a Single Career Path**
   - **Problem**: Fear of choosing "wrong" and closing doors; restlessness; a desire to do *all* the things.
   - **Solution**:
     - Choose a career that integrates multiple fields (e.g., science communication, education, design, fieldwork).
     - Use values-based decision-making to identify

which parts of your polymath self must be honored.

- o Embrace a *portfolio career*—one made up of evolving roles over time.

2. **The Vocation–Avocation Model**
   - ▪ **Concept**: Vocation fulfills core survival and purpose needs; avocation nourishes creativity, curiosity, or long-range dreams.
   - ▪ **Application**:
     - o Choose a day job that reflects your strengths, values, or interests.
     - o Maintain a parallel passion that doesn't need to "pay" to be meaningful.

Avocation ideas:
   - o Volunteer at a nature center or museum
   - o Write fiction, blogs, or articles
   - o Tinker with design, mechanics, or software
   - o Host a podcast, club, or local event
   - o Garden, build, create—just because it lights you up

3. **Overwhelm in Choosing a College Major**
   - ▪ **Problem**: College demands early commitment and narrow focus.
   - ▪ **Solution**:
     - o Choose inherently interdisciplinary majors (e.g., environmental science, anthropology, cognitive science).
     - o Explore double majors or themed minors.
     - o Design a self-directed or advisor-supported custom path.
     - o Prioritize programs with fieldwork, experiential learning, or independent research.

Your story might not fit the mold. But it might just build a better one.

If your brain works like a constellation, not a checklist, you are not broken. You are just a different kind of navigator.

Start by noticing:

- What themes keep showing up?
- What questions won't leave you alone?
- What lights you up—even if no one else understands why?

Build your life around those signals.
You don't have to choose one thing.
But you do have to choose on purpose.

@ Sidebar: Where to Aim Next—A Signal-Based Career Forecast

In a fractured world, ADHD polymaths may feel like misfits.

In a changing world, they become signal receivers—and system designers.

The best future careers for ADHD minds will require:

- High flexibility and rapid learning
- Pattern detection, synthesis, and interdisciplinary agility
- Tolerance for ambiguity, complexity, and emotional intensity
- Purpose-driven motivation and connection to real-world impact

Watch for growth in fields like:

- Climate resilience and environmental design
- Neurodiverse learning, mental health, and coaching
- Storytelling, podcasting, experience architecture
- Biotech, UX, and human-centered AI
- Social innovation and grassroots organizing
- Field science, ecological restoration, and future systems research

And many of these careers don't exist yet.

Which means ADHD polymaths may be the ones who create them.

Case Study: Zayn

Zayn is a 22-year-old returning to college after academic suspension. Diagnosed with ADHD (Predominantly Inattentive Type) and a learning disability in written expression, he had long been dismissed as underperforming.

But beneath the overwhelm was a deep, polymathic intelligence—an explorer of marine ecosystems, fossils, biodiversity, and climate systems. He didn't just love information. He connected it across domains.

Here's how Zayn rebuilt his structure:

- o Designed an interdisciplinary major blending life sciences, geology, and ecological history
- o Interned at a fossil lab and a coastal research center
- o Used voice-to-text tools to bypass writing blocks
- o Built signal-based schedules aligned with energy and interest
- o Externalized task structure with color-coded boards and executive function coaching

He stopped trying to "fit in"—and started designing a future that honored his brain's wiring.

🔑 Closing Thought

In a world that rewards fitting, ADHD polymaths are born to shape.

They're not here to master one thing.

They're here to weave across things—to build bridges where others see boundaries.

For some polymath minds, the best way to honor all these signals isn't through one job—but by building a system of their own. That's where we go next

When you follow the signal, structure follows you.

And the world, whether it knows it or not, is waiting for your map.

✧

For Parents, Educators, Clinicians, Coaches, and Curious Readers

Polymath ADHD learners are often misdiagnosed as distracted, defiant, or disorganized—when in truth, they're juggling too much meaning, not too little focus.

Support Strategies for Polymath ADHD Learners

Polymath ADHD students often struggle with executive function not because they're unfocused—but because they're trying to juggle too many deeply meaningful ideas at once. They are driven by intense internal motivation but often lack the structural tools to turn curiosity into consistent, sustainable action.

Support strategies include:

- o **Normalize divergence and validate the polymath identity**
  Help them see wide-ranging interests not as distraction, but as a powerful way of engaging the world.
- o **Use values cards and signal tracking tools**
  Clarify what they care about most right now and align action with deeper motivation.
- o **Design flexible scaffolds**
  Use visual timelines, interest boards, signal stacks, and sprint-based schedules to externalize structure.
- o **Encourage integrative reflection**

Ask: "What themes connect your favorite classes or projects?"

- **Teach emotional pacing and energy restoration**
  Polymaths often burn bright—and burn out. Help them build rhythms that sustain momentum.
- **Frame structure as support, not limitation**
  Let plans feel like containers, not cages.
- **Reframe success**
  Success isn't about narrowing. It's about threading diverse passions into a coherent life.

Understanding Fractal Intelligence

Fractal intelligence is the capacity to think in patterns and networks rather than straight lines. ADHD minds often make connections across domains and revisit themes at different scales. These minds operate in nested cycles of learning—like spirals rather than ladders—continually returning to ideas with new depth and perspective.

✧

🎨 Multiple Intelligences and ADHD

Howard Gardner's theory of Multiple Intelligences offers a helpful lens for understanding polymath learners. Many ADHD students exhibit strong abilities across several areas, including:

- Naturalistic (ecology, biology, systems)
- Verbal-Linguistic (storytelling, language)
- Logical-Mathematical (patterns, systems)
- Interpersonal (collaboration, empathy)

- o Intrapersonal (self-reflection)
- o Musical (sound patterns, rhythm)
- o Bodily–Kinesthetic (hands-on, physical learners)

Rather than forcing these learners to conform to a single-track intelligence, our goal should be to build environments that reflect and affirm their cognitive diversity.

✧

References for Further Reading

o **Armstrong, T.** (1999). *ADD/ADHD Alternatives in the Classroom.* Alexandria, VA: ASCD.
Armstrong explores strengths-based strategies for ADHD students, emphasizing creativity, curiosity, and learning diversity—essential for supporting polymath learners.

o **Gardner, H.** (1983). *Frames of Mind: The Theory of Multiple Intelligences.* New York, NY: Basic Books.
Gardner's landmark theory highlights the cognitive diversity of polymath minds, particularly the value of interweaving multiple intelligences.

o **Root-Bernstein, R. & Root-Bernstein, M.** (1999). *Sparks of Genius: The 13 Thinking Tools of the World's Most Creative People.* Boston, MA: Houghton Mifflin.
This book offers a deep dive into the habits of creative polymaths across disciplines—pattern spotting, analogizing, modeling—aligning beautifully with fractal intelligence.

o **Thomas, J. L.** (2019). *Thriving at the Edge of Chaos: Making ADHD a Superpower in College and Career.* Sleepy Creek Press.
The foundational work introducing the

Visionary–Producer–Editor model, emotional pacing, and signal-based strategies now expanded in *Beyond the Edge of Chaos.*

🔄 Handoff from Chapter 19: *The Polymath Mind—ADHD and the Power of Fractal Intelligence*

The polymath mind doesn't just collect knowledge—it weaves meaning across disciplines. But what happens when that drive for meaning collides with a world that demands structure, stability, and a clear career path?

In the next chapter, we zoom in on the tension between signal and structure as it plays out in the world of work. Whether you're choosing a major, rethinking a career, or just trying to make peace with your path, this chapter reframes what it means to work with purpose—not just pressure.

Chapter 20

Job, Career, Calling— Reframing Work and Meaning Through the ADHD Lens

"I love my work. It's a calling. I'm working till noon on the day of my funeral."
—Jon Thomas

"Work is not always required. There is such a thing as sacred idleness."
—George MacDonald

🪧 How to Use This Chapter

This chapter is designed with three perspectives in mind. You don't have to read it all at once—and you're free to skip to what's most relevant for you.

- o 🧠 **For People with ADHD—Students, workers, and curious minds:** This section reframes how ADHD minds approach work—not as a ladder to climb, but as a signal to follow. You'll learn how to spot the difference between a job, a career, and a calling—and how to design a path that fits
your energy, values, and evolving sense
of self.
- o 🖊️ **For Parents, Educators, Clinicians, and Coaches:**

If you support someone with ADHD who is struggling to find their path, this section offers tools to decode motivation, normalize career zigzags, and scaffold emotional pacing in early adult work discovery.

- ○ ♀ **Key Concepts and Takeaways:** Throughout the chapter, you'll find metaphors (like the Shaper vs. Fitter model), practical tools (like signal mapping and values cards), and reflection prompts to help guide real-world decision-making around career and purpose.

💡 You can read this chapter straight through—or return to it anytime you're at a crossroads, rethinking your direction, or trying to make sense of what work should feel like.

🧠 For People with ADHD—Students, Workers, and Curious Minds

💼 In This Chapter—What You'll Discover

- ○ Why ADHD minds crave meaning at work—and burn out without it
- ○ How the classic "Job–Career–Calling" model breaks down through the ADHD lens
- ○ Why ADHD folks often zigzag through early adulthood—and why that's not failure
- ○ The hidden difference between "fitters" and "shapers"— and how education mislabels us
- ○ How to spot signal-rich work that energizes instead of drains
- ○ How to support ADHD learners as they navigate the messy early stages of career discovery

Most people think of work as a necessary means to an end—paying the bills, getting ahead, building security. But for individuals with ADHD, work tends to function less as a destination and more as a signal receiver. It must be meaningful, aligned, and emotionally resonant to sustain attention. When it's not, motivation collapses. And when it is—even briefly—it lights up the brain like a pinball machine.

In this chapter, we'll reframe the traditional idea of work as a linear progression and instead explore the three lenses through which people often view their professional lives: Job, Career, and Calling. We'll also explore why ADHD individuals are more sensitive to these distinctions, how mismatches can cause stagnation or burnout, and how finding signal-rich alignment can turn work into a source of growth and energy rather than depletion.

1. The Three Frames of Work

Psychologist Amy Wrzesniewski describes three main orientations toward work:

- o **Job**: A means to an end. You do it for a paycheck.
- o **Career**: A path of progress and achievement. It carries personal investment.
- o **Calling**: A deeply felt purpose. Work as meaning. Work as identity.

While all three roles are valid and can coexist across different life stages, ADHD individuals often find it hard to stay engaged in the first two without some degree of the third.

Why?

Because the ADHD brain isn't simply "under-stimulated."

It's under-signaled. And meaning—real, felt meaning—is one of the most powerful internal signals available.

2. Misfit at Work: What Burnout Looks Like with ADHD

When ADHD individuals find themselves in roles that are low on meaning or alignment, the cost is more than boredom. It's burnout, disengagement, and sometimes even a crisis of self-worth.

You may hear the internal monologue:

- ○ "I know I should be able to do this."
- ○ "Everyone else seems to be okay with it."
- ○ "What's wrong with me that I can't just push through?"

But what if the issue isn't grit—it's signal? What if your brain is rejecting the role not because it's too hard, but because it's too empty?

3. Meaning as a Career Signal: Why ADHD Brains Can't Fake It for Long

The ADHD mind is a meaning-seeking engine. While many people can persist in jobs that are dull, misaligned, or purely practical, individuals with ADHD often experience an internal resistance to such roles. It's not laziness. It's neurological integrity.

When a task, role, or field aligns with deeper values—curiosity, justice, creativity, connection—it activates intrinsic motivation. That spark isn't optional; it's structural. ADHD learners can learn discipline, but not in a vacuum. Meaning is the ignition switch.

This is why someone with ADHD can go from total disengagement in a classroom to obsessive focus in a hobby project. It's not about effort—it's about signal clarity.

Helping students and young adults identify and track the signals of meaning—and not just status or salary—can create an entirely different arc to their professional development.

So what does this mean in the real world? Let's look at where ADHD minds not only thrive, but where the future of work is heading."

Sidebar: ADHD-Friendly Career Fields— And Why They're a Good Bet

🎨 Creative & Design Professions

- Graphic design, writing, film, marketing, product design
- **Why ADHD fits**: Reward novelty, storytelling, and visual thinking. Often project-based with bursts of intensity.
- **Why it's a good bet**: Content creation, branding,

and digital storytelling are booming globally. Companies can't automate creativity, so demand for fresh ideas continues to grow.

⚡ Emergency & High-Stakes Work

- o Paramedics, ER nurses, firefighters, journalists (media and storytelling), trial lawyers.
- o **Why ADHD fits**: Urgency and adrenaline cut through distraction; decisions matter in the moment.
- o **Why it's a good bet**: Healthcare, crisis response, and information flow are all expanding fields—aging populations, climate events, and real-time news cycles guarantee demand.

🛠 Skilled Trades & Hands-On Work

- o Carpentry, electrical, welding, mechanics, construction
- o **Why ADHD fits**: Tangible, physical work with visible progress. Built-in variety and problem-solving.
- o **Why it's a good bet**: Skilled trades are in shortage across the U.S. and globally. Infrastructure rebuilding, clean energy construction, and retirements in the workforce make this one of the most reliable paths.

🌱 Entrepreneurship & Startups

- o Founding a business, freelancing, consulting
- o **Why ADHD fits**: Freedom to design your own systems, pursue passion projects, and pivot quickly when interests shift.
- o **Why it's a good bet**: The gig economy and remote work trends favor self-starters. Tech platforms make it easier than ever to launch niche businesses with low overhead.

🧑‍🏫 Teaching, Coaching & Counseling

- ○ ADHD coaching, education, therapy, social work
- ○ **Why ADHD fits**: Relationship-driven, improvisational, and fueled by empathy—strengths many ADHD folks carry naturally.
- ○ **Why it's a good bet**: Mental health and education are critical shortage areas. Rising awareness of ADHD and neurodiversity creates new opportunities in coaching and support services.

💻 Technology & Innovation

- ○ Software development, data visualization, UX/UI, AI applications
- ○ **Why ADHD fits**: Combines problem-solving, creativity, and fast-moving environments. Constant learning keeps boredom at bay.
- ○ **Why it's a good bet**: Tech remains one of the fastest-growing sectors. AI, cybersecurity, and user-centered design are exploding fields where demand far outpaces supply.

🌍 Advocacy & Mission-Driven Work

- ○ Nonprofits, activism, sustainability, community organizing
- ○ **Why ADHD fits**: Meaning and purpose help sustain long-term motivation. Often flexible, dynamic, and people-centered.
- ○ **Why it's a good bet**: Even in politically turbulent times, social and environmental advocacy keeps expanding. Global markets and younger generations continue to push for sustainability, equity, and impact-driven work.

4. From Shapers to Fitters: How We Lost the Plot

In the Napoleonic era, battles were often won not by the best weapons, but by the best shapers. Shapers were the armorers who could take a broken cannon or mangled musket and—using skill, intuition, and a few spare parts—shape raw materials to fit and function again.

Then came the Industrial Revolution. Mass-produced parts. Tight tolerances. Workers didn't need to shape anymore—they needed to fit. Just take the piece and click it in. The rise of the fitter had begun. Education followed.

For the past 150 years, we've trained fitters—not shapers. The curriculum became standard. The answers pre-formed. The goal was replication, not re-creation.

ADHD students are shapers. They improvise solutions, think across categories, tinker until things click, and thrive in ambiguity and pressure. But in a system that rewards only fitting—right part, right place, right time—shapers get labeled as distractible, defiant, or disorganized.

The tragedy isn't that they don't fit. The tragedy is that we forgot how much we need them. Jobs often reward fitting. Careers may demand upskilled fitting. But callings? Those demand shaping. And shaping can't be taught in rows. It's learned in the margins—in the spaces where signal meets story.

5. Navigating the Early Career Chaos

Early adulthood is messy, nonlinear, and often filled with job hopping, false starts, and zigzagging priorities. This isn't a failure—it's data collection.

ADHD learners may feel discouraged by the perception that they're behind or unstable. But these experiences often help them refine their sense of alignment. They're not just chasing work—they're learning to listen for signal.

Encouraging this approach—and supporting students in reflecting on what worked and what didn't—helps shift the narrative from "failure" to "discovery."

One way to reframe the zigzags is by asking: am I in a job, building a career, or listening for a calling?

6. Building Toward a Calling Without the Pressure of Having One

"Calling" is a loaded term. Not everyone discovers theirs early. Some never do in a singular form. That's okay.

Instead of pressuring ADHD individuals to find their "one true path," we can help them recognize the emotional and cognitive signals that tell them when they're on the right track:

- o Do you lose time when you're doing it?
- o Do you talk about it even when no one's asking?
- o Does it energize you—even when it's hard?

are signs you're moving toward calling. And they matter more than any job title or resume.

7. ADHD Strengths at Work

Finally, it's important to note that when ADHD individuals do find the right match, they often outperform expectations. Creativity, risk tolerance, humor, and hyperfocus can become extraordinary assets—not liabilities.

But these strengths need the right ecosystem to emerge. The right role. The right team. The right mission.

That's not entitlement—it's alignment.

Closing Reflection

Instead of asking "What do you want to be when you grow up?", we might ask ADHD learners:

- o "What kind of problems do you feel called to solve?"
- o "What kind of work doesn't feel like work?"
- o "What feels like a signal—not just a task?"

The question isn't "Where can I fit?"—but rather: **"What future needs my kind of mind?"** Because for people with ADHD, **the signal is the strategy**.

Whether you start with a job, build into a career, or lean into a calling, the key for ADHD minds is to track the signal— not just the paycheck.

✧

For Parents, Educators, Clinicians, Coaches—and Curious Readers

Many ADHD students or emerging adults get stuck trying to choose a path that sounds good on paper but feels lifeless in practice. Others jump impulsively into jobs or majors that align with external rewards (status, income, approval), but offer no internal signal.

The following strategies help support ADHD young adults in developing self-awareness and career clarity:

- o **Normalize divergence.** Validate the wide interests of ADHD learners and affirm that nonlinear paths are often richer.
- o **Use values cards and signal tracking tools.** Help clarify what kinds of work create resonance and meaning.
- o **Design flexible scaffolds.** Visual timelines, interest boards, and sprint-based scheduling help poly-math thinkers stay grounded while remaining fluid.
- o **Encourage integrative reflection.** Ask guiding questions like: "What themes connect your favorite classes or jobs?"
- o **Teach emotional pacing and energy restoration.** Many ADHD students burn out by chasing peak engagement. Help them balance intensity with rest.
- o **Reframe success.** Instead of narrowing choices, help them learn to thread their unique story across diverse experiences.

Note for Supporters

As outlined earlier, certain career fields—like tech, healthcare, skilled trades, creative industries, and advocacy—tend to be especially good bets for ADHD learners because they combine urgency, variety, and meaning. But the bigger takeaway isn't the specific job titles. It's the **patterns**: environments that offer rapid feedback, room for adaptability, and work that feels connected to values are far more likely to sustain motivation than rigid, repetitive roles. As a parent, educator, or clinician, you don't need to steer someone toward one "right" career field—you need to help them notice these underlying conditions, so they can choose (and stick with) work that truly fits.

 Sidebar – Careers for a Changing World: What ADHD Students Should Be Watching

In a world shaped by AI, remote work, climate disruption, and global flux, ADHD minds have a powerful advantage—adaptability.

They should keep an eye on:

- Creative industries, content design, and storytelling
- Mental health, coaching, and peer support
- Renewable energy, sustainability, and climate resilience
- Hybrid technical roles that allow for rapid learning and reinvention
- Fields that welcome freelancers, creators, or solopreneurs

📖 References for Further Reading

o **Barkley, R. A. (2012).** *Executive Functions: What They Are, How They Work, and Why They Evolved.*
Explains why ADHD individuals struggle with time, planning, and delayed gratification—vital when supporting young adults in long-haul career paths or linear job systems.

o **Brown, T. E. (2013).** *A New Understanding of ADHD in Children and Adults: Executive Function Impairments.*
Highlights the role of emotional and motivational impairments, helping us understand why ADHD minds often disengage from "empty" or misaligned roles.

o **Hallowell, E. M., & Ratey, J. J. (2021).** *ADHD 2.0: New Science and Essential Strategies for Thriving with Distraction.*
Offers a strengths-based approach, emphasizing stimulation, connection, and meaningful environments—essential for coaching students toward calling-aligned careers.

o **Wrzesniewski, A., McCauley, C., Rozin, P., & Schwartz, B. (1997).** *Jobs, Careers, and Callings: People's Relations to Their Work.* Journal of Research in Personality, 31(1), 21–33.
The original source for the "job, career, calling" framework—foundational to understanding identity-based work alignment for ADHD individuals.

o **Thomas, J. L. (2019).** *Thriving at the Edge of Chaos: Making ADHD a Superpower in College and Career.*
Introduces the signal-based model of motivation and decision-making, offering a roadmap for career alignment rooted in identity, emotion, and energy.

➡️ Handoff to Chapter 21: *The ADHD Entrepreneur—Building Systems That Fit Your Brain*

Some ADHD minds find their match in existing jobs or careers. But others feel the signal only when they start building something of their own.

In the next chapter, we explore the ADHD entrepreneur—someone who stops looking for a job that fits and starts designing one that aligns. Whether you're launching a business, creating a side hustle, or dreaming up systems that work for your brain, this chapter offers tools to turn ideas into sustainable action.

Chapter 21

The ADHD Entrepreneur— Building Systems That Fit Your Brain

"I couldn't work for anyone else—so I hired myself."
(ADHD Entrepreneur, probably)

I still remember the moment one of my clients—let's call him Marcus—walked in and announced, "I finally figured it out. I'm not unmotivated. I'm unemployable."

He said it like a confession, but I heard it like a breakthrough.

Marcus had cycled through five jobs in two years. Fired once, ghosted another, rage-quit the third. "I get ideas," he told me, "but I can't do them on other people's timelines." When I asked what changed, he grinned and slid a scrappy notebook across my desk.

Inside was a half-baked blueprint for a mobile detailing business. He'd already made the name, the logo, and a hand-drawn map of every high-traffic neighborhood within twenty miles. Not because anyone told him to. But because at 2am—after watching a YouTube video of a guy restoring a grimy pickup to showroom shine—he felt something in his chest light up.

That something is what we're here to talk about.

Why ADHD Minds Gravitate Toward Entrepreneurship

Most people think ADHD folks are too scattered, too disorganized, too impulsive to run a business. That's a neat little theory—until you realize how many wildly successful founders, creatives, and bootstrappers either have ADHD or show every trait of it.

We're not allergic to work. We're allergic to meaningless work.

We're not bad at focus. We're bad at faking it on command.

We're not lazy. We're energy-efficient—we wait for the signal.

Entrepreneurship offers ADHD minds the freedom to structure life around internal logic—not clock time, not external systems, not neurotypical expectations of linear progress. The key is learning how to build scaffolding around your signals, not your "shoulds".

Building Your Business Around Signals, Not Schedules

Forget what the productivity gurus told you: most of their advice was written for brains that aren't yours.

- o Block scheduling? Feels like a trap.
- o Five-year plans? Anxiety in bullet-point form.
- o Early morning routine with cold plunges? You lost me at morning.

What most ADHD entrepreneurs need is not more discipline—it's better alignment. Alignment with when you think best. Move best. Connect best. When you feel moved to act—by meaning, urgency, curiosity, or vision.

Those are signals, and they are the natural fuel of ADHD productivity.

Visionary–Producer–Editor: The ADHD Business Blueprint

You've already met the Visionary, the Producer, and the Editor back in Chapter 15. But here's the twist: for entrepreneurs, this isn't just a metaphor. It's survival strategy.

Most ADHD entrepreneurs don't fail because they lack ideas—they fail because they try to be all three at once:

- o The Visionary who dreams it
- o The Producer who builds it
- o The Editor who organizes, refines, and sustains it

The VPE model lets ADHD founders stop blaming themselves for being "inconsistent" and start designing workflows that flex with how they think.

 Mini vignette: One founder I worked with loved the thrill of pitching ideas but dreaded contracts and bookkeeping. Once she brought in a partner who thrived in "Editor mode," her startup stopped stalling. She didn't need to change her wiring—she needed to
honor it.

You don't have to be all three at once. You just need to know when to step into each role—and who to bring in when you can't.

✧

Real-World Tools That Fit ADHD Brains

You don't need fancy systems—just systems that speak your signal language.

Think of tools not as rules—but as externalized signals. The best systems aren't built to control you. They're built to catch you when your brain zigzags.

Try:

- o **Signal-aligned Kanban boards**—visual task boards (physical sticky notes or digital cards) where you move tasks from "to-do" → "doing" → "done," here organized by energy states.
- o **Emotion-tagged CRMs**—a client-tracking tool (basically a smart address book for business contacts) set up so reminders pop based on the *feeling* you noted last time, not just a calendar date.

- o **Task batching by energy type**—grouping similar tasks so you can ride one energy wave (creative flow vs. admin grind) instead of constantly switching gears.
- o **Hiring or partnering with an Editor-type person**—someone who actually loves structure, details, or finishing touches, so you don't have to do it all.

 Mini vignette: A graphic designer I coached set up two Kanban boards: one for "creative flow" projects and one for "admin grind." On low-energy days she hit the admin board. On high-energy days, she rode the creative one. For the first time, she stopped calling herself "inconsistent."

✧

The Burnout Trap—When the Signal Becomes a Siren

Hyperfocus can turn into a supernova cycle:

1. Signal hits → excitement
2. You go all in → skip recovery
3. You ignore warning signs → spiral
4. Crash → collapse or shame loop
5. Shame loop → Doubt your ability → Start over with even more pressure

The fix? Create off-switches, embed recovery rituals, and separate your self-worth from your output.

The Inner Dashboard: Why ADHD Entrepreneurs Must Monitor Emotion, Energy, and Balance

Your business depends not just on what you do—but on your ability to monitor the status of your persona resources.

Quick reminders from earlier chapters:

- o **Stress Wagon (Ch.18):** Are you overloaded? Drop the nonessential.
- o **Energy rhythms (Ch.18):** What restores vs. drains you?
- o **Crystal, Steel, Plastic (Ch.4):** Are you protecting what really matters?

These aren't new tools—but as an entrepreneur, you'll need them more than ever.

Your Business Is Not Your Worth: Emotional Intelligence for ADHD Entrepreneurs

One of the hardest truths for ADHD entrepreneurs to internalize is this: **your business is not your worth.**

For many of us, rejection sensitivity and belief loops can become traps. A single lost client, a failed pitch, or a slow sales week can quickly spiral into:

"I failed at this project → that means I'm not cut out for business → which means I'm not good enough as a person."

That's a dangerous loop. It blurs the line between identity and outcome.

Think of your business like a lab experiment: every result is data, not destiny. Outcomes are feedback. Identity is who you are—and that is not up for negotiation.

Using the "Three E's" to Break the Loop
(Quick refresher from Chapter 18.)

The **Three E's model** offers a simple, portable way to step back and untangle the mess:

1. **Experience**: What happened?
   - "A potential investor didn't return my call."
   - "My first product launch only got a few sales."
2. **Evaluation**: What did I tell myself it meant?
   - "They're not interested because my idea isn't worth anything."
   - "Nobody bought because I'm not capable of running a business."
3. **Emotion**: What feeling did that create?
   - Shame.
   - Fear.
   - Hopelessness.

Notice the pattern: the *experience* itself is neutral, but my *evaluation* loads it with meaning—and that meaning generates the painful *emotion*.

Challenge the Loop
The next step is to **close the loop with truth.**

- The investor didn't call back → *that's data, not destiny.*
- A weak launch → *that's one iteration, not the final verdict.*
- Fewer clients than you hoped for → *that's a signal to adjust your offer, not a reflection of your character.*

Separating identity from outcome lets you stay in the game. Outcomes are feedback. Identity is who you are—and that is not up for negotiation.

A Practical Reframe
Instead of letting rejection sensitivity turn every "no" into a character judgment, practice this shift:

- **Old loop:** "They said no → I must not be good enough."
- **New loop:** "They said no → I learned something about fit, timing, or messaging. Now I can adjust."

One way to reinforce this reframe is to actually write it down in two columns: *What Happened* vs. *What I Made It Mean.*

This simple act of seeing your thought process on paper often breaks the spell.

Remember

Your business is an experiment. You are not.

Your worth does not rise and fall with quarterly profits. And the entrepreneurs who thrive are not the ones who never get rejected—they're the ones who refuse to confuse rejection with identity.

Final Reflection: Build the System That Loves You Back

What are you building that will still love you on your worst day?

What scaffolding will hold you up?

What truths will remind you who you are, even when your energy is gone?

The most sustainable business is the one shaped like you.

ADHD Entrepreneur Self-Check

1. **Energy Check**
   - Have I eaten in the last 4 hours?
   - Moved my body today?
   - Green/yellow/red zone?
   - What can I unload today?

2. **Signal Awareness**
   - What wants to be worked on right now?
   - Interest / urgency / relationship?
   - Need cue or accountability?
3. **Loop Awareness**
   - What happened?
   - What did I tell myself it meant?
   - What emotion followed?
   - Is that story true, or just familiar?

↻ Closing Reflection: What If This *Is* the Road?

Not everyone is built to follow a map. Some of us are built to draw them.

In this section, we've explored the ADHD mind not as something that *fails* to fit, but as something that *reimagines* the world—through interdisciplinary curiosity, signal-driven work, and creative independence. The polymath mind doesn't pick one lane. It sees the landscape. The calling-driven worker doesn't just chase a paycheck—they chase alignment. And the ADHD entrepreneur? They don't just launch a business. They build a system that lets them breathe.

This is the part of the journey that feels expansive. Possibility-rich. Sparked by signal. But what happens when the spark fades? When the plan doesn't land? When things fall apart?

That's where we're headed next.

→ Handoff to Part VI: *Failing Forward— What Happens When the System Breaks (and How You Grow Anyway)*

Part VI begins with a truth most ADHD learners know too well: Sometimes the scaffolding cracks. The sprint stalls. The signal vanishes.

In the next chapters, we'll explore what it means to fail—and how to reframe failure not as a verdict, but as a vital part of signal-based growth. We'll unpack shame spirals, burnout, self-doubt, and derailment. But more importantly, we'll show you how to track patterns, intervene early, and build antifragile systems that get stronger under stress.

Because thriving with ADHD doesn't mean never crashing.

It means learning how to rise better, smarter, and more aligned than before.

✸ Part VI: Failing Successfully— How to Fall, Learn, and Get Back Up Stronger

From Breakdown to Breakthrough— Learning to Fall Without Falling Apart

> *"If at first you don't succeed...*
> *congratulations. You're human."*
> —Somewhat Disappointed, Wildly Insightful Mentor

> *"You don't run into problems by standing still—*
> *you hit them when you're moving forward."*
> —Someone finally being honest about progress

Failure isn't optional. It's not a detour from the path—*it is the path*.

If you've lived with ADHD (or honestly, if you've lived at all), you've probably built an impressive résumé of false starts, flamed-out projects, lost passwords, and mysterious deadlines that were ... last week?

But here's the twist: people with ADHD don't just fail more *often*—they often fail *faster, harder,* and with more dramatic side effects. The stakes are higher. The consequences stick longer. And the shame can burrow deep.

But that's not the end of the story.

It's the beginning of a new one.

Over the course of this book, we've explored tools for signal awareness, emotional intelligence, motivation, and executive function—piece by piece, building a more complete picture of how the ADHD mind works. But once you bring all of those pieces into real life—with all its complexity, unpredictability, and demands—one thing becomes clear:

You're still going to fail.

That's not a flaw in the system.
That *is* the system.

We're often told that failure is part of growth.
That you have to fail to succeed.
That everyone fails, and failure builds resilience.
And that's all true. But here's the part most people leave out:

NO ONE EVER TEACHES YOU *HOW* TO FAIL!!!

How to notice when you're heading for a breakdown.

How to catch yourself in the early stages.

How to recover quickly—and how to mine the failure for useful data instead of self-loathing.

That's what this section is for.

Learning to deal with failure isn't just about enduring it—it's about *engaging* with it. That includes:

o **Averting failure** where possible—by spotting early signs and redirecting course
o **Recovering quickly** when the crash comes anyway
o **Learning deeply** from the experience, so the next time you stumble, you fall smarter ... or not at all.

This is where everything comes together.

This is where thriving becomes *resilient*—and eventually, *antifragile.*

And this is your opportunity to do some of the most important work any of us are called to do in life:

To face the hard parts without flinching.
To take the lessons, not the shame.
And to turn falling down into getting stronger.

Chapter 22

Failing Successfully—Why Failure Isn't Optional

*"The only real mistake is the one
from which we learn nothing."*
—Henry Ford

How to Fail at the System Level (and Get Stronger)

Failure isn't just something that happens to us. It's a critical part of how we learn, how we grow, and how we adapt to a world that doesn't come with clear instructions. This is doubly true for people with ADHD whose minds are wired not for perfect execution, but for *experiential learning*—trial, error, adjustment, and repeat.

📄 How to Use This Chapter

This chapter explores how failure—far from being a sign of weakness—is often the gateway to growth, especially for people with ADHD. It introduces the concept of antifragility and walks readers through the mindset and methods for failing early, recovering skillfully, and integrating feedback into future action.

As with other chapters in this book, the content is structured for three types of readers:

- o 🧠 For people with ADHD—to understand their own experiences and strategies
- o 🤝 For parents, educators, clinicians, and coaches—to better support others with ADHD
- o 💡 For curious minds—to explore the broader implications for learning and growth

🧠 For People with ADHD—Students, Workers, and Curious Minds

People with ADHD often struggle with delayed rewards, abstract rules, and purely theoretical instruction. They learn best through immediate feedback, real-world consequences, and hands-on experience. In short: **trial and error**.

This doesn't mean ADHD minds are broken—it means they're designed to engage directly with the world, to learn by doing (and sometimes by crashing). The downside? This learning style tends to rack up more visible failures, especially in systems that punish mistakes instead of embracing them.

But seen differently, this is a superpower. Trial-and-error learning isn't a flaw—it's a powerful feedback loop. People with ADHD, when supported well, can become masters of creative problem-solving and innovation, precisely because they've lived through more real-world iterations than most. They learn by doing, adjusting, and trying again—and that resilience becomes a strength.

You're not just wired to survive stress. You're wired to adapt—*if* you can break the shame loop that says failure is proof of unworthiness.

So if you:

- o Overthink every choice because you fear doing it wrong
- o Self-sabotage or procrastinate when the risk of failure feels too high
- o Avoid new challenges because past failures still sting

Then this chapter is your guide to breaking that cycle. The goal isn't to be fearless—it's to become **failure-wise.**

⚖️ The Real Cost of Avoiding Failure

In an effort to avoid pain, many people try to engineer their lives to be as risk-free as possible. Parents often do this too—with the best of intentions. Wanting to protect their children from disappointment, rejection, or consequences, they may create bubble-wrapped lives where failure is minimized or even eliminated. But in doing so, they may also be eliminating the child's opportunity to learn how to fail well—and how to recover.

SAVING OUR KIDS FROM DISAPPOINTMENT, REJECTION, OR CONSEQUENCES

This is especially true for those with a history of shame, perfectionism, or high sensitivity to rejection—common companions to ADHD. But in trying not to fail, we often cut ourselves off from the very conditions required for growth.

Avoiding failure looks like:

- ○ Only doing what feels safe or familiar
- ○ Holding back effort to protect your ego
- ○ Waiting until conditions are perfect before starting

But the hidden cost is enormous: stagnation, missed opportunities, and a fragile sense of self that can't withstand even small disruptions. In trying to avoid one kind of pain, we guarantee another.

◑ ◑ Fragile, Resilient, and Antifragile

Philosopher and statistician Nassim Taleb offers a model that reframes how systems (including people) respond to stress and failure:

- **Fragile systems** break when stressed. They depend on stability.
- **Resilient systems** withstand stress. They return to baseline.
- **Antifragile systems** actually grow stronger under stress. They use disruption to evolve.

A helpful metaphor:

A fragile system is like a **candle in the wind**—the wind blows, and the flame goes out.

- A resilient system is like a **camping lantern**—the wind blows, and the flame holds steady.
- An antifragile system is like a **campfire**—the wind blows, and the flames burn brighter.

Real-Life Student Examples

- **Fragile (Candle):**
  A student studies all night for one exam and depends on getting an "A" to feel okay about themselves. When the professor gives them a C, they shut down completely: *"I'll never succeed in college. I'm not cut out for this."* One bad outcome feels like the end of everything.
- **Resilient (Lantern):**
  Another student also gets a C, but instead of collapsing, they regroup: *"That stung. But I'll review my notes differently next time and maybe get tutoring."* They bounce back, returning to baseline.
- **Antifragile (Campfire):**
  A third student gets the same C and uses it as fuel: *"Okay, I clearly misunderstood the way this professor tests. Now I know I need to practice their style of questions. Next time, I'll be better prepared."* The failure doesn't just leave them standing—it makes them sharper and stronger.

Why All Three Matter

Each system has its place:

- **Fragility** can be important when something *must* be preserved exactly (like your GPA meeting a scholarship minimum). In those cases, you protect it—extra studying, backup reminders, asking for accommodations.

- o **Resilience** is crucial for everyday setbacks. You won't always ace things—bouncing back quickly keeps you moving forward.
- o **Antifragility** is how you grow long-term. Every stumble becomes feedback that refines your system. Instead of just recovering, you improve.

The Bigger Point
Learning how to fail means learning these three modes— when each is necessary, and how to move between them. Sometimes you protect (fragile), sometimes you endure (resilient), and sometimes you adapt and grow (antifragile).

This chapter isn't about becoming bulletproof. It's about becoming adaptive—using stress, mistakes, and breakdowns as fuel in the feedback loop that makes you stronger. Not just surviving difficulty, but growing through it.

🌱 Why Small Failures Beat Big Crashes
Here's a pattern a lot of people with ADHD know all too well: You miss a few early signs. You tell yourself you'll catch up. You push through. And then—crash. You're behind, burned out, or feeling like you blew it completely.

But those crashes rarely come out of nowhere. They usually start small:

- o You show up late to class a few times.
- o You forget to turn in an assignment.
- o You convince yourself the quiz "doesn't really count."

- o You miss a class because you feel behind—and now feel more behind.
- o You stop checking your email or syllabus because it's just too much.

Each of these moments might seem small on its own—but they're signals. And stacked together, they form a pattern. A pattern the Success Curve (coming in Chapter 25) is designed to help you recognize and interrupt.

That Curve shows how people with ADHD often move from "doing okay" into "struggling silently" then into a tailspin—often without realizing how fast it's happening.

But here's the good news: the earlier you catch the signal, the easier it is to fix.

One missed assignment is a chance to notice your planning system isn't working. One skipped class might reveal something's off with sleep, motivation, or structure. These aren't moral failures—they're course corrections in disguise.

When we ignore them? The cost goes up. More stress. More shame. More clean-up. Small failures are data you can use. Big crashes are what happen when you ignore the data too long.

That's why learning to pay attention early—to your own early-warning signs—is one of the smartest, most self-respecting things you can do.

⚒ Building Antifragility (Without Reading a Textbook)

Nassim Taleb outlines several habits that help systems (including people) become stronger under stress. Here's what those ideas sound like in real life:

- o Cut the crap that's not working. Don't just keep adding

planners, apps, or hacks. Start by removing what's draining you. (Taleb calls this *via negativa*—getting stronger by subtracting.)

- o Leave margin. Give yourself extra time, wiggle room, or backup plans. Don't schedule your day so tight that one delay topples everything.
- o Bet small, but bet often. Try things that might fail—but in low-stakes ways. Test study techniques, time routines, or conversation openers. Learn fast and adjust.
- o Build for bounce-back. Don't aim for perfect performance. Aim for recoverability. If something knocks you down, how quickly can you get up and try again?
- o Put some skin in the game. You learn better when the outcome matters to you. Make your goals personal, not just required.

These are antifragile moves—and the ADHD brain is often accidentally wired for them. It's already living in a world of trial and error. The trick is learning how to use that as a strength instead of treating it like a flaw.

And one last thing: you'll get an even clearer picture of how this all plays out in Chapter 25, when we introduce the Success Curve—a visual map that shows how breakdowns happen, what the early warning signs look like, and how to reroute before you crash.

⤨ Reframing Failure as Feedback

Failure is not a moral statement. It's not proof of inadequacy. It's a **signal**. Something didn't work. Something needs adjusting. And that's *all* it means—until we load it up with shame and self-judgment.

When failure is seen as information rather than identity, it becomes one of the most powerful tools in your personal toolkit. Ask:

- What didn't go as planned?
- What signal did I miss or ignore?
- What might I do differently next time?

These aren't punishment questions. They're design questions. You're building your system—not judging your worth.

✦

Antifragility as a Mindset

Antifragility isn't just a trait—it's a mindset. A way of relating to mistakes with curiosity instead of condemnation. It's the belief that you're *not finished yet.* That you can become wiser, stronger, and more skillful with every iteration.

It means being open to stress—not recklessly, but *strategically.* It means building a system (and a life) that welcomes feedback instead of fearing it. It means recognizing that failing doesn't make you a failure. It makes you a *learner.*

And sometimes, to become antifragile, you first have to allow yourself to become fragile.

✦

A Personal Story: Learning to Be Fragile

"Vulnerability sounds like truth and feels like courage."
—Brené Brown

My father died in 1997. It was very painful. I had never experienced loss like this.

My way of dealing with his death was to focus on caring for my grieving mother and my siblings ... pretty much everyone else who was experiencing the pain of this loss. I conveniently overlooked the fact that I was one of those. It didn't go well for me.

Organizing my mom's financial, social, and living circumstances took a lot of my attention. When I returned to my counseling practice, I threw myself into work in a new way that I attributed to appreciating life after seeing the alternative.

Several friends reached out to me during this time, encouraging me to join them for dinner, concerts, or just to come by and talk. I always found myself too busy and made that my standing excuse.

And one day out of the blue, I woke up and wondered if I wanted to continue being a therapist. I began to seriously think of a career change. A friend suggested I attend a men's weekend retreat called "The New Warrior Training Adventure."

The weekend was brilliantly designed to be a place where men could be safely fragile. They could drop down into the raw spaces of their deepest unmet needs and most painful sadness of unhealed wounds … openly. I did that. And it was very hard. And very good.

It seemed that I had allowed myself to consciously become Fragile for the first time in a very long time … maybe ever. And after that I continued to find occasion to be effectively Fragile. Not just with the deep rooted and hidden stuff, but with the day-to-day difficulties and discouragements that life brings as well.

I began to feel more alive. And I decided to continue to be a therapist. I'm glad I did that.

The road to antifragility almost always passes through vulnerability. And the work of becoming whole often begins at the exact moment we let go of pretending we already are.

👥 For Parents, Educators, Clinicians, Coaches, and Curious Minds

If you support someone with ADHD—as a parent, coach, educator, or therapist—your relationship with failure shapes theirs more than you might realize.

People with ADHD already live with a heightened sensitivity to perceived judgment, a tendency toward shame, and often a long history of being misunderstood. If failure is treated as a character flaw, they will learn to hide it. If it's treated as feedback, they will learn to learn from it.

What helps most?

- **Normalize failure.** Talk openly about your own. Share how you got through it—or didn't—and what you learned.
- **Ask engineering questions.** What didn't work? What can we try next? This helps move the focus from blame to iteration.
- **Value effort over outcome.** Especially when risk-taking or novelty is involved.
- **Don't bubble-wrap their life.** It's tempting to prevent failure, especially in kids you love. But safe, supported failure is essential for building antifragility. If they never fall, they never learn how to get up.
- **Coach the recovery.** Help them name what went wrong, what they felt, and what their next experiment will be.

Support doesn't mean protecting them from every stumble—it means walking with them *through* the stumbles and helping them gather wisdom as they go.

📑 References for Further Reading

o **Brown, B. (2012).** *Daring greatly: How the courage to be vulnerable transforms the way we live, love, parent, and lead.* **Gotham Books.**
Brown emphasizes that failure and vulnerability are not weaknesses but pathways to connection and growth. Her insights help ADHD students see that admitting struggle or rejection is part of building resilience rather than proof of inadequacy.

o **Ford, H. (1922).** *My life and work.* **Garden City Publishing.**
Ford's reflections on experimentation and persistence illustrate resilience in action. His well-known belief that "failure is only the opportunity to begin again more intelligently" captures the antifragile spirit—mistakes as raw material for improvement.

o **Sinek, S. (2009).** *Start with why: How great leaders inspire everyone to take action.* **Portfolio.**
Sinek's work complements the antifragile model by showing how a strong sense of purpose provides stability when external outcomes falter. For ADHD learners, anchoring in "why" helps separate identity from temporary failure and sustains momentum through setbacks.

o **Taleb, N. N. (2012).** *Antifragile: Things that gain from disorder.* **Random House.**
Taleb's concept of antifragility provides the backbone for this chapter—systems that don't just withstand stress but actually improve because of it. His model reframes failure as fuel for growth, a message especially vital for ADHD students learning to fail successfully.

Coming up next: Of course, failing successfully isn't only about systems and strategies. Sometimes failure doesn't just knock over your plans—it knocks you over. You might even say it gets personal. That's where we turn next: the emotional side of failure—the shame spirals, the identity hits, and the long road back to rising stronger.

Chapter 23

The Fall and the Fire—When Failure Gets Personal

Sometimes the fire burns everything down—and that's how we discover what can't be destroyed."
—Jon Thomas

How to Use This Chapter

In the last chapter, we explored how failure functions at the system level—how habits, feedback, and antifragile design help you grow through setbacks.

This chapter goes deeper. What happens when failure doesn't just wreck your plans, but wrecks your confidence? When shame creeps in and whispers that *you are the failure*?

Here, we turn inward—to the emotional and identity side of falling down. You'll learn how shame spirals form, how to break them, and how to rebuild a sense of self that can grow even through the fire.

✧

For People with ADHD—Students, Workers, and Curious Minds

When Failure Feels Like Identity

The ADHD mind is wired for intensity—in effort, in emotion, in experience. Which means when failure comes, it doesn't just topple your plans. It can knock you flat.

What was an external stumble a moment ago suddenly feels internal: not *"I failed"* but *"I am a failure."* Shame hits faster. Self-doubt cuts deeper. And if those stories aren't challenged, they begin to rewrite identity itself.

This chapter is about that deeper fire—the one that burns hot enough to test who you think you are. It's about what happens when failure gets personal, and how to walk through the ashes to find what still remains.

 In this chapter, you'll learn:

- o   How to recognize and disrupt patterns of shame
- o   Why vulnerability is a strength, not a weakness
- o   How to build bounce-back capacity with intention
- o   How to rise again with identity intact and purpose clearer

The Shame Spiral Map

Failure is painful enough. But shame adds fuel to the fire. Here's how it often plays out:

1. **Trigger** → Something goes wrong. (You bomb a test. Your boss criticizes your work. A friend ghosts you.)
2. **Story** → You explain it with self-attack. ("I'm stupid." "I'll never get this right." "I always screw things up.")
3. **Emotion** → Shame, hopelessness, anger at yourself.
4. **Avoidance** → You pull back—procrastinate, hide, stop trying.
5. **Reinforcement** → The avoidance creates new problems, which confirm the story. The spiral tightens.

Breaking the Spiral: The 4 N's

- o **Notice** → "I just bombed that quiz."
- o **Name** → "The story I'm telling myself is that I'm stupid."
- o **Normalize** → "Everyone fails sometimes. One quiz doesn't define my intelligence."
- o **Next Step** → "Email the professor for feedback. Make a new study plan."

☞ Think of this as a **firebreak**—a line you draw so the flames don't spread. The failure still happened, but the shame doesn't get to burn everything down.

Narrative Rewriting
Shame thrives on rigid stories. Resilience thrives on reframing them.

- o Old story: *"I bombed that exam, so I'm not college material."*
- o New story: *"I didn't study the professor's way. Now I know how to prepare differently next time."*
- o Old story: *"My business launch flopped—I'm not cut out for this."*
- o New story: *"That version didn't connect. Now I have data to adjust my offer."*

📖 **Journaling prompts:**

- o What happened?
- o What did I tell myself it meant?

- o What else could it mean?
- o What's one small action I can take from here?

Mini Recovery Stories

- o **College Student:** After dropping a class, she told herself she "wasn't cut out for college." With support, she reframed it as a *course mismatch*, not a personal failure. She re-enrolled, got tutoring, and graduated on time.
- o **Young Entrepreneur:** A product launch flopped, and he decided it meant he wasn't "meant for business." Coaching helped him see it as iteration. The next launch worked. Same person, new story.

🜕 From Fragile to Antifragile—Learning to Rise Again

In Chapter 22, we explored how systems can be fragile, resilient, or antifragile. The same pattern shows up in our *sense of self*. Failure isn't just about what we do—it's about who we believe we are.

- o **Fragile self** → collapses under shame.
- o **Resilient self** → bends, feels pain, but bounces back.
- o **Antifragile self** → grows stronger because of stress, not in spite of it.

The shift happens when you stop asking, *"What does this*

failure say about me?" and start asking, *"What can this failure teach me?"*

Fragile

To be fragile is to break under pressure. Early experiences of failure—especially if tied to humiliation or punishment—can teach us that mistakes are dangerous, even shameful.

Signs of fragility in identity:

- o   Believing one mistake invalidates all progress
- o   Avoiding challenges for fear of looking stupid
- o   Overidentifying with old failure stories

Resilient

Resilience is the ability to bend without breaking. It starts with permission to feel pain—followed by tools for recovery.

Tools that build resilience:

- o Narrative reframing: *"What's another way to tell this story?"*
- o Emotional processing: journaling, therapy, or trusted conversation
- o Small action planning: one concrete next step

Antifragile

Antifragility is more than recovery—it's transformation. Instead of just bouncing back, you bounce forward.

Questions that build antifragility:

- What did this failure teach me?
- What strengths did I discover under pressure?
- How can I redesign my system to grow from this?

When failure is metabolized in this way, it becomes fuel. Not the kind that burns you down—the kind that fires you up.

Your Story Isn't Over

There's a quiet moment after the fire when you realize: *I'm still here.*

The plan failed. The relationship ended. The attempt back-fired. But something remains. That ember—wiser, humbler, maybe a little singed—is real.

Fragility isn't a flaw. It's often the most honest place you can be. But with support, fragility can become resilience. And with practice, resilience can become antifragility.

✧

👥 For Parents, Clinicians, Educators, and Curious Minds

People recovering from failure—especially people with ADHD—don't just need solutions. They need space to be fragile, support to be resilient, and guidance to become antifragile.

This chapter helps you:

○ Understand the emotional cost of public failure and private shame
○ Offer reflective listening instead of advice too soon
○ Support bounce-back practices without minimizing pain
○ Model your own relationship with failure and growth

Your role isn't to shield them from fire—it's to help them discover what remains when the smoke clears. That's the foundation they'll build from.

Helping someone move from fragility to resilience—and eventually to antifragility—requires more than encouragement. It takes modeling, mirroring, and careful permission to be vulnerable without being undone by it.

ADHD minds are often intensely sensitive and emotionally reactive. They may bounce between feeling overexposed and defensive, especially after setbacks. For these individuals, **failure is not just an event—it's often interpreted as evidence of unworthiness**.

Here's what helps most in guiding someone through this emotional terrain:

○ **Model emotional recovery out loud.** Share your own stories of failing, feeling worthless, and finding your footing again.

- o **Respond to shame disclosures with calm.** If a student says "I'm a failure," meet it with empathy: *"I can hear how painful this feels. Failing at something doesn't mean you are a failure."*
- o **Expand emotional vocabulary.** Help name feelings like disappointment, grief, or embarrassment so they don't all collapse into "I suck."
- o **Create safe disclosure spaces.** If failures are met with panic, criticism, or quick fixes, the sharing stops.
- o **Don't over-rescue.** Support repair, but let them experience natural consequences. Strength is built not from never falling, but from learning how to rise with help.

Your role isn't to shield them from fire—it's to help them discover what survives when the smoke clears.

Finally, remember that **fragility is not a flaw—it's a phase.** Being fragile is sometimes the most honest place a person can be. And with the right kind of support, it can become the launchpad to strength.

✦

References for Further Reading

o **Brown, B. (2012). *Daring greatly: How the courage to be vulnerable transforms the way we live, love, parent, and lead.* Gotham Books.**
Complements *Rising Strong* by focusing on why vulnerability is not weakness but strength. Encourages readers—and those supporting ADHD learners—to see openness about failure as a critical step in building antifragility.

o **Brown, B. (2015). *Rising strong: The reckoning. The rumble. The revolution.* Spiegel & Grau.**
Brown offers a framework for moving through failure by first acknowledging pain, then "rumbling" with the hard emotions, and finally rewriting the story in a way that restores strength. Especially useful for ADHD readers who equate mistakes with identity collapse—Brown normalizes vulnerability as a prerequisite for resilience.

o **Goleman, D. (1995). *Emotional intelligence: Why it can matter more than IQ.* Bantam.**
Introduces the idea that recognizing and regulating emotions is key to long-term success. His model highlights why ADHD individuals, who often feel emotions intensely, need tools for reframing failure rather than letting shame define them.

o **Linehan, M. (2015). *DBT skills training manual.* Guilford Press.**
Provides practical tools for managing overwhelming emotions and breaking destructive cycles. Skills like distress tolerance and emotion labeling can help ADHD minds interrupt shame spirals and return to resilience after setbacks.

o **Van der Kolk, B. (2014). *The body keeps the score.* Viking.**
Explains how unresolved trauma and shame "live in the body" and can freeze forward motion. For ADHD learners, this helps make sense of why failure sometimes feels like more than disappointment—it feels visceral. Healing begins with safe vulnerability and identity repair.

o **Up next: Chapter 24—Standing Tall Before the Man: The Heuristics of Accountability.**
Rising again isn't always just about private resilience.

Sometimes it means facing another kind of failure—not just personal stumbles or hidden shame, but the kind that calls you to stand tall before others. That's where we turn next: accountability as a sacred confrontation with failure.

Chapter 24

Standing Tall Before the Man— Accountability as a Sacred Confrontation With Failure

"... Now answer my question or you'll be
standing tall before the man!"
—Full Metal Jacket

📜 How to Use This Chapter

This chapter is about the rare and underrated skill of taking responsibility. We'll explore what accountability means—not just as punishment, but as a practice that builds identity, earns trust, and enables real learning from failure.

You'll see what restorative justice looks like in real life, how ADHD impulsivity can lead to trouble, and what it means to come back into integrity after making a mistake. You'll also learn why avoiding accountability leads to fragility—and how facing the music builds antifragile character.

🧠 For People with ADHD—Students, Workers, and Curious Minds

ADHD impulsivity, emotional intensity, and rejection sensitivity can all make accountability feel terrifying. But learning to face consequences, own your impact, and restore trust is one of the most powerful things you can do for your future.

In this chapter, you'll:

- Understand the difference between punishment and accountability
- See how restorative justice can lead to healing—not just guilt
- Learn how to apologize, make amends, and regain integrity
- Recognize that real strength is built through honest repair

Accountability isn't about perfection. It's about growth. And it's a core piece of becoming antifragile.

✦

For Parents, Educators, Clinicians, Coaches, and Curious Minds

Too often, young people are either over-punished or let off the hook. Neither teaches accountability. What works is restorative responsibility—a process that includes acknowledging harm, repairing it, and rejoining the community with trust rebuilt.

In this chapter, you'll:

- Learn how shame disrupts the development of accountability
- Discover how to use natural consequences as learning tools
- Understand the role of community in restorative justice
- See the long-term benefits of allowing young people to face the impact of their actions—and make them right

Support doesn't mean shielding. It means walking with someone as they face what's hard, and helping them stand tall.

✦

⚖️ A Very Personal Case Study: My Encounter with ADHD Impulsivity, Foolishness, and Restorative Justice

> *"... he cried, 'Somebody help me.' I can't help you ... you brought this shit upon yourself ..."*
> —From a song by Jim Fredo and Dwyne Chambers

I had my greatest lesson in accountability and restorative justice during the peak of my hyperactive adolescence in my very small rural hometown. One fine day, a group of my bored ADHD friends and I decided it would be great fun to drive down select country roads hitting mailboxes with bottles thrown from our moving car.

It started with a few empty beer bottles, and we got skilled pretty quickly. But there were plenty of bottles lying about in those days. And plenty of mailboxes. So, we got even better. And knocked down several of the mailboxes as a result of our improved skills and foolish intent.

In the high stimulation and adrenaline of our excitement, we reinforced each other in our anti-social pact increasingly into the recursion of destructiveness. It was a great deal of fun.

And then we got caught.

In our small town we had a Justice of the Peace official and tiny local system of law enforcement. They all knew us by name and considered us good kids (at heart). Most importantly, they knew our parents – and called them up. See, though we were good kids (at heart), we had been in trouble before. They advised us that our parents had each told them to "do what they need to do with us" and declined to come to the proceedings. We didn't realize the proceedings were "informal" and included secret input from our absent parents. We did know, however, that we were pretty much screwed.

The justice of the peace brought us into his office where a U.S. Postal official arrived later to advise us as to the cost of our actions. We listened in horror as he explained that the law provides a penalty of two to ten years in prison and a fine of up to $10,000 FOR EACH MAILBOX! As to total number of mailboxes we had destroyed? I'd have to rely on that Clint Eastwood statement, "... Well, to tell you the truth, in all this excitement, I've kinda lost count myself." Let's just say it was – several.

The room began to smell bad as at least one of our group lost bowel and/or bladder function. The justice of the peace went on to explain that they knew we were good kids, but the law was unfortunately pretty clear. And they would do all they could to help us.

And then they left us there alone. With all that bad smell. And fear.

They came back periodically, offering us small particles of hope. Like a plea deal that involved only two years in prison for each mailbox ... which later became only two years in prison for the total of the damage done.

Eventually; (just short of forever), they came back with a plan. If we were to go out and replace all the mailboxes with an even better mailbox, speak to each homeowner to "satisfactorily explain our actions" and pay a fine – we might find redemption in the eyes of the law.

We collectively and spontaneously fell to our knees expressing our gratitude and willingness to do this noble work.

And work we did. In the hot Texas sun, we built some of the most beautiful mailboxes seen in this part of the world. We decorated with artwork and landscaped with drought resistant plants.

After speaking with the first three or four families about our misdeeds, we began to understand that there really was no sensible explanation for what we had done. In the fullness of a healthy, community-building shame, we stood tall before these great men and women and humbly asked their forgiveness.

Now here's the unexpected part. These folks were firm and let us know clearly that they didn't appreciate what we had done. But they indicated they understood people make mistakes and that young people make rather stupid mistakes at times. I remember one elderly farmer saying something to the effect of "it takes a village to raise an idiot." They were understanding and forgiving. And they also appreciated our work.

But most importantly, we could meet these people in town on Saturday mornings and look them in the eye. They shook hands with us and asked how we were doing in such a way that we knew they really wanted to know. They cared that we were on the good side of things and were doing something with our lives.

We were blessed by this justice.

Working with adolescents and young adults with ADHD, I frequently encounter many who run afoul of the law. The combination of ADHD impulsivity, hyperactivity, and youthful poor judgment delivers them bound and chained to difficult challenges in today's world of high-cost temptations.

At these times, I wonder what I'd be doing now if I had not experienced the restorative justice of enlightened community leaders. What might my life be like now if I'd been sent to prison as punishment? Or where would my values have led me if my parents had intervened and paid my way out of the trouble I had created for myself and others? Or what would have happened if I hadn't been apprehended – and had instead gotten completely away with it?

At these times, I wish all young people who get themselves into trouble could have the extraordinary opportunity I had. It truly changed my life.

Imagine what society might be like if more young people were held truly accountable for their actions as opposed to punished, overlooked, or excused from responsibility? If they could experience the opportunity to heal the people and institutions wronged by their impulsive actions? Imagine the benefits if more of our youth had the opportunity to learn that can only come from "standing tall before the Man?"

For my part, I never felt taller in my life than the moment I righted my wrongs, was forgiven, and was back into full integrity with people I had wronged.

It might not serve the bottom line of the private prison industry, but imagine how much more empowered and connected our communities could be—if we saw ourselves as part of the solution. Raising, guiding, and correcting young people through restorative justice, so they could grow up not just in society, but *of* it. In integrity. In belonging.

📑 References for Further Reading

• **Braithwaite, J. (2002).** *Restorative Justice and Responsive Regulation.* Oxford University Press.
A foundational text in restorative justice, exploring how flexible, community-based approaches to accountability can promote healing over punishment.

• **Karp, D. R. (2015).** *The Little Book of Restorative Justice for Colleges and Universities.* Good Books.
A practical guide for applying restorative principles in academic communities. Offers language and examples particularly useful for supporting young adults in school settings.

• **Regier, N. (2023).** *Compassionate Accountability: The Art of Connection and Getting Results.* Berrett-Koehler Publishers.
Explores how accountability rooted in empathy can strengthen relationships and fuel personal growth. Highly accessible for young adults learning to move from shame to self-responsibility.

• **Zehr, H. (2015).** *Changing Lenses: Restorative Justice for Our Times.* Herald Press.
A deeply compassionate reimagining of justice as a process of repair, not retribution. Zehr's storytelling approach makes abstract concepts tangible and personally meaningful.

Up Next: Chapter 25—The Anatomy of a Crash: Understanding the Success Curve

Accountability closes the loop on failure. But what if you could see the failure coming—before the crash? In the next chapter, we'll map the invisible warning signs that lead to breakdown, and how to chart your path back toward thriving.

Chapter 25

The Anatomy of a Crash— Understanding the Success Curve

*"You don't drown by falling in the water.
You drown by staying there."*
—Edwin Louis Cole

Failure often feels like it comes out of nowhere. One minute you're keeping up. The next, you're buried under overdue tasks, missed deadlines, broken promises, or lost momentum you can't seem to get back.

But here's the truth: failure is almost never sudden. It's a process. A pattern. And most of us live it again and again.

The Success Curve is a visual framework for understanding how people with ADHD (and many others) drift from thriving to barely-holding-on to full collapse. It draws inspiration from relapse prevention models in addiction recovery, but it applies just as easily to school, work, motivation, and mental health.

This isn't just a failure map. It's a dashboard—a way to track signals *before* they escalate. A way to see the patterns that repeat in your life, and then shift them.

And it all started with a story.

The Origin Story: Jabo and the Curve

Years ago, I was working with a client I'll call Jabo—a reflective, rough-edged member of a motorcycle club who was trying to stay sober after years of addiction. He was smart, capable, and genuinely trying to get his life together. But he kept falling off track.

Every time he relapsed, he'd describe the same cycle: things would be going fine, then something would shift, and within weeks (sometimes days) he'd spiral. Not because he didn't see it coming, but because he didn't *recognize* what he was seeing until he was already at the bottom.

One day, in session, I grabbed a piece of paper and drew a simple slope:

- A curved line, starting high and gradually dipping downward.
- At the peak: high functioning, routines, clarity.
- In the middle: stress rising, priorities slipping, life looking "tine" from the outside.
- At the bottom: collapse.

Jabo stared at it, then nodded slowly. *"That's it. That's exactly what it feels like."*

We started adding markings—emotional shifts, warning signs, turning points. It wasn't just a diagram anymore. It was a mirror.

Since then, I've shared versions of the curve with students, parents, teachers, doctors, creatives, and professionals across fields. Again and again, they point at it and say the same thing: *"That's me."*

What began as a scribble became a powerful tool to predict, recognize, and reverse downward spirals. But more importantly, it revealed something deeper:

 We succeed and fail in patterns. And once we can see those patterns, we can shift them.

✧

The Shape of Collapse: Zones of the Curve

The Success Curve, inspired in part by Terence Gorski's relapse prevention model, adapts that insight to the everyday breakdowns of ADHD life.

It's divided into three zones:

Zone 1: Thriving

Here, things work. You have structure, rhythm, clarity. Energy feels renewable. Mistakes are recoverable. You're in motion, and that motion is forward.

- You know what you're doing and why it matters.
- Your habits support your goals.
- You have margin to recover from stress.
- Other people may comment on how "together" you seem.

Zone 2: Slipping

The danger zone—and the hardest to recognize. Outwardly, you may still look fine. But underneath, you're compensating.

- o Skipping tasks and telling yourself it's no big deal
- o More reactive, less intentional
- o Self-care drops off
- o Anxiety and shame creep in, but you mask it well

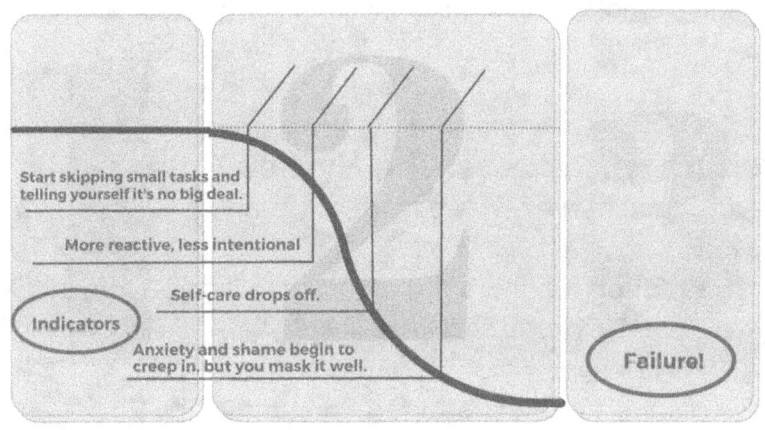

Zone 2 is so dangerous because it feels survivable. You

convince yourself you'll catch up later. But these aren't random slips. They're **patterns in motion**.

Zone 3: Crashing

This is when the bill comes due. Deadlines are missed. Sleep is erratic. Communication collapses. You isolate. Tasks feel impossible. You start to believe *you are the failure*.

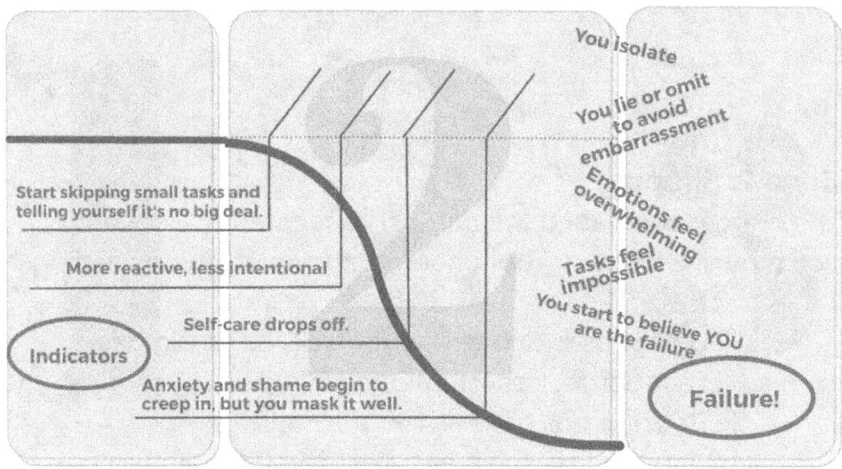

Sometimes no one else even sees it—people with ADHD often mask remarkably well. But the crash always comes.

Product vs. Process: The Hidden Split

In every zone, there are two kinds of data:

o **Product:** What are the outcomes? Did you turn in the paper? Did you show up?
o **Process:** How did you get there? Were you rested, steady, supported—or hanging by a thread?

Zone 2 often fools us, because product can still look okay while process is falling apart. You're still turning things in... but you're pulling all-nighters, ghosting people, living on caffeine and shame.

That's why tracking **process** is essential. If you only measure outcomes, you'll miss the curve until it's steep.

Failure Isn't Random—It's Patterned

When people say they "suddenly crashed," what really happened was a chain of ignored signals. A missed assignment → guilt → procrastination → skipped class → unprepared test → failing grade → shame → avoidance.

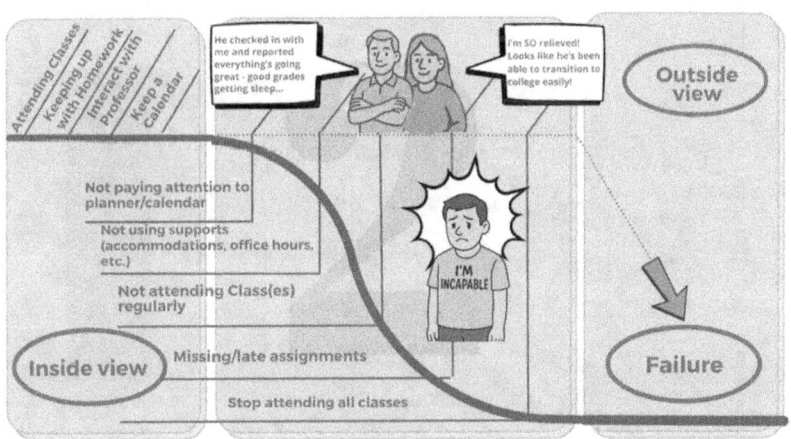

From the outside, it looks like a sharp drop-off. From the inside, it was a pattern all along.

☞ This is the heartbeat of the Success Curve: failure is not a single event. It's a repeating sequence. If you can learn your sequence, you can learn where to step in and change it.

Relapse, Recovery, and the Road Back

Psychologist Terence Gorski mapped relapse as a predictable series of stages. We've adapted his framework for ADHD and everyday breakdowns:

1. **Warning Phase**—skipped meals, sleep disruption, rising stress
2. **Avoidance & Rationalization**—"I'm fine, it's just a busy week"
3. **Loss of Structure**—routines unravel, coping fades
4. **Disconnection**—shame, isolation, avoidance of feedback
5. **Acting Out**—impulsivity, meltdowns, collapse of responsibilities
6. **Crash**—the full breakdown

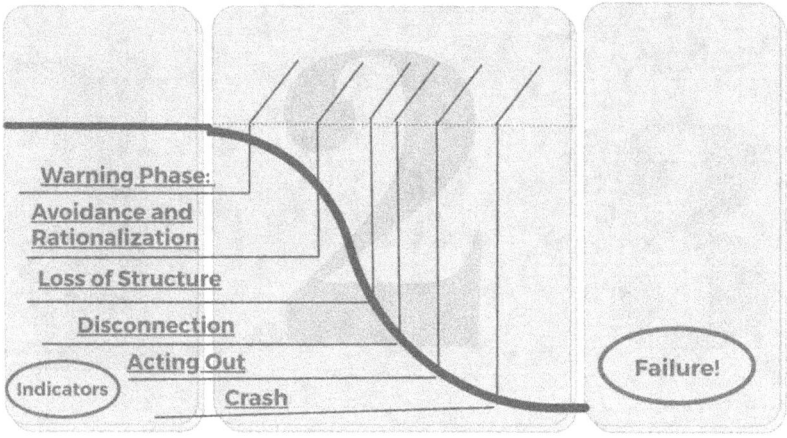

The genius of Gorski's model is this: relapse doesn't begin with the drink or the drug. It begins with the first ignored signal.

The same is true here.

And the earlier you notice, the smaller the correction you need.

✦

Indicators and Antidotes

 Indicators = the "check engine" lights of your life. Early, small signals.
Examples:

- Snoozing repeatedly and skipping morning structure
- Avoiding messages or responsibilities
- Feeling low-level guilt or anxiety without action
- Dropping restorative habits like exercise or journaling

🏷️ **Antidotes** = targeted course corrections.
Examples:

- Reset your calendar for 10 minutes
- Text a friend and set up a short check-in
- Open the assignment and write for 15 minutes
- Go to bed on time *tonight* instead of planning a "perfect reset" tomorrow

Principle: The earlier you act, the smaller the antidote. Delay, and the solution must be bigger, harder, more uncomfortable.

✦

The Sooner, the Simpler

The beauty of catching early indicators is that antidotes can be light, even enjoyable:

- Indicator: "I skipped my usual planning session."

→ Antidote: Spend 10 minutes resetting your to-do list.
o Indicator: "I haven't had a good conversation in a few days."
→ Antidote: Text a friend to grab coffee.
o Indicator: "I keep putting off this paper."
→ Antidote: Open the doc and write for 15 minutes.

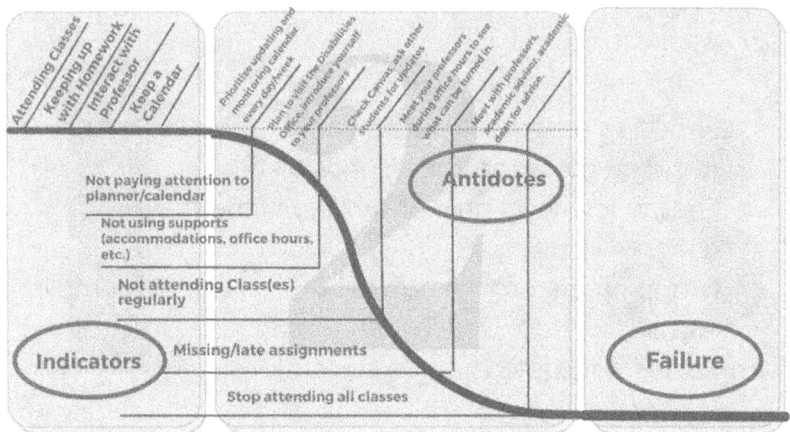

But if you ignore these? The curve steepens. Antidotes must become heavier: accountability meetings, advisor interventions, even crisis triage.

☞ *Key principle: the sooner you respond, the simpler the antidote.*

✧

A Relapse Story, Revisited

Remember Jabo? His early indicator might be subtle: *"I'm not having fun anymore."* His antidote? Spend time with sober friends fishing.

But when he ignored that, the pattern deepened. He hit the turning point: *"I think I can go back to the bar and just have one."* That's when small antidotes no longer worked. He needed big ones: sponsor support, emergency meetings, full resets.

Same curve. Same process. Different arena.

Your Success Curve, Your Antidotes

What are *your* early indicators?

What slips first when you're drifting?

What antidotes actually work for you?

At the end of this chapter, you'll find a worksheet to map your personal curve—naming your indicators and pairing them with antidotes. This is one of the most powerful tools you can build, and it only gets stronger with use.

Why It Works in the Real World

In every ADHD College Success workshop, we have students map their Success Curve before the semester begins. They identify early indicators and design antidotes in advance.

And again and again, we hear the same feedback:

"That curve saved my butt."

Not because it prevents all failure—but because it makes the invisible visible. When the crash begins, they already know what to do. Because they wrote the plan themselves.

That's the power of learning from failure before it happens.

Designing a System That Catches You Early

Most people don't crash because they never had a system. They crash because the system they had was too slow to notice the drift.

Especially for people with ADHD, success depends less on motivation and more on **signal detection.** Build a system that catches the small stuff:

1. **Make the Invisible Visible**—use habit trackers, dashboards, or weekly signal check-ins.
2. **Map Your Curve**—keep it somewhere visible, like a fire drill plan.
3. **Weekly Checkpoints**—ask: What zone am I in? What indicators showed up? Did I apply antidotes?
4. **Recruit a Support Team**—peers, mentors, coaches who reflect your patterns back.
5. **Treat It Like a Skill**—every cycle of recognition and adjustment makes you more antifragile.

☞ The earlier you respond, the easier the recovery.

Putting It All Together

By now, you've seen that success isn't a mystery—it's a pattern. And so is failure.

The Success Curve gives you a **map of what breakdown looks like** and a **toolkit for turning it around**. But more than that, it's an invitation to start seeing your life as a series of **signals**, **choices**, and **adjustments**—not just outcomes.

Let's recap the core ideas:

You Have a Pattern

Failure rarely shows up out of nowhere. Most people with ADHD experience early warning signs—slipping routines, missed responsibilities, rising anxiety, disconnection from values—long before the crash. But without a system for tracking those signs, they can go unnoticed until it's too late.

The Success Curve turns that pattern into something visible, trackable, and actionable.

✦

You Can Learn to Read the Signals

By identifying **indicators** (the behaviors, thoughts, and feelings that show you're sliding) and matching them with **antidote behaviors** (targeted actions that lift you back up), you give yourself a way out of the downward spiral. The key is acting early—while the distance back to stability is still short.

✦

You Can Build a System That Recovers

Your success isn't about never slipping. It's about **slipping less often**, **recovering faster**, and **learning every time**. A personal system—built on weekly check-ins, visual cues, and trusted people—helps you do exactly that. When used consistently, your Success Curve becomes a kind of **dashboard for life**: a way to monitor your energy, behavior, and emotional state in real time.

✦

🌐 You Can Reroute at Any Point

Even if you're deep in Zone 2 or already feeling the crash of Zone 3, the curve can still help. It shows you *where you are* and gives you a way back. You're never too far gone to start noticing, naming, and responding. That's the power of signal-based self-awareness.

Your Success Curve Worksheet
Spot the signals. Apply the antidotes. Shift the pattern.

Step 1. Map Your Zones
Think about your life in three states. Write down how each looks for **you**:

Zone 1: Thriving (Success Line)

- What routines, habits, and feelings show you're steady?
- What "green zone" behaviors keep you grounded?

Zone 2: Slipping (Danger Zone)

- What are the *first little signals* you're drifting?
- Think: skipped habits, hidden stress, avoidance, rationalizations.

Zone 3: Crashing (Red Zone)

- What does crisis look like for you?
- What behaviors or emotions mean you've bottomed out?

Step 2. Identify Your Indicators

List 3–5 **early warning signs** that usually show up in Zone 2.

(Examples: hitting snooze repeatedly, procrastinating small tasks, avoiding emails, stopping exercise, withdrawing socially.)

1. _____
2. _____
3. _____
4. _____
5. _____

✦

Step 3. Match Antidotes

For each indicator, write one **antidote behavior**—a small action that helps you course-correct before things worsen.

(Examples: reset to-do list, text a friend, write for 15 minutes, go to bed early.)

Indicator → Antidote

_____ → _____

_____ → _____

_____ → _____

✦

Step 4. Weekly Dashboard Check

At least once a week, ask yourself:

1. What zone am I in right now? ☐ Thriving ☐ Slipping ☐ Crashing

2. What indicators showed up this week?

   _____

3. Did I use my antidotes? ☐ Yes ☐ No—If no, what blocked me?

4. What's one adjustment for the coming week?

   _____

✧

Step 5. Recruit Support

Who can help reflect your signals back to you? (friend, coach, advisor, parent, mentor)

Write their name(s): _____

✧

🔁 Reminder

The sooner you act, the simpler the antidote.

Delay—and the fix gets harder.

Your curve is not a test. It's a **map**.

Chapter Wrap-Up: You're Not Broken— You're Building a Dashboard

You've just learned something that many people go their whole lives without ever realizing: **failure follows a pattern.** And once you can see the pattern, you can interrupt it. Rewire it. Recover from it. Even grow stronger because of it.

The Success Curve isn't just a tool for avoiding breakdown. It's a way to become *more adaptive, more aware,* and *more in control* of your own life. And for people with ADHD—who often feel like they're at the mercy of invisible forces—this kind of clarity is priceless.

When you can spot the signals early...

When you can act with intention instead of shame...

When you can adjust your process before your product falls apart…

That's not just success. That's mastery.

For Parents, Educators, Clinicians, Coaches, and Curious Minds

This chapter is more than a theory—it's a lens. If you support someone with ADHD, you've likely watched them slip from thriving to struggling without any obvious "event." One day things seem fine. The next, there's a crisis. But as this chapter outlines, the slide into breakdown is rarely sudden. It follows a predictable curve—with early indicators that often go unnoticed.

The Success Curve gives people with ADHD a framework to spot trouble before it spirals. But it also gives *you* a framework to support more compassionately:

- o When students go quiet, withdraw, or drop a ball—you'll know it may not be laziness, but a signal.
- o When a client or loved one starts to "look fine" but feels off—you'll have language for what's really happening.
- o When you want to help but don't know how—you can guide them back to their own curve, their own plan, and their own tools.

This chapter teaches pattern awareness. In the next, we'll show how to turn that awareness into a thriving system—one that parents and professionals can help reinforce, without taking over.

📑 References for Further Reading

○ Brown, T. E. (2013). *A new understanding of ADHD in children and adults: Executive function impairments.* Routledge.
Explains how ADHD impairs self-regulation of attention, emotion, and motivation—the same skills that falter in Zone 2 of the curve.

○ Duckworth, A. (2016). *Grit: The power of passion and perseverance.* Scribner.
Research on sustained effort and recovery from setbacks. Reinforces the importance of antidote behaviors and persistence.

○ Gorski, T. T. (2001). *Relapse prevention counseling: Clinical strategies to guide addiction recovery and reduce relapse.* Independence Press.
A foundational relapse model that inspired the Success Curve. Shows why breakdowns follow predictable patterns.

○ Maté, G. (2008). *Scattered minds: The origins and healing of attention deficit disorder.* Vintage Canada.
Highlights the emotional and regulatory dimensions of ADHD, emphasizing subtle early warning signs—exactly what the Success Curve helps track.

○ Sapolsky, R. M. (2004). *Why zebras don't get ulcers: The acclaimed guide to stress, stress-related diseases, and coping.* Holt Paperbacks.
Explains how chronic stress wears down resilience, illuminating why prolonged Zone 2 drift leads to collapse.

○ Thomas, J. L. (2019). *Thriving at the Edge of Chaos: Making ADHD a Superpower in College and Career.* CreateSpace.
The first appearance of the original "Jabo Curve." This book laid the foundation for the Success Curve by showing how ADHD breakdowns follow predictable arcs—and how those arcs can be shifted.

➡️ Coming Up Next: The Success Curve in Action—A Meta-Framework for Thriving

So far, you've seen how breakdown happens. You've mapped the curve. You've learned to spot your patterns.

In the next chapter, we zoom out. We'll bring together every tool in this book—signal mapping, stress tracking, emotional intelligence, the VPE model, beliefs and identity—and show how the Success Curve becomes the dashboard that unifies them all.

This isn't just a model of how you fall.

It's a map of how you thrive.

And it's where everything comes together.

Chapter 26

The Success Curve in Action—A Meta-Framework for Thriving

"Everything should be made as simple as possible, but no simpler."
—Albert Einstein

Most people only discover the Success Curve when they've already crashed. But the real power of the curve isn't in diagnosing failure—it's in designing the climb.

This chapter is where everything comes together: your energy, your signals, your focus, your emotions. Not as separate hacks, but as one dashboard that shows you where you are and how to move forward.

Because thriving with ADHD isn't about perfection or never falling. It's about recognizing your signals, working your system, and recovering faster each time you drift off course. It's about building the kind of life where thriving isn't a lucky streak—it's something you've engineered.

✳ What You'll Learn in This Chapter

- How the Success Curve becomes your personal dashboard for thriving
- How to map and monitor your signals across five key domains

- o How to use the curve to track breakdown, recovery, and growth
- o How to design your own custom early-warning system and antidotes
- o How to move from reactive to proactive, from fragile to antifragile
- o How to live with direction, not perfection

1. Why Integration Matters

Most people with ADHD don't lack tools. They lack a unifying system.

Think about it: You may have a planner, a to-do app, sticky notes, energy hacks, coping strategies, self-talk scripts. But when stress hits, they scatter. The very moment you need them, they fall apart.

The Success Curve fixes that. It's not one more strategy—it's the framework that tells you when and how to use the strategies you already have.

- o Your **energy levels**—the Life Bar from Chapter 18
- o Your **motivation patterns**—tracked with Method–Motive–Opportunity
- o Your **beliefs and inner dialogue**—decoded in Chapters 16 and 17
- o Your **emotions**—mapped with the Three E's and Emotional Compass
- o Your **executive function flare-ups**—interpreted with the Visionary–Producer–Editor model
- o Your **identity shifts and nested selves**—giving context to shame, collapse, and recovery

Instead of managing all of these separately, the Success

Curve brings them into one conversation. Once you can see the pattern beneath the noise, your ability to self-correct multiplies.

2. The Curve as Dashboard

Imagine waking up one day and feeling just slightly off. Not enough to call it burnout—but not quite your best either.

With the Success Curve as your dashboard, you don't panic. You check in:

- What zone am I in right now?
- What indicators have been showing up this week?
- How's my Life Bar?
- Do I still have Method, Motive, and Opportunity in place?
- What does my Emotional Signal Compass say—is this frustration, fatigue, fear, or something else?

Instead of spiraling into shame or confusion, you start gathering data. Not "what's wrong with me?" but "what's shifting, and what needs attention?"

That's the power of a dashboard: it helps you intervene early, course-correct compassionately, and stay aligned with your real priorities.

3. Real Life Implementation

Let's walk it out.

You've missed a couple classes. That's your first indicator. Your energy bar's been dipping, you've avoided friends, and your to-do list is growing cobwebs. You check the curve. You're in early Zone 2. Time to act.

Your antidote behaviors might look like this:

- o Text your academic coach.
- o Schedule a restorative activity (Zone 1 behavior).
- o Do a quick 5-minute Signal Mapping scan and emotional check-in.
- o Use MMO to figure out why class was hard to get to (was it motive? method? opportunity?).

You take one corrective action. Then another. Slowly, you inch back toward balance. That's not failure—that's antifragility in action.

And the best part? You didn't wait for the crash. You listened to the signal—not just the crisis.

4. When Tools Talk to Each Other

Here's the magic: when your tools start talking to each other.

- o Signal Mapping shows a dip in motivation. MMO helps diagnose whether it's motive, method, or opportunity.
- o Emotional flooding hits—the Three E's help you name the feeling, and your Nested Selves help you respond with compassion.
- o You notice your Visionary is spinning out ideas while your Editor is asleep—time to recruit support, not shame yourself.

Case in point: A student I worked with felt antsy and angry every time she sat down to study. Normally she would've called it laziness. Instead, she paused. Three E's: her *experience* was studying, her *evaluation* was "I'm behind and hopeless," and her *emotion* was anger. That pointed her back to MMO: the problem wasn't motive (she cared about passing) or method (she had a study plan). It was opportunity—she was trying to study in a noisy apartment. The fix? Relocate to the library. One tool led to another, and the dashboard lit up a path back to alignment.

This is the point: the Success Curve isn't frozen. It's dynamic. It doesn't just show you where you are—it shows you how your tools interconnect in real time.

5. The SignalWorks App: A Living Extension of the Curve

Everything in this book can be done on paper. But many of us know the reality: we forget. We lose the map. We miss the signals until they've piled too high.

That's why we're building SignalWorks—a living dashboard that extends the Success Curve into daily life.

Imagine opening your phone and seeing your week not as a to-do list, but as a snapshot of your energy, focus, and signals. Imagine nudges that don't nag, but remind you of what you already know matters.

The app will help you:

- Track indicators and antidotes in real time
- Log energy, emotion, and motivation using tools like the Life Bar, Signal Compass, and MMO
- Visualize your curve over weeks or months to spot repeating patterns
- Get nudges tailored to your actual signals, not generic advice

Over time, it adapts to you. If your Producer is strong but your Editor keeps dropping the ball, it supports your Editor. If your burnout patterns hit mid-semester, it starts flagging early.

The app won't replace your agency. But it will make remembering your own wisdom easier. It will help your system love you back.

6. A Theory of Everything (Important)

Einstein spent the last decades of his life searching for a Theory of Everything—one elegant framework to connect the universe's forces. He never found it. But his search revealed a profound truth: simplification doesn't mean reduction. It means connection.

That's what the Success Curve—and this whole book—has been about. Not reducing your life to one diagram, but showing how the parts connect:

- Your beliefs and your burnout.
- Your shame and your scheduling.
- Your feelings and your focus.
- Your identity and your executive function.

When those things drift apart, you feel it—that quiet hum of misalignment. When they move back together, something clicks.

Call it meaning. Call it momentum. Call it your compass. Whatever you call it, it's alignment.

You're not finished. But you're no longer flying blind.

✧

✴ Your Success Curve Dashboard
A one-page check-in for energy, signals, and alignment

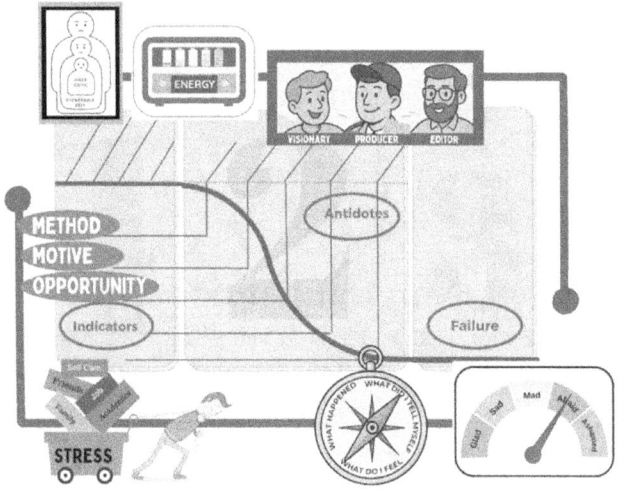

1. Where Am I on the Curve?

- ○ **Zone 1: Thriving** → Habits in place, energy renewable, clear direction
- ○ **Zone 2: Slipping** → Small cracks, missed cues, compensating but drifting
- ○ **Zone 3: Crashing** → Collapse, overwhelm, disconnection

Circle your current **zone** before diving into the rest.

✧

2. Check Your Signals (The Core Tools)

Domain	Tool	Quick Prompt	Signal Example
Energy	Life Bar (Ch. 18)	"Green, yellow, or red?"	Skipping meals, sleep debt
Motivation	Method–Motive–Opportunity	"Which piece is missing?"	Bored (no motive), bad strategy (no method)
Emotion	Three E's + Emotional Compass	"What happened → what did I tell myself → what do I feel?"	Event: missed deadline → Eval: "I'm hopeless" → Emotion: shame
Executive Function	Visionary–Producer–Editor	"Who's in charge right now?"	Visionary spinning, Editor asleep
Identity	Nested Selves (Ch. 19)	"Which 'me' is showing up?"	Child-self retreating, future-self unheard

3. Indicators & @Antidotes

- **Indicator** = small signal something's drifting.
- *Examples: avoiding email, skipping class, snapping at people.*
- **Antidote** = specific action that steers back to Zone 1.
- *Examples: write for 15 minutes, text a friend, reset planner.*

☞ Write one **indicator you've noticed** + one **antidote you'll try.**

4. Weekly Dashboard Questions

1. What zone am I in?
2. What indicators did I notice this week?
3. Did I act on antidotes—or do I need to adjust?

5. Your Support Team
Who can reflect your curve back to you when you can't see it?

- Accountability partner
- Mentor/coach
- Peer group

Reminder

The earlier you respond, the lighter the fix.

This dashboard isn't about perfection. It's about awareness, alignment, and recovery.

✧

👥 For Parents, Educators, Clinicians, Coaches, and Curious Minds

This chapter might feel like a technical deep dive. But at its heart, it's an invitation to empathy.

People with ADHD don't just need accountability—they need *dashboards*. They need systems that speak their language, reflect their real experience, and support early correction instead of delayed punishment.

If you support someone with ADHD:

- Learn to spot early indicators. They won't always say "I'm crashing." But their energy, motivation, and behavior will whisper it first.
- Encourage proactive antidotes. Waiting until they've failed a class or dropped out of school isn't support— it's cleanup.
- Help them build their own dashboards. Whether with a pen and notebook or an app, the earlier they see their own curve, the sooner they can respond.
- Normalize nonlinear growth. The curve isn't straight. Neither is thriving. But there *is* a pattern—and it's learnable.

And remember: You don't need to be their compass. You just need to help them find their own.

🗐 References for Further Reading

• **Barkley, R. A. (2008). *ADHD in Adults: What the Science Says*. Guilford Press.**
A comprehensive summary of ADHD research in adults by one of the foremost experts in the field. Particularly helpful in understanding patterns of impairment and executive dysfunction that make proactive monitoring tools—like the Success Curve—essential for long-term functioning.

• **Brown, B. (2012). *Daring Greatly: How the Courage to Be Vulnerable Transforms the Way We Live, Love, Parent, and Lead*. Gotham Books.**
Explores the role of vulnerability and shame resilience in human growth—foundational to the emotional self-awareness required to respond skillfully to early signals of breakdown.

• **Gorski, T. T. (1989). *Passages Through Recovery: An Action Plan for Preventing Relapse*. Hazelden.**
A landmark in relapse prevention literature, Gorski's work outlines predictable stages of relapse and recovery. This model served as the original inspiration for the Success Curve's design and its staged response to failure indicators.

• **Ratey, J. J. (2001). *A User's Guide to the Brain: Perception, Attention, and the Four Theaters of the Brain*. Vintage.**
Accessible neuroscience that links attention, motivation, and self-regulation—critical in understanding why the integration of emotion, signal awareness, and executive function (as modeled in the Success Curve) is so essential for ADHD management.

• Taleb, N. N. (2012). *Antifragile: Things That Gain from Disorder.* Random House.
Introduces the concept of antifragility—systems that grow stronger through stress. The Success Curve embodies this idea by helping individuals not just recover from breakdown but evolve more adaptive, personalized systems of support over time.

Chapter 27

A Theory of Everything Important

*"I've worn the faces off all the cards. I'm
gonna take it with me when I go."*
—Tom Waits

Imagine for a moment that your mind is not yours alone.

That your thoughts, talents, instincts—even your struggles—are signals within a much larger pattern of intelligence. Not because we are neurologically wired into one shared brain, but because we are biologically, socially, and ecologically interwoven.

The "you" reading this page is not a static, separate entity, but a node in a living network—a nested self within a repeating pattern, from the cellular to the relational, from your neural circuitry to the family, school, or culture you help shape.

This chapter isn't about strategies or symptoms. It's not about college or career.

It's about what happens when we zoom out—way out. Beyond the brain, the diagnosis, the GPA. Beyond even the individual organism—and into the possibility that minds, plural, may exist in dynamic relation.

Howard Gardner's theory of multiple intelligences opened the door to viewing intelligence as multidimensional. But what if those dimensions also have depth?

What if each intelligence—musical, spatial, interpersonal, existential—is not just a personal strength, but a signal role within a broader ecosystem?

Like fractals, these intelligences may echo across scales: an individual mind, a group dynamic, a cultural norm, even something resembling an ecological intelligence—a kind of planetary nervous system, not literally but metaphorically.

In this view, someone with ADHD may not be disordered, but differently tuned—a kind of specialist in scanning for novelty, responding to emerging signals, and disrupting systems when they become stagnant.

ADHD becomes less about dysfunction and more about functional uniqueness—a particular pattern of signal sensitivity—within a diverse ecology of minds.

Maybe the purpose of minds like ours—wired for pattern, tuned to signal, restless in the face of stillness—isn't to conform, but to reveal. To sense what others overlook. To press at the edges where new truths live.

Albert Einstein was one of us. Not in diagnosis, but in divergence. A mind that struggled with school, spoke late, resisted rote learning—yet saw the hidden architecture of space and time.

He didn't just solve problems; he reimagined the shape of reality itself.

And yet, for all his brilliance, he was also a man who wrestled deeply with meaning, humanity, and his place in the moral order of the world. He knew things—and yet, he still wondered about what really mattered.

Which is why it feels right to end here—with a thinker who reached for the stars, but never stopped asking what it means to be human.

In his later years, Albert Einstein walked the halls of Princeton in soft slippers, famously avoiding socks and publicity when he could. Despite the awe in which the world held him, he once described himself as "an old man mainly known as a crank who doesn't wear socks."

He spent much of those years working alone on a Unified Field Theory—a single framework to explain all the forces of nature.

It never quite came together. Not because he lacked brilliance, but perhaps because he was chasing the wrong everything.

And maybe, in that relentless pursuit, he lost something else: the balance of a fuller life. He became more solitary, more withdrawn, consumed by an idea that resisted completion. A genius, yes—but one increasingly alone with his equations.

There's a lesson in that.

Especially for those of us whose minds run a little hot, a little fast, a little sideways.

We're often told to get organized. To find structure. To focus on what matters.

But what matters doesn't always fit on a blackboard.

And it certainly doesn't always fit in a planner.

Maybe the real theory of everything isn't mathematical—it's metaphorical.

Not about explaining the universe but aligning with it.

Not about reducing life to a formula but expanding into a role—your role—in a nested, intelligent cosmos.

We've covered a lot in this book—motivation, executive function, emotional intelligence, beliefs, energy, recovery.

We've drawn maps and curves, built dashboards and compasses.

We've tried to make what's overwhelming feel simpler—without losing its meaning.

But here's the deeper truth: when you use these tools together, something new happens.

The Compass, the Curve, the Wagon, the VPE, the Nested Selves—they're not just strategies. They're parts of a living system. And when they interact, they create something more powerful than the tools alone.

That "more" is emergent intelligence.

Like a jazz ensemble, like an ecosystem, like fire catching from spark to ember to flame—the integration itself creates a pattern larger than the sum of its pieces. You're not just managing symptoms. You're cultivating an emergent way of thinking, acting, and aligning that makes you bigger than your distractions, stronger than your setbacks, and wiser than your impulses.

This is the real point: you are building a system that grows with you. A system that doesn't just catch you when you fall, but one that learns, adapts, and evolves alongside your own story.

But let me be clear: this was never just a book about ADHD.

It was always a book about you.

About how you make sense of yourself in a world that often misunderstands you.

About how you build a life that works—not just on paper, but in motion, in feeling, in meaning.

This isn't a theory of disorder.

It's a theory of design.

A theory of how attention and meaning intersect.

A theory of how we thrive—at the edge of chaos, in the middle of mess, in the beauty of the in-between.

Writing this book took me many years. Not because I couldn't figure out what to say—but because I kept learning.

Every time I worked with a student who took one of these tools and made it their own, I realized I had more to say.

Not because the book wasn't finished—but because they were the ones finishing it. In real time. With their lives.

So that's what I want for you, too.

Take what's here. Use what works. Forget the rest.

Rebuild it. Remix it. Repurpose it.

Pretend you thought of the ideas yourself.

Or better yet, imagine you once heard them in an old story, and are now remembering them in your own way, in your own time.

This is your system now. Your compass. Your map.

Not just a way to manage symptoms—but a way to live.

It's not just about thriving at the edge of chaos.

It's about choosing how you want to live, learn, love, and contribute—even when the world feels noisy, even when your path feels nonlinear, even when you're still figuring it out.

So, in closing, let me ask you one last time—not as a writer, but as a fellow traveler:

What will you do with your one wild and precious mind?

Jon Thomas

Acknowledgments

This book, like all books, is not the work of one person alone. It is the product of patience, encouragement, and the gifts of others who walked beside me in the process.

First, to my wife, **Pamela**. These pages carry your fingerprints in every way. You gave shape and color to the words through your illustrations, and you gave the book its cover—the first impression by which it will travel into the world. But more than that, you gave me the steady presence, care, and inspiration without which this book, or the two before it, could never have been completed. You are, in every sense, the quiet artist of my life.

To **Danilo Salli**, **Sebastian Soto**, and **Gabriel Blake**—thank you for your careful editorial work. Each of you strengthened this manuscript with clarity, insight, and attention to detail. You caught what I missed, sharpened what was soft, and helped these words stand taller than they could have on their own.

I am also grateful to friends, colleagues, and early readers who encouraged me along the way, to those who asked hard questions, and to those who reminded me why this work matters. If these pages speak to others, it is because of the conversations we shared.

Finally, to every student, client, and reader who has walked with me "at the edge of chaos"—thank you. Your courage, struggles, and stories have been my greatest teachers. This book is for you.

About the Author

Jon L. Thomas, EdD has been called a counselor, educator, ADHD coach, writer, woodworker, and beekeeper. He prefers "fellow traveler at the edge of chaos."

For more than 30 years, Jon has worked with students, adults, and families to reimagine ADHD—not as a flaw, but as a different way of paying attention with its own kind of brilliance. His first book, *Thriving at the Edge of Chaos: Making ADHD a Superpower in College and Career*, gave students and educators practical tools for harnessing strengths. His second, *Beyond the Edge of Chaos: ADHD, Identity, and the New Art of Thriving*, expands that vision into a deeper guide for meaning, identity, and resilience.

The journey continues with his forthcoming third book, *Human Emergent Intelligence: Evolving Beyond the Edge of Chaos*, which explores how human intelligence is shifting in a world increasingly shaped by AI, networks, and collective learning.

Jon also trains educators, clinicians, and coaches in applying these models and devotes time to men's work, supporting programs that help men grow into purpose and accountability beyond early challenges and trauma. A singer-songwriter and occasional extra in indie films, he lives in the hills of West

Virginia with his wife, Pamela—who now manages the bee-keeping business—where they enjoy quiet mornings, big ideas, and projects that usually take twice as long but end up twice as interesting, with a healthy dose of creative chaos along the way.

Stay connected: **www.ADHDCollegeSuccess.com | JonThomas@ADHDCollegeSuccess.com**

Looking Ahead

At the close of *Beyond the Edge of Chaos*, we saw how individuals can thrive by noticing signals, aligning with values, and building resilience in the face of breakdown. But the story does not end with the self. Just as no brain thrives in isolation, no person thrives outside the currents of culture. That is where the third book begins.

For hundreds of thousands of years, the human brain has been evolving slowly, carefully, beautifully. It was shaped for scarcity of signal: a rustle in the grass, a flicker of firelight, a familiar face across the camp. But in just the last century—and especially since the digital revolution—technology has raced ahead, flooding us with abundance. Our brains, designed for trickles, now face torrents: infinite feeds, relentless alerts, even entire industries built to capture attention through pornography, compulsive gaming, and algorithmic stimulation. The result has been predictable: stress, distraction, addiction, disconnection, and breakdown.

And now, history is repeating on a larger stage. As our individual brains struggle to keep pace with digital signals, our cultures now risk falling behind the pace of artificial intelligence. Artificial General Intelligence (AGI) is advancing at breakneck speed, scaling faster than our collective wisdom can keep up. Without a parallel evolution of what I call *Human Emergent Intelligence (HEI)*, AGI will simply amplify whatever dominates: distraction, division, or dysfunction.

But there is hope. Emergence is what happens when the whole becomes greater than the sum of its parts. Water is not just hydrogen and oxygen; consciousness is not just firing neurons; a forest is not just trees, but soil and fungi and weather woven together into resilience. In the same way, when humans pool perspective, integrate signals, and co-create meaning, something new appears: an intelligence that is not reducible to any individual, but that belongs to us together. That is Human Emergent Intelligence. Where AGI expands raw capacity, HEI expands context, values, and wisdom. Where AGI risks isolating us in a flood of noise, HEI has the power to reconnect us—to one another, to meaning, and to a future worth building.

This project is more than just a book. It is an adventure in connectivity—a call to help shape what comes next. If these pages have stirred something in you, I invite you to join the dialogue as *Human Emergent Intelligence: Evolving Beyond the Edge of Chaos* comes to life. Updates, early insights, and opportunities to be part of the conversation are available at **www.ADHDCollegeSuccess.com**. I would love to have you walk with me in this exploration—because emergence, by its very nature, is never a solo act.

Glossary of Key Terms & Metaphors

- **Accountability**—Facing the consequences of actions and restoring integrity, beyond punishment.
- **Antifragile**—A system that grows stronger under stress (Taleb).
- **Belief loops**—The repeating cycle of experiences, evaluations, and emotions that can trap or liberate behavior.
- **Beginner's Mind**—Staying open to new solutions, even when experienced.
- **Cauldron (of emotions)**—A metaphor for what happens when feelings are suppressed instead of expressed.
- **Crystal–Steel–Plastic model**—A way to prioritize commitments: crystals (can't drop), steel (can bend), plastic (can be dropped).
- **Default Mode Network (DMN)**—The brain's resting-state network, linked to wandering thoughts.
- **Emergence / Human Emergent Intelligence (HEI)**—Intelligence that arises when many parts of a system interact, producing results greater than the sum of their parts. In this book, ADHD minds are seen as uniquely tuned to contribute to collective, emergent intelligence.
- **Emotional Signal Compass**—A tool for decoding emotions as directional signals.
- **Energy bar (Life Bar)**—A video-game-style metaphor for tracking energy and restoration.
- **Executive function**—The brain's self-management system: planning, working memory, impulse control, shifting, and monitoring.

- **Fragile / Resilient / Antifragile**—Taleb's three system responses to stress.
- **Fractal Intelligence**—Seeing intelligence as recursive and patterned across scales.
- **Gorski Relapse Curve**—Model of relapse adapted for ADHD breakdowns.
- **Job, Career, Calling**—Three levels of work orientation: paycheck, profession, or purpose.
- **Kanban boards**—Visual project-tracking tools adapted for ADHD energy states.
- **Method–Motive–Opportunity (MMO)**—A triad for diagnosing motivational blocks.
- **Nested Selves**—The multiple internal roles or versions of self we shift among.
- **Non-specific amplifier**—A force that magnifies whatever signal is present (e.g., ADHD, AI).
- **Producer (VPE)**—The doer role, focused on execution.
- **Shame loop**—A self-reinforcing cycle of mistake → meaning → identity → shame.
- **Signal Mapping**—The process of noticing, labeling, and responding to inner and outer signals.
- **SignalWorks App**—The digital extension of the Success Curve and related tools.
- **Social Mirror**—The way emotions and self-concept are reflected by others.
- **Sprint Thinking**—ADHD-friendly bursts of focused work.
- **Stress Wagon**—A metaphor for carrying (and unloading) burdens.
- **Success Curve**—A framework for recognizing early signs of breakdown and recovery.
- **Visionary–Producer–Editor (VPE)**—Three roles for balancing ADHD strengths.

References

Anticevic, A., Cole, M. W., Murray, J. D., et al. (2012). The role of default network deactivation in cognition and disease. *Trends in Cognitive Sciences, 16*(12), 584–592.

Armstrong, T. (1999). *ADD/ADHD alternatives in the classroom.* ASCD.

Bandura, A. (1997). *Self-efficacy: The exercise of control.* Freeman.

Barkley, R. A. (2008). *ADHD in adults: What the science says.* Guilford Press.

Barkley, R. A. (2008). The nature of executive functioning and its role in ADHD: A response to critiques. *Psychological Bulletin, 134*(6), 835–868. https://doi.org/10.1037/a0012768

Barkley, R. A. (2012). *Executive functions: What they are, how they work, and why they evolved.* Guilford Press.

Beck, A. T. (1976). *Cognitive therapy and the emotional disorders.* International Universities Press.

Beck, K., et al. (2001). *Manifesto for Agile Software Development.* https://agilemanifesto.org/

Boroditsky, L. (2000). Metaphoric structuring: Understanding time through spatial metaphors. *Cognition, 75*(1), 1–28.

Braithwaite, J. (2002). *Restorative justice and responsive regulation.* Oxford University Press.

Brown, B. (2012). *Daring greatly: How the courage to be vulnerable transforms the way we live, love, parent, and lead.* Gotham Books.

Brown, B. (2015). *Rising strong: The reckoning, the rumble, the revolution.* Spiegel & Grau.

Brown, T. E. (2005). *Attention deficit disorder: The unfocused mind in children and adults.* Yale University Press.

Brown, T. E. (2009). *ADHD comorbidities: Handbook for ADHD complications in children and adults.* American Psychiatric Publishing.

Brown, T. E. (2013). *A new understanding of ADHD in children and adults: Executive function impairments.* Routledge.

Burns, D. D. (1980). *Feeling good: The new mood therapy.* William Morrow.

Coker, T. R., Elliott, M. N., Toomey, S. L., Schwebel, D. C., Cuccaro, P., & Schuster, M. A. (2016). Racial and ethnic disparities in ADHD diagnosis and treatment. *Pediatrics, 138*(3). https://doi.org/10.1542/peds.2016-0107

Csikszentmihalyi, M. (1990). *Flow: The psychology of optimal experience.* Harper & Row.

Damasio, A. (1994). *Descartes' error: Emotion, reason, and the human brain.* Putnam.

Deci, E. L., & Ryan, R. M. (2000). *Self-determination theory: Intrinsic motivation and self-determination in human behavior.* Plenum.

Dilts, R., Hallbom, T., & Smith, S. (1990). *Beliefs: Pathways to health and well-being.* Meta Publications.

Dodson, W. (2021). Rejection sensitivity dysphoria and ADHD. *ADDitude Magazine.*

Duckworth, A. (2016). *Grit: The power of passion and perseverance.* Scribner.

Dweck, C. S. (2006). *Mindset: The new psychology of success.* Random House.

Engel, S. (2011). Children's need to know: Curiosity in schools. *Harvard Educational Review, 81*(4), 625–645.

Ford, H. (1922). *My life and work.* Garden City Publishing.

Gardner, H. (1983). *Frames of mind: The theory of multiple intelligences.* Basic Books.

Gershon, M. D. (1998). *The second brain.* HarperCollins.

Gilbert, P., & Choden. (2013). *Mindful compassion.* New Harbinger.

Goleman, D. (1995). *Emotional intelligence: Why it can matter more than IQ.* Bantam Books.

Gopnik, A., Meltzoff, A. N., & Kuhl, P. K. (1999). *The scientist in the crib: Minds, brains, and how children learn.* William Morrow.

Gorski, T. T. (1989). *Passages through recovery: An action plan for preventing relapse.* Hazelden.

Gorski, T. T. (2001). *Relapse prevention counseling: Clinical strategies to guide addiction recovery and reduce relapse.* Independence Press.

Hallowell, E. M., & Ratey, J. J. (2011). *Driven to distraction* (Rev. ed.). Anchor Books.

Hallowell, E. M., & Ratey, J. J. (2023). *ADHD 2.0: New science and essential strategies for thriving with distraction—from childhood through adulthood.* Ballantine Books.

Hengen, K. B., et al. (2024). Criticality and adaptive learning in cortical networks. *Nature Neuroscience.*

Hinshaw, S. P., & Scheffler, R. M. (2014). *The ADHD explosion: Myths, medication, money, and today's push for performance.* Oxford University Press.

James, W. (1890). *The principles of psychology.* Henry Holt and Company.

Jensen, E. (2009). *Teaching with poverty in mind: What being poor does to kids' brains and what schools can do about it.* ASCD.

Kahneman, D. (2011). *Thinking, fast and slow.* Farrar, Straus and Giroux.

Kaufman, S. B. (2013). *Ungifted: Intelligence redefined.* Basic Books.

Kirmayer, L. J. (2007). Psychotherapy and the cultural concept of the person. *Transcultural Psychiatry, 44*(2), 232–257. https://doi.org/10.1177/1363461506070794

LeDoux, J. (1996). *The emotional brain: The mysterious underpinnings of emotional life.* Simon & Schuster.

Levine, M. (2003). *A mind at a time.* Simon & Schuster.

Medina, J. (2014). *Brain rules: 12 principles for surviving and thriving at work, home, and school.* Pear Press.

Mischel, W. (2014). *The marshmallow test: Mastering self-control.* Little, Brown.

Morgan, P. L., Staff, J., Hillemeier, M. M., Farkas, G., & Maczuga, S. (2013). Racial and ethnic disparities in ADHD diagnosis from kindergarten to eighth grade. *Pediatrics, 132*(1), 85–93. https://doi.org/10.1542/peds.2012-2390

Nadeau, K. G., Littman, E. B., & Quinn, P. O. (2020). *Understanding girls with ADHD: How they feel and why they do what they do.* Advantage Books.

Nigg, J. T. (2017). *Getting ahead of ADHD: What next-generation science says about treatments that work—and how you can make them work for your child.* Guilford Press.

Oyserman, D., & Destin, M. (2010). Identity-based motivation: Implications for intervention. *The Counseling Psychologist, 38*(7), 1001–1043.

Pink, D. H. (2009). *Drive: The surprising truth about what motivates us.* Riverhead Books.

Ratey, J. J. (2001). *A user's guide to the brain.* Vintage.

Ratey, J. J. (2008). *Spark: The revolutionary new science of exercise and the brain.* Little, Brown Spark.

Regier, N. (2023). *Compassionate accountability: The art of connection and getting results.* Berrett-Koehler Publishers.

Reif, S. F. (2005). *How to reach and teach children with ADD/ADHD: Practical techniques, strategies, and interventions.* Jossey-Bass.

Rogers, C. R. (1961). *On becoming a person: A therapist's view of psychotherapy.* Houghton Mifflin Harcourt.

Ross, L. (1977). The intuitive psychologist and his shortcomings. In L. Berkowitz (Ed.), *Advances in experimental social psychology* (Vol. 10, pp. 173–220). Academic Press.

Royaards, W., & Drevitch, G. (2025, July 21). Your brain speaks three languages. *Psychology Today.*

Russell, J. A. (2003). Core affect and the psychological construction of emotion. *Psychological Review, 110*(1), 145–172. https://doi.org/10.1037/0033-295X.110.1.145

Russell, M., & Zentall, S. (2012). Supporting executive function in ADHD learners. *Educational Psychologist Review.*

Sapolsky, R. M. (2004). *Why zebras don't get ulcers* (3rd ed.). Holt Paperbacks.

Satir, V. (1988). *The new peoplemaking.* Science and Behavior Books.

Seli, P., et al. (2015). Mind wandering in ADHD. *Journal of Attention Disorders, 19*(8), 627–638.

Siegel, D. J. (2010). *Mindsight: The new science of personal transformation.* Bantam Books.

Siegel, D. J. (2010). *The mindful therapist: A clinician's guide to mindsight and neural integration.* W. W. Norton & Company.

Siegel, D. J. (2012). *The developing mind* (2nd ed.). Guilford Press.

Siegel, D. J., & Bryson, T. P. (2012). *The whole-brain child.* Bantam Books.

Sinek, S. (2009). *Start with why: How great leaders inspire everyone to take action.* Portfolio.

Sleeper-Triplett, J. (2010). *Empowering youth with ADHD.* Specialty Press.

Stevens, E. A., et al. (2022). Predicting academic success for students with ADHD or learning disabilities. *Journal of Learning Disabilities, 55*(3), 179–192.

Taleb, N. N. (2012). *Antifragile: Things that gain from disorder.* Random House.

Thomas, J. L. (2019). *Thriving at the edge of chaos: A guidebook for ADHD and highly creative people.* Sleepy Creek Press.

Thomas, J. L. (2025). *Beyond the edge of chaos: ADHD, identity, and the new science of thriving*. Sleepy Creek Press.

Tuckman, A. (2009). *More attention, less deficit: Success strategies for adults with ADHD*. Specialty Press.

Tuckman, A. (2012). *Understand your brain, get more done: The ADHD executive functions workbook*. Specialty Press.

Vaihinger, H. (1924). *The philosophy of "as if"*. Harcourt, Brace & Company.

Van Der Kolk, B. (2014). *The body keeps the score: Brain, mind, and body in the healing of trauma*. Viking.

Wrzesniewski, A., et al. (1997). Jobs, careers, and callings. *Journal of Research in Personality, 31*(1), 21–33.

Yochman, A., Alon-Beery, O., & Parush, S. (2022). Sensory processing and its relation to emotional regulation in children with ADHD. *Research in Developmental Disabilities, 124*, 104196.

Zentall, S. S. (2005). Theory- and evidence-based strategies for children with attentional problems. *Psychology in the Schools, 42*(8), 821–836.

Zehr, H. (2015). *Changing lenses: Restorative justice for our times*. Herald Press.

📄 Index of Key Terms, Authors, and Works

www.ingramcontent.com/pod-product-compliance
Lightning Source LLC
Chambersburg PA
CBHW060401130626
46555CB00005B/1962